PERSPECTIVES IN PSYCHIATRY VOLUME 2

The Diagnosis of Depression

J.P. Feighner and **W.F. Boyer**

JOHN WILEY & SONS

Chichester · New York · Brisbane · Toronto · Singapore

Other Wiley Editorial Offices

John Wiley & Sons, Inc., 605 Third Avenue,
New York, NY 10158-0012, USA

Jacaranda Wiley Ltd, G.P.O. Box 859, Brisbane,
Queensland 4001, Australia

John Wiley & Sons (Canada) Ltd, 5353 Dundas Road West,
Fourth Floor, Etobicoke, Ontario M9B 6H8, Canada

John Wiley & Sons (SEA) Pte Ltd, 37 Jalan Pemimpin 05-04.
Block B, Union Industrial Building, Singapore 2057

Library of Congress Cataloging-in-Publication Data

Diagnosis of depression / [editors] J.P. Feighner and W.F. Boyer.
        p.   cm.—(Perspectives in psychiatry ; v. 2)
    Includes bibliographical references and index.
    ISBN 0 471 92891 7
    1. Depression, Mental—Diagnosis.   I. Feighner, John Preston,
1937–   .   II. Boyer, W. F.   III. Perspectives in psychiatry
(Chichester, England)
    [DNLM: 1. Depression—diagnosis.   2. Depressive Disorder—
diagnosis.   WM 171 D536]
    RC537.D475   1991
    616.85′27′075—dc20
    DNLM/DLC
    for Library of Congress   91–24508
                                                                    CIP

British Library Cataloguing in Publication Data

A catalogue record for this book is
available from the British Library

ISBN 0 471 92891 7

Typeset by Inforum Typesetting, Portsmouth
Printed in Great Britain by Biddles Ltd, Guildford

Dedication

To Anne, Jennifer, J.D. & Scott

Contents

Contributors

H.S. Akiskal   *Department of Affective Disorders, University of Tennessee, Memphis, TN 38163, USA*

H. Beckmann   *Department of Psychiatry, University of Würzburg, Füchleinstrasse 15, 8700 Würzburg, Germany*

W.F. Boyer   *Feighner Research Institute, 15725 Pomerado Rd, Suite 206, Poway, CA 92064, USA*

J.P. Feighner   *Feighner Research Institute, 15725 Pomerado Rd, Suite 206, Poway, CA 92064, USA*

A. Frances   *New York State Psychiatric Institute, 722 West 168th St, New York, NY 10032, USA*

W. Hall   *New York State Psychiatric Institute, 722 West 168th St, New York, NY 10032, USA*

Y. Kasahara   *Department of Psychiatry, Nagoya University Medical School, Nagoya 466, Japan*

M.M. Katz   *Department of Psychiatry, Albert Einstein College of Medicine, Montefiore Medical Center, 111 East 210th St, Bronx, NY 10467, USA*

D.J. Kupfer   *Department of Psychiatry, Western Psychiatric Institute and Clinic, 3811 O'Hara St, Pittsburgh, PA 15213, USA*

M. Lanczik   *Department of Psychiatry, University of Würzburg, Füchleinstrasse 15, 8700, Würzberg, Germany*

J.J. López-Ibor Jr   *Department of Psychiatry, Ramon y Cajal Hospital, University of Alcala de Henares, Madrid, Spain*

S. Montgomery   *Academic Department of Psychiatry, St Mary's Hospital, Praed St, London, UK*

N. Sartorius   *Division of Mental Health, World Health Organization, 1211 Geneva, Switzerland*

A.L. Smith   *College of Physicians and Surgeons of Columbia University, 722 West 168th St, New York, NY 10032, USA*

H.M. van Praag   *Department of Psychiatry, Albert Einstein College of Medicine, Montefiore Medical Center, 11 East 210th St, Bronx, NY 10467, USA*

J. Wålinder   *Department of Psychiatry, Linköping University, S-581 85 Linköping, Sweden*

M.M. Weissman   *College of Physicians and Surgeons of Columbia University, 722 West 168th St, New York, NY 10032, USA*

S. Wetzler   *Department of Psychiatry, Albert Einstein College of Medicine, Montefiore Medical Center, 111 East 210th St, Bronx, NY 10467, USA*

Preface

The modern era of symptom-oriented psychiatric diagnosis is now twenty years old. During this time there has been a tremendous amount of effort on the part of thousands of people around the world in developing, refining, testing and fine-tuning psychiatric diagnostic systems.

Depression is an extremely common, debilitating, but treatable psychiatric illness which therefore has received a considerable portion of this attention. It is a multi-faceted symptom, syndrome and disease which reveals important parts of itself to those who approach it from different perspectives.

This book contains a variety of views of the diagnosis of depression. Included are its history as it developed from ancient times through Mid-Eastern and European traditions, examination of current issues in Western and non-Western cultures, and proposals for future improvements. The authors bring a variety of backgrounds, methods and disciplines to the task. It has been rewarding, and educating, to help in the development of this book. In addition to the wealth of factual knowledge contained in the chapters, the book emphasizes that psychiatric diagnosis is not static. A diagnostic system reflects the current state of knowledge of symptoms, longitudinal course, genetics, biochemistry and psychology. As new information is gathered in each of these areas, diagnostic systems must, and should be, revised.

This book focuses on a comprehensive and systematic global approach to the diagnosis of depression. We believe it will have significant value for both clinical and research purposes.

1

Historical aspects of affective disorders

M. Lanczik and H. Beckmann

Introduction

'Each piece of information given with understanding about an object must proceed from its definition so that it becomes clear what is actually being spoken about.' This claim of Cicero (106–43 B.C.) is easier said than done. Friedrich Nietzsche (1844–1900) objected to this. He said that none of the terms in which a process is semiotically summarized can be defined: we can only define something that has no history. Therefore we find ourselves in the middle of a dilemma concerning psychiatric classification. A perfect classification of psychic illnesses, especially of the endogenous psychoses, has not yet been realized. The present-day classification reflects the development of an ongoing process. It is a historical object that is always presented in its current state and which does not yet appear in final form. Therefore a historical consideration of the classification of affective disorders seems to be justified.

Terms such as melancholy, depression and mania are considerably older than contemporary psychiatric nosology. Since they were first used to describe psychopathological phenomena, syndromes or diagnoses they have experienced fundamental changes in meaning.

Since the end of the seventeenth century psychiatry has tried to establish itself as a biological discipline similar to other medical spheres with the theory of psychogenic causation. Psychiatry has moved away from a purely phenomenological description of psychopathological conditions to nosological units. The pathological–anatomical, pathophysiological or pathobiochemical grounding of this has been considered a matter of time (Glatzel, 1981). Karl

The Diagnosis of Depression. Edited by J.P. Feighner and W.F. Boyer
© 1991 John Wiley & Sons Ltd

Ludwig Kahlbaum (1828–1899) called for psychiatric diagnoses in his work *Die Gruppirung der Psychischen Krankheiten* (Kahlbaum, 1863). According to Kahlbaum a diagnosis should describe patients with an identical symptom pattern, aetiology, therapeutic response, prognosis and biochemical or pathological anatomical findings. To date we have not succeeded in combining biological pathology with the psychopathological phenomena. Therefore the current classification system of endogenous psychoses remains a construction that is by no means 'natural' and whose origin can only be understood in its historical connection.

The development of the current classification systems and the operationalized diagnostic criteria of affective illnesses can be traced to Ancient Greek medicine. The modern classification systems have their immediate origins in French, German and English psychiatry of the late nineteenth and early twentieth centuries. Up until then aetiological classification principles alternated with the symptomatological description. Some classifications were more organ localized or functional. Others were more phenomenologically oriented.

Since the turn of the century, two diametrically opposed conceptions have dominated the scientific dispute on psychiatric nosology. One is the research trend intent on dividing the endogenous psychoses and the other is the concept of a uniform nosological and pathogenetic interpretation.

Melancholy and mania in ancient medicine

While in our times mania and melancholia are seen as two opposing psychopathological conditions, in ancient times confusion dominated both terms. A striking feature was the emphasis on somatic factors in the pathogenesis of psychic illnesses. The term melancholy was first mentioned in the last third of the fifth century B.C. in one of the oldest Hippocratic scripts. The concept of melancholy (black bile) was an expression of humoralism in ancient medicine, which considered mental illness as being the clinical expression of biological or organic pathology. Hippocrates considered epilepsy and melancholia to be closely related. The term mania is also of Greek origin and is mentioned as a psychiatric illness in the *Corpus Hippocraticum*. However, it was only vaguely defined and was used in the sense of a psychomotor state of excitement or madness.

Manic as well as depressive moods were attributed to melancholy. Fischer-Homberger (1983) pointed out that in the Hippocratic and pseudo-Hippocratic scripts (fifth and fourth centuries B.C.) the terms mania and melancholia were used as synonyms.

Soranus of Ephesus (c. 100 B.C.) thought of disease as due to organ pathology rather than 'ill' humours. According to Soranus mania and melancholia were different illnesses. Melancholy was an illness of the oesophagus and mania was in the head. However, Soranus did not contrast the symptoms of both disorders (Fischer-Homberger, 1968; Flashar, 1966).

Soranus differentiated among three mental illnesses with affective symptoms, as did other compilers of that period (e.g. Celsus, c. A.D. 30):

1. Phrenitis (mental disorder with fever).
2. Mania (disorder of reason without fever).
3. Melancholy (sadness without fever).

Alexander Trallianus (sixth century A.D.) thought of mania as melancholy that had escalated to frenzy; in other words as an advanced stage of melancholy (Berrios, 1988). This view was modernized by Hermann Boerhaave (1668–1738) and later by representatives of the unitary psychosis school.

Systematic nosological thinking on the subject of affective illnesses can be found only after the first century A.D. Aretaeus of Cappadocia (second or third century A.D.) described melancholy as caused by rising black gall in the stomach or diaphragm. It had physical symptoms as well as sadness, tendency to suicide, feelings of indifference and psychomotor retardation. He described patients whose depression changed to a euphoric mood and so indicated that melancholy can represent the beginning or part of mania (Lewis, 1934). He also drew attention to the periodic course of the illness.

Aretaeus thought primarily of aetiology and not symptomatology. He localized the origin of mania and melancholy in the hypochondrium. Melancholy was caused by black gall and mania by an additional affectation of the head. According to Aretaeus mania represented an advancing organic process. Fischer-Homberger therefore refused to recognize Aretaeus as the initial depictor of manic-depressive illness (Fischer-Homberger, 1968). Although Aretaeus knew about the change from depressed to a cheerful mood and vice versa, he understood this to be a characteristic of mania and melancholy, and not as a nosological unit of a manic-depressive illness (Pauleikoff, 1983; Ackerknecht, 1985).

Galenos (A.D. 129 or 130–199) proposed a similar aetiologically oriented concept. He described melancholy in three stages:

1. Black gall in the blood of the stomach region.
2. Rising black gall vapours to the brain
3. Distribution of black gall in the whole body.

In the first stage somatic complaints arise, called hypochondria. In the second stage symptoms are added such as fear, delusion and hallucinations. The term hypochondria was first coined by Galenos to describe physical illnesses that were always accompanied by psychological symptoms. The close connection of melancholy and hypochrondria in later conceptions is based on this galenic humoral pathology. This basic idea can be found up to the nineteenth century, for example with Philippe Pinel (1809) and Wilhelm Griesinger (1845). Hypochondria was usually interpreted as a mild form of melancholy. But if according to Galenos the brain suffers too, Galenos described under melancholia clearly 'schizophrenic' symptoms.

Melancholia in the Middle Ages and the Renaissance

The doctors of Islam handed down the heritage of ancient science, philosophy and medicine but only a few developed it further. Science in the Middle Ages both advanced this knowledge and produced reversals that unfavourably affected mental patients. The somatic aspect of melancholy was given up again. The psychic patient was regarded from a theological viewpoint as either obsessed or damned (Leibbrand and Wettley, 1961). Nosological problems were superfluous, even though the terms melancholy and mania continued to be used. At times melancholy was thought of as a result of deadly sin, in polar contrast to Christian life, the so-called vita activa.

With the Renaissance the somatic viewpoint once more became superior. We can recognize a return to the ancient nosological conceptions of affective conditions. The division between melancholy and mania was again indistinct. Psychiatry in the Renaissance, as so often in the history of medicine, lagged behind the other medical disciplines.

An example of the reorientation at the beginning of the New European Age is Theophrastus Bombastus von Hohenheim (1391–1431). He is generally known by the name he chose, Paracelsus. He connected ancient humoral pathology and theology in the aetiology and nosology of psychic illnesses (Pauleikoff, 1983). He pointed out the periodic course of mania. He also differentiated, according to present-day terminology, between endogenous (endotoxic), exogenous causation (Pauleikoff, 1983) and obsession as etiopathogenetic factors. In this formulation biological–dynamic thinking resumed its influence on the classification of psychic diseases.

Melancholia and mania in the nosology of the eighteenth century

Since ancient times psychic diseases were regarded as intellectual disorders. Emotional disorders were epiphenomena. Madness with sadness were the signs of melancholy. Mania was characterized by madness without this sadness. This was to be different now. In the seventeenth and eighteenth centuries they gradually turned away from the aetiological definition of melancholy and concentrated more on symptomatology. *However, the terms mania and melancholy were still not used as they are today.* Philippe Pinel (1745–1826), representative of 'moral treatment' in French psychiatry, and Johann Christian August Heinroth (1773–1843), representative of 'Romantic Psychiatry' in Germany, described as melancholy what we would today diagnose as a schizophrenic residual syndrome (Heinroth, 1818; cf. Schmidt-Degenhard, 1983). Pinel's and Heinroth's concept of mania corresponded to the excited state of schizophrenia.

Until then mania and melancholy had been described as extremely varied and very different conditions. The terms were now more closely defined. Sadness as a symptom of melancholy came to the fore. However, mania was still an intellectual disorder that accompanied psychomotor excitation. The affective component was not yet a part. For example William Cullen (1710–1790) defined melancholy as an affective disease with depressive and euphoric moods. He identified mania as madness. The apothecary John Haslam (1763–1833) reserved the terms mania and melancholy for affective disorders but he didn't regard them as opposite diseases (Haslam, 1798; cf. Lewis, 1934).

Melchior Adam Weikard (1742–1803) compared 'mood diseases' with 'mental diseases' in his book *The Philosophical Doctor* (1790). But it took another hundred years until psychiatry actually dealt with valid nosological entities. At the time of Weikard, as since antiquity, there were philosophical attempts to solve psychiatric classification. For example, the East Prussian philosopher Immanuel Kant (1724–1804) presented in 1798 a nosological system which was oriented toward older standards. It did not contrast melancholy with mania or count hypochondria as one of the mood disorders.

We are only able to read about the problem of nosological separation of melancholy and its connection with mania in the works of the French Provenience after the French Revolution. Jean Etienne Dominique Esquirol (1772–1830) rejected the term melancholy as a nosological entity and only wanted it to distinguish a temperament (Esquirol, 1838; cf. Freud, 1967; Tellenbach, 1961; Kretschmer, 1951). He introduced two new terms:

1. Monomanie—melancholy complicated by mania.
2. Lypemanie—melancholy in the traditional sense.

Esquirol emphasized that melancholy was a matter of mood and not an impairment of intellect (Esquirol, 1838; Walser, 1968). He also pointed out the seasonal nature of mood disorders.

The influence of neurology on psychiatric classification

Neurology also influenced psychiatric nosology. Albrecht von Haller (1708–1777) differentiated between reduced and increased neural excitability. This fostered the origin of neuropathological or neurophysiological explanations of mental illnesses. Psychiatry took over the terms irritability and excitability and distinguished between increased or diminished psychic irritability.

William Cullen (1710–1790) was among the most significant representatives of this neurologically orientated psychopathology. His ideas of sadness, fear and depression assumed a depression of the brain vessels with a resulting atonia or diminished excitability of nerve fibres. In 1983 Schmidt-Degenhard correctly wrote that the term 'depression' in its historical origins was not a psychopathological but a physiological phenomenon, i.e. a functional change in the organic substrate.

Before the term depression became a synonym for melancholy in the nineteenth century it was applied in the sense of an unspecific diminution and general impairment of psychic functions. In the first half of the nineteenth century depression was used as a designation for heterogeneous nosological groups that only had a negative symptom (i.e. any psychic subfunction) in common.

An example of this is *melancholia attonita*. In the description of Emil Kraepelin (1856–1926) melancholia attonita contained features of a depressive stupor. Kahlbaum's description included elements of catalepsia. Pinel listed melancholia attonita in his 1874 dissertation *Catatonia* (Kindt, 1980). Esquirol called stupor and numbed state typical symptoms of melancholy. He took catalepsia to be a phenomenon of dementia (Esquirol, 1838). Like Kahlbaum, Carl Wernicke (1848–1905) classified melancholia attonita among the recurrent motility psychoses that were repeatedly cured (Leonhard, 1986). Heinroth compared the term depression to hypersthenia (Heinroth, 1818). He therefore used terms that go back to Cullen's pupil John Brown (1735–1788). Brown simplified Cullen's ideas and differentiated between sthenic and asthenic forms of mental disorders (Brown, 1795; cf. Leibbrand and Wettley, 1961). These corresponded to depression and exaltation.

Mania was therefore identified with psychic over-excitation and melancholy with psychic paralysis. Through these neurological interpretations the terms mania and melancholy corresponded more to their present-day position as opposites (Fischer-Homberger, 1968). Wilhelm Griesinger (1817–1878) accentuated the psychomotor phenomena of melancholy rather than the pathological mood (Griesinger, 1845). The pair of terms were now finally in a polar position to each other. At this point, however, we still cannot speak of two diagnostic entities. Movement in this direction came from the French psychiatric school.

The nosology of affective diseases in the nineteenth century: on the way to describing manic-depressive illness

Psychic disorders were subdivided according to symptoms until the middle of the nineteenth century. Then, with Pinel, there developed a movement to describe psychopathological syndromes with equal emphasis on the course of the disease.

In 1851 Pierre Falret (1794–1870) formulated the term folie circulaire. He described the cyclic succession of exultant and depressive moods. His contribution does not lie in the initial description of mania alternating with melancholia. Others had done that before him. It lay rather in having described this as a diagnostic entity. Falret was oriented by the model of progressive paralysis. In the transition from the melancholic phase to a manic one he saw one illness rather than a metamorphosis of one illness into another. Therefore he is considered the initial describer of manic-depressive illness as it is understood today.

Falret's opponent Jules Gabriel Franois Baillarger (1809–1890) postulated in 1854 that the symptomless intervals between a melancholic and manic period prevent one of talking of a single diagnostic entity. Surely two different diseases were alternating. Through this Baillarger claimed credit for describing a new psychiatric diagnosis. This was the folie double forme in which one affective condition alternates with the other. Anticipating Kraepelin's later synthesis, both these descriptions focused on chronic illness with poor prognosis (Falret, 1851; Baillarger, 1854).

The concept of unitary psychosis

Falret credited Wilhelm Griesinger (1817–1869) as the initial describer of folie circulaire. In his work *Pathology and Therapy of Psychic Diseases* (1845) Griesinger described the alternating manic and melancholic affective disorders. He also supported a more unitary interpretation of a variety of psycho-pathological phenomena (Vliegen, 1980).

In this Griesinger was preceded by Vicenzo Chiarugi (1789–1820; Chiarugi, 1793). Chiarugi had seen melancholy as a partial mental illness and mania as the complete stage. *As can be seen*, ancient models influenced Chiarugi in this formulation (Roccatagliata, 1973).

The concept of a unitary nosological and pathogenetic process also may be traced back to Joseph Guislain (1797–1860; Guislain, 1833) and Ernst Albert Zeller (1803–1877). Zeller in turn was influenced by the writings of Thomas Sydenham (1624–1689). Sydenham saw psychic illness as a single process that progressed in phases and appeared different in each stage. Zeller distinguished four stages of madness (Zeller, 1838):

1. Melancholy.
2. Mania
3. Paranoia.
4. Amentia.

Melancholy was regarded as the initial stage of psychic illness by Guislain (1852), Zeller (1838) and later by both Griesinger (1845) and Henry Maudsley (1835–1918; Maudsley 1848). It no longer had the character of a distinct nosological entity.

Griesinger took over this doctrine of a unitary psychosis, according to which melancholy and mania are only stages of a mental illness. That means that Griesinger, in contrast to Falret, did not see a nosological entity in the alternating melancholic and manic syndromes. Heinrich Neumann (1814–1884), the most radical advocate of the unitary concept in Germany, recognized neither mania nor melancholy as individual types of illness. He went further than Griesinger with the view that melancholy could not even be regarded as a criterion for stage classification because depressive syndromes could occur with any one of the mental illnesses (Vliegen, 1980; Lanczik, 1989).

However, it is less well known that Neumann considered his views temporary. Conscious that psychiatric nosology is the weak point of the field, he suggested two ways of classifying psychic illness, longitudinal course and neuropathology. Kraepelin followed the first way and his opponent Wernicke took the latter.

Between the unitary and the differentiated concept we find Kahlbaum, who has been mentioned. He reserved melancholy as a designation for an initial or transitional depressive mood, but he regarded dysthymia as a separate variety of mental disease. Kahlbaum's dysthymia corresponds to unipolar endogenous depression in the modern sense (Kahlbaum, 1863).

The nosological compromise: Kraepelin's dichotomy of the endogenous psychoses

Present-day classification systems owe much to Emil Kraepelin (1856–1926). For this reason his classification system for affective illnesses should be presented here in more detail. The development from the first (1833) to the sixth edition (1899) of his psychiatric textbook goes from a differentiated classification up to a summary of all affective syndromes within one diagnosis. With Kraepelin the term melancholy fell from use as a word to describe a diagnosis, a syndrome or a symptom. The term depression took over to describe a mood disorder as part of manic-depressive illness, but not an independent diagnostic entity.

In the first editions of his textbook Kraepelin retained the term melancholy and postulated a nosological entity under this name. He distinguished three subforms:

1. Melancholia simplex.
2. Melancholia activa.
3. Melancholia attonita.

Kraepelin regarded melancholia simplex in the fourth edition (1893) as the simplest form of melancholy. It was distinguished by an unmotivated sadness. In melancholia activa, also called anxiety melancholia, anxious excitation was the prominent symptom. Kraepelin saw melancholia attonita as the polar opposite of melancholia activa in terms of psychomotor state. He used the term stupor as a synonym.

In the third edition (1889) circular insanity can be found as an independent nosological unit beside the periodic psychoses. In 1893 Kraepelin put monopolar periodic mania, periodic melancholy and circular insanity under the periodic psychoses. He understood circular insanity to be the alternating occurrence of manic and melancholic conditions. The difference between this and the 'simple psychoses' of pure melancholy and pure mania was that the periodic psychoses showed 'quite regular intervals'.

In the fifth edition (1896) the endogenous psychoses were simplified into manic-depressive illness and dementia praecox. Melancholy attonita was a part of dementia praecox because of similarities in prognosis. The term melancholy changed to depression and periodic melancholy was no longer a subgroup of the periodic psychoses. In the following editions melancholy included the involutional depressive disorders. These were still called depressive insanity (see Table I). Schmidt-Degenhard wrote in this connection of a growing tendency towards the expansion of the term 'depression' and restriction of the term 'melancholy' (Schmidt-Degenhard, 1983) until the latter was integrated into manic-depressive insanity. In the sixth edition (1899) we find the term manic-depressive insanity as a collective name for all forms of recurrent psychoses. They are therefore regarded as a unitary illness process. *There was no fundamental distinction between bipolar and unipolar disorders.*

The dispute between Falret and Baillarger in the definition of manic-depressive insanity was not significant for Kraepelin. In his opinion depression

Table I. Division of the pure affective psychoses according to Leonhard (1986).

1.1 Manic-depressive disease

2.1 Pure melancholia
2.2 Pure mania

Pure depression:
3.1 Harried depression
3.2 Hypochondriacal depression
3.3 Self-torturing depression
3.4 Suspicious depression
3.5 Non-participatory depression

Pure euphorias:
3.1 Unproductive euphorias
3.2 Hypochondriacal euphoria
3.3 Enthusiastic euphoria
3.4 Confabulatory euphoria
3.5 Non-participatory euphoria

and mania could be interrupted by symptomless intervals but could also switch to one another without interruption. In this Kraepelin did not, as was customary in psychiatry up to Pinell, use symptoms to differentiate manic-depressive insanity from dementia praecox. The principle of his classification instead was the prognosis.

Like Weikard, Karl Friedrich Flemming (1799–1880) in his book *Pathology and Therapy of Psychoses* foresaw in parts Kraepelin's dichotomy of endogenous psychoses. He distinguished between a primary mood disorder that he called deuteropathic psychosis and protopathic psychosis, which was primarily an intellectual deficiency (Flemming, 1844). Deuteropathic psychosis could have secondary effects on the intellect and protopathic psychosis could have secondary affective symptoms.

This discussion illustrates that the integration of affective diseases into a single nosological entity cannot be attributed primarily to any one researcher. It is merely the provisional conclusion of a development. Kraepelin's very simple but extremely pragmatic classification of endogenous psychoses into manic-depressive illness and dementia praecox therefore also had its forerunners.

The differentiated concept

The psychiatric school named after Carl Wernicke, Karl Kleist (1879–1960) and Karl Leonhard (1908–1988) continues to oppose the Kraepelinan system (Beckmann and Lanczik, 1990). Kleist was not able to prevail with his opinion that mania and depression are two different diseases (Kleist, 1953). Nevertheless Leonhard continued to stress the basic difference between bipolar and unipolar psychoses (Neele, 1949; Leonhard, 1962, 1972). He tried to validate this difference in terms of symptoms, genetics and prognosis. For example, Leonhard (1962) and von Trostorff (1968) found a lower hereditary factor among unipolar than bipolar affective psychoses.

The distinction between mania and depression had only been propagated through the works of Carlo Perris (1966) and Jules Angst (1966). In these writings unipolar manias were regarded as artefacts of the course of bipolar disorder (Angst, 1978). Perris and Angst each independently denied the unitary concept of manic-depressive psychosis and therefore supported Leonhard's idea. DSM-III and ICD-10 recently reconsidered these views.

According to Leonhard the difference between bipolar and unipolar affective psychoses is not the only basis for a differentiated classification. Leonhard proposed a fivefold division of endogenous psychoses, in which he separated manic-depressive illness, the monopolar phasic psychoses, the cycloid psychoses, unsystematic schizophrenia and systematic schizophrenia. Within these five groups he distinguished among subtypes with the same prognosis, heredity and therapeutic response. With the unipolar affective psychoses Leonhard differentiated between pure melancholy and mania, in which only the mood is pathologically changed and depressions and euphorias, which show an affective disorder plus psychomotor or paranoid symptoms. The basis for this division was Wernicke's separation of an affective melancholy with prominent pathological mood from depressive melancholy distinguished by marked psychomotor inhibition (Wernicke, 1906).

Leonhard therefore revived the separation between mania and melancholy that Kahlbaum presented with the terms dysthymia and hyperthymia (Leonhard, 1986; cf. Schmidt-Degenhard, 1983) and which had been given up since Kraepelin. With this classification Leonhard tried both to accommodate the prognostic principle of Kraepelin as well as apply Wernicke's differentiated description of psychotic syndromes.

Wernicke distinguished in his textbook of psychiatry (1906) five depressive syndromes that can be found in Leonhard's classification:

1. Melancholia agitata—Wernicke regarded this as a subform of anxiety psychosis. It was classified by Leonhard as an anxiety–happiness psychosis or harried depression.
2. Melancholia depressiva—this was distinguished by hypokinesis and amimia as an expression of abulia which with Leonhard corresponds to pure melancholia.
3. Melancholia affectiva—the Leonhard diagnosis of a pure melancholia is also contained in this term.
4. Melancholia hypochondria—the symptoms of this are described in the name and which Leonhard called hypochondriacal depression.
5. Melancholia attonita—this is identified by Wernicke (1906) and later by Leonhard (1979) as the akinetic pole of the motility psychoses.

From Wernicke's example it is again clear that the term melancholy was used for a heterogeneous nosological group, as it is today.

Leonhard, like Kraepelin, at first distinguished 16 different nosological entities among the affective psychoses (see Table II). Leonhard described 'pure' forms of phasic psychoses that in each episode offered a repeatedly similar picture. He compared these pure forms with a 'kaleidoscopic' psychopathological picture in the phasic psychoses, manic-depressive illness and the cycloid psychoses. In these descriptions Leonhard referred to Wernicke.

Kraepelin had also planned a finer subdivision beyond his dichotomy of endogenous psychoses into the affective psychoses and schizophrenia. This has remained largely unnoticed (see Table I). Only after the sixth edition of his famous textbook did he drop the independent status of his phenomenological subtypes.

Table II. The affective psychoses in
Kraepelin's system (1893).

1.	Deliria
1.1	Fever delirium
1.2	Intoxication delirium
2.	Acute states of exhaustion
2.1	Collapse delirium
2.2	Amentia
2.3	Dementia acuta
3.	Mania
4.	Melancholia
4.1	Melancholia simplex
4.2	Melancholia activa
4.3	Melancholia attonita
5.	Insanity
5.1	Hallucinatory insanity
5.3	Depressive insanity
6.	Periodic mental disorders
6.1	Delirious forms
6.2	Manic forms
6.3	Circular forms
6.4	Depressive forms
7.	Paranoia
7.1	Depressive paranoia
7.2	Expansive paranoia
8.	Psychic deterioration processes
8.1	Dementia praecox (hebephrenia)
8.2	Catatonia
8.3	Dementia paranoides
9.	Neuroses
10.	Chronic intoxications
11.	Dementia paralytica
12.	Acquired dementia
13.	Psychic development anomalies

From Kraepelin to ICD-10 and DSM-III-R

The Kraepelinian dichotomy of endogenous psychoses with emphasis only on prognosis therefore stands as a compromise between the differentiated concept of the Wernicke–Kleist–Leonhard school and the unitary concept that is connected with Chiarugi, Guislain, Zeller, Griesinger and Neumann. Eugen Bleuler

(1857–1939) took over the Kraepelinian dichotomy but rejected the exclusive emphasis on prognosis. He emphasized validation by symptomatology. Current classification systems like ICD-10 and DSM-III attempt to synthesize the prognostically oriented Kraepelinian classification scheme and the symptom-oriented Bleulerian classification order.

The Kraepelinian concept seems to have been so far confirmed by modern pharmacopsychiatry. However, in the initial description of the antidepressive effect of imipramine in 1957 (Kuhn, 1970) and the monoamine oxidase inhibitor iproniazid by Nathan Kline in 1958 (1970) Kraepelin's classification was put aside.

The summary of bipolar and unipolar forms of affective psychoses gained fundamental worldwide significance but also experienced a lot of contradiction. The question of manic-depressive illness as a nosological entity was and is posed as before. The reception of the Kraepelinian nosology in North American psychiatry determined nearly all international classification systems today. On the other hand, in France and Japan the Kraepelinian interpretation never completely took hold (Pichot, 1983, 1990).

The separation of nosological entities and subforms among endogenous psychoses has never stopped and has been encouraged, for example, by Kasanin's description of schizoaffective psychoses (Kasanin, 1933). Bleuler classified these as schizophrenia. Because of the considerable affective symptoms and the more favourable prognosis they were an affective disease according to Kraepelin.

Kleist (1953) pointed out this disagreement. He did not try, as Leonhard after him, to attribute these illnesses either to schizophrenia or manic-depressive illness but regarded them as separate forms. According to Leonhard's classification schizoaffective psychosis is one of the cycloid psychoses, suspicious depressions, or affect-laden schizophrenias. Present-day classification systems also accommodate this. ICD-9 and DSM-III cling to the dichotomy of endogenous psychoses as coined by Kraepelin, but in their newer editions they consider the discussion between Kasanin and Leonhard.

The authors of DSM-III also adopted a series of nosological terms which were suppressed in the Kraepelinian system and believed to be on the decline. Among these were melancholia, cyclothymia, dysthymia and affective psychoses.

Melancholy had only rarely been found in modern psychiatric literature since Kraeplin replaced the term in favour of depression. Melancholia described a form of psychosis only in Leonhard's system. Sigmund Freud (1856–1939) considered melancholy to be a result of disturbed early childhood development that reduced feelings of self-esteem. Hubertus Tellenbach used the term melancholy to describe a type of personality (typus melancholicus; Tellenbach, 1961). In DSM-III melancholia can be found as an operationally defined subtype of a major depressive disorder.

The term 'cyclothymia' also underwent changes in the past century. Kahlbaum presented the term cyclothymia as a milder form of mania circularis. Kurt Schneider (1887–1967) suggested cyclothymia as a synonym for manic-depressive illness (Schneider, 1980). At that time cyclothymia was not a generally accepted term, because it was often confused with a temperament following the typology of Ernst Kretschmer (1888–1963; Kretschmer, 1919, 1951; see also Glatzel, 1981, 1990). In DSM-III cyclothymia is a milder form of bipolar disorder.

The reintroduction of 'dysthymia' in the psychiatric vocabulary dates back to Flemming. However, he understood dysthymia to be an affective disorder that could present as a depressive, hypomanic or a bipolar syndrome (Flemming, 1844; cf. Lewis, 1933; Schmidt-Degenhard, 1983). Modern classification systems like DSM-III have also revived this term.

In 1911 Theodor Ziehen (1862–1950) introduced the title affective psychosis. For example, the German version of DSM-III has readopted this title for all psychoses that are distinguished by a considerable and lasting mood-disorder.

With ICD-10 and DSM-III-R we can again recognize the tendency towards a differentiated system. That is emphasized in the revival of almost forgotten nosological terms in the modern psychiatric vocabulary. We are justified in speaking of a trend in psychiatric nosology from increasing simplification back to further differentiation.

References

Ackerknecht EH (1985) *Kurze Geschichte der Pschiatrie.* Stuttgart: Enke.

Alexander FG and Selesnick T (1966) *The History of Psychiatry.* New York: Harper & Row.

Angst J (1966) *Zur Etiologie und Nosologie endogener depressier Psychosen.* Berlin: Springer.

Angst J (1978) The course of affective disorders. II. Typology of bipolar manic-depressive illness. *Arch Psychiatr Nervenkr* **226**, 65–73.

Aretaeus von Kappadocien (1828) In: Kuhn CG (ed.) *Medicorum graecorum opera*, Vol. XXIV, pp. 74–78. Leipzig.

Aretaeus of Cappadocia (1856) *The Extant Works of Aretaeus.* Adams F (ed.) London.

Baillarger JGF (1854a) Note sur un genre de folie dont les acces sont caractrises par deux periodes regulieres, l'une de depression et l'autre d'excitation. *Bull Acad Imp Med* **19**.

Baillarger JGF (1854b) De la folie a double forme. *Ann Med-Psychol Paris.*

Beckmann H and Lanczik F (eds) (1990) Leonhard classification of endogenous psychoses: Cycloid psychoses, differentiated nosology, differentiated therapy and historical aspects. *Psychopharmacology* (Suppl.), 4–6.

Berrios GE (1988) Melancholia and depression during the 19th century: Conceptual history. *Br J Psychiatry* **153**, 298–304.

Boerhaave H (1709) *Aphorismi de Cognoscendis et Curandis Morbis.* J. vander Linden: Lugduni Batavorum.

Brown J (1795) *The Elements of Medicine.* London.

Chiarugi V (1793) *Della pazzia in genere, e in specie*. Firenze.
Corpus Hippocraticum: Oevres completes d'hippocrate. Littre E (ed.) Paris, 1839–1861.
de Boor W (1953) *Psychiatrische Systematik. Ihre Entwicklung in Deutschland seit Kahlbam*. Berlin: Springer.
Esquirol E (1838) *Des Maladies Mentales*. Paris: Raillire.
Falret J (1851) *De la folie circulaire ou forme de la maladie mentale caracterisee par alternative reguliere de la manie et de la melancholie*. Paris.
Fischer-Homberger E (1968) *Das zirkulare Irresein*. Zurich: Juris.
Flashar H (1966) *Melancholie und Melancholiker in den medizinischen Theorien der Antike*. Berlin: Walter de Gruyter.
Flemming CF (1844) Uber Classification der Seelenstrungen. *Allg Zeitsch Psychiat* **1**, 97–103.
Freud S (1967) Traver und Melancholie. In: *Gesammelte Werke* (4th edn) Vol. 10. Frankfurt am Main: Fischer.
Galenus C (1821–1833) *Opera omnia*, Vol. VIII. Kuhn CG (ed.) Leipzig.
Glatzel J (1981) Zum Problem der Krankheitseinheiten in der Psychiatrie seit Jaspers. In: Burchard (ed.) *Psychopathologie*. Stuttgart: Schattauer.
Glatzel J (1990) Psychiatric diagnosis in the German-speaking countries. In: Sartorius N, Jablensky A, Regier DA, Burke JD and Hirschfeld RMA (eds) *Sources and Traditions of Classification in Psychiatry*. Toronto: Hogrefe & Huber.
Griesinger W (1845) *Die Pathologie und Therapie der psychischen Krankheiten* (1st edn). Stuttgart: Krabbe.
Guislain J (1833) *Traité sur les phrénopathies*. Bruxelles.
Guislain J (1852) *Lecons orales sur les Phrenopathies*. Gand.
Haslam J (1798) *Observations on Insanity*. London: Rivington.
Heiberg JL (1927) Geisteskrankheiten im klassischen Altertum. *Arch Psychiatr* **86**, 1–44.
Heinroth JC (1818) *Lehrbuch der Strungen des Seelenlebens*. Leipzig: Vogel.
Jaspers K (1913) *Allgemeine Psychopathologie*. Berlin: Springer.
Kahlbaum KL (1863) *Die Gruppirung der psychischen Krankheiten und die Eintheilung der Selenstorungen*. Danzig: Kafemann.
Kant I (1798) *Anthropologie*. Konigsberg.
Kasanin J (1933) The acute schizoaffective psychoses. *Am J Psychiatry* **90**, 97–126.
Kindt H (1980) *Katatonie. Ein Modell psychischer Krankheit*. Stuttgart.
Kleist K (1953) Die Gliederungen der neuropsychischen Erkrankungen. *Monatsschr Psychiatr Neurol*, 526–554.
Kline NS (1958) Clinical experience with iproniacid (Marsilid). *J Clin Exp Psychopathol* **19** (Suppl.): 72–78.
Kline NS (1970) Monoanine oxidase inhibitors: An unfinished picaresque tale. In: Ayd FJ and Blackwell B (eds) *Discoveries in Biological Psychiatry*, pp. 193–194. Philadelphia: Lippincott.
Kotsopoulos S (1986) Aretaeus the Cappadocian on mental illness. *Compr Psychiatry* **27**, 171–179.
Kraepelin E (1883) *Compendium der Psychiatrie*. Leipzig: Abel.
Kraepelin J (1889) *Psychiatrie* (3rd edn). Leipzig: Barth.
Kraepelin J (1893) *Psychiatrie* (4th edn). Leipzig: Barth.
Kraepelin J (1896) *Psychiatrie* (5th edn). Leipzig: Barth.
Kraepelin E (1899) *Pschiatrie* (6th edn). Leipzig: Barth.
Kretschmer E (1919) Gedanken zur Fortentwicklung der psychiatrischen Systemitik. *Z Ges Neurol Psychiat* **48**, 370–377.
Kretschmer E (1951) *Korperbau und Charakter* (20th edn). Berlin: Springer.

Kuhn R (1957) Uber die Behandlung depressiver Zustaende mit einem Iminodibenzylderivat (G 22355). *Schweiz Med Wschr* **36**, 1135–1140.

Kuhn R (1970) The imipramine story. In: Ayd FJ and Blackwell B (eds) *Discoveries in Biological Psychiatry*, pp. 205–217. Philadelphia: Lippincott.

Lanczik M (1989) Heinrich Neumann und seine Lehre von der Einheitspsychose. *Fundamenta Psychiatrica* **3**, 49–54.

Leibbrand W and Wettley A (1961) *Der Wahnsinn. Geschichte der abendlandischen Psychopathologie.* Freiburg: Alber.

Leonhard K (1979) *The Classification of Endogenous Psychoses* (5th edn) New York: Irvington.

Leonhard K (1986) *Aufteilung der endogenen Psychosen und ihre differenzierte Atiologie.* Berlin: Akademie.

Leonhard K, Korff L, Schulz H (1962) Temperament in families with monopolar and bipolar phasic psychoses. *Pschiatr Neurol* **143**, 316.

Lewis AJ (1934) Melancholia: historical review. *J Ment Sci* **80**, 1–3.

Maudsley H (1848) *The Physiology and Pathology of Mind.* London.

Neele E (1949) *Die phasischen Psychosen nach ihrem Erscheinungs- und Erbbild.* Leipzig.

Neumann H (1859) *Lehrbuch der Psychiatrie.* Erlangen: Enke.

Pauleikoff B (1983) *Das Menschenbild im Wandel der Zeit. Ideen-geschichte der Psychiatrie und klinischen Psychologie.* Hurtgenwald: Pressler.

Perris C (1966) A study of bipolar (manic-depressive) and unipolar recurrent depressive psychoses. *Acta psychiat Scand* (Suppl.), 194.

Pichot P (1983) *Ein Jahrhundert Psychiatrie.* Paris: Dacosta.

Pichot P (1990) The diagnosis and classification of mental disorders in the French-speaking countries: Background, current values and comparison with other classifications. In: Sartorius N, Regier DA, Burke JD and Hirschfeld RMA (eds) *Sources and Traditions of Classification in Psychiatry.* Toronto: Hogrefe & Huber.

Pinel Ph (1809) *Traits medico-philosophique sur l'alienation mentale ou la mania* (2nd edn) Paris.

Schmidt-Degenhard M (1983) *Melancholie und Depression.* Stuttgart: Kohlhammer.

Roccatagliata G (1983) *Le radici storiche della psicopatologia.* Naples: Liguori.

Schneider K (1980) *Klinische Psychopathologie* (13th edn) Stuttgart: Thieme.

Sedler MJ (1983) Falret's discovery: The origin of the concept of bipolar affective illness. *Am J Psychiatry* **130**, 1127–1133.

Teichmann G (1990) The influence of Karl Kleist on the nosology of Karl Leonhard. *Psychopathology* **23**, in press.

Tellenbach H (1961) *Melancholie.* Berlin: Springer.

Vliegen J (1980) *Die Einheitspsychose.* Stuttgart: Enke.

von Trostorff S (1968) Uber die hereditre Belastung bei den bipolaren und monopolaren phasischen Psychosen. *Schwiez Arch Neurol Neurochir Psychiatr* **102**, 235–243.

Walser H (1968) Melancholie aus medizingeschichtlicher Sicht. *Rev Ther* **25**, 17–21.

Weikard MA (1790) *Der Philosophische Arzt.* Frankfurt: Kornfeld.

Wernicke K (1906) *Grundriss der Psychiatrie* (3rd edn) Leipzig: Thieme.

Zeller EA (1838) *Vorwort und Zusatze zu L. Guislain, Abhandlung uber die Phrenopathien.* Stuttgart and Leipzig.

Ziehen Th (1911) *Psychiatrie* (4th edn). Leipzig: Hirzel.

2

The epidemiology of depressive disorders: national and international perspectives

A.L. Smith and M.M. Weissman

Introduction

Significant advances in systematic psychiatric diagnosis and case assessment occurred in the mid-1970s and were applied to epidemiological studies in the following decade. This chapter presents results from these studies in the USA, Puerto Rico, Canada, Italy, Korea and Taiwan. All studies used the Diagnostic Interview Schedule (DIS) and DSM-III criteria. These studies are described in greater detail in Table I. For the first time these surveys provide independent cross-national comparisons with data obtained by similar methods. We believe that these community survey data provide the most unbiased estimates of rates of illness because they avoid counting only those who have sought professional help. This review focuses on three major categories of depressive disorders: major depression, dysthymia and bipolar disorder.

Major (unipolar) depression

Table II shows the six-month, one-year and lifetime rates per hundred of major depression found in the community surveys. The largest of these was the Epidemiologic Catchment Area (ECA) study in the USA. The ECA study yielded a six-month rate per hundred of 2.2 and a one-year prevalence of 2.7. The annual rates were higher in Florence and New Zealand and lower in Taiwan.

The Diagnosis of Depression. Edited by J.P. Feighner and W.F. Boyer
© 1991 John Wiley & Sons Ltd

Table I. Epidemiological community surveys of psychiatric disorders using DSM–III.

Place	Year	N	Age (years)	Reference
USA–ECA	1980–83	18572	18+	Weissman *et al.* (1988a,
New Haven	1980	5034		1988b)
Baltimore	1981	3481		
St Louis	1981	3004		
Durham, NC	1982	3921		
Los Angeles	1983	3132		
Edmonton, Canada	1983	3258	18+	Bland *et al.* (1988a, 1988b, 1988c)
Puerto Rico	1984	1551	17–64	Canino *et al.* (1987)
Florence, Italy		693	18+	Faravelli *et al.* (1985)
Seoul, Korea	1984	5100	18–65	Lee *et al.* (1987)
Taiwan	1982	11004	18+	Hwu *et al.* (1989)
Urban		5005		
Small towns		3004		
Rural villages		2995		
New Zealand	1986	1498	18+	Joyce *et al.* (1990)

Table II. Rate per hundred of major depression.

	Six-month	One-year	Lifetime
USA–ECA	2.2	2.6	4.4
New Haven	2.8	3.4	5.8
Baltimore	1.7	1.9	2.9
St Louis	2.3	2.7	4.4
Durham, NC	1.5	1.7	3.5
Los Angeles	2.6	3.2	5.6
Edmonton, Canada	3.2	–	8.6
Puerto Rico	3.0	–	4.6
Florence, Italy	–	5.2	–
Seoul, Korea	–	–	3.4
Taiwan			
Urban	–	0.6	0.9
Small towns	–	1.1	1.7
Rural villages	–	0.8	1.0
New Zealand	5.3	5.3	12.6

The lifetime rate per hundred of major depression in the ECA was 4.4. This was considerably lower than the rate of 18 per hundred found in the 1975 New Haven study (Weissman and Myers, 1978). Most of the discrepancy may be due to the relatively limited probing for lifetime episodes allowed by the DIS (used in the ECA) compared with the Schedule for Affective Disorders and Schizophrenia (SADS, used in the New Haven study).

The lifetime rates in the ECA study are similar to Puerto Rico's (4.6) and Seoul's (3.4). The lifetime rates are considerably higher in New Zealand (12.6) and in Edmonton, Canada (8.6) but again lower in Taiwan.

Risk factors

Sex

An increased rate of major depression in women has been well documented in previous studies. Weissman and Klerman (1977, 1985) reviewed these studies more than ten years ago and concluded that this 'gender gap' was not simply due to women reporting distress or seeking help more than men. They pointed to the higher rates of major depression among women in community samples, which avoid the bias of counting only those who seek help.

Higher rates of major depression in women were found again in the community surveys reviewed in this chapter (Figure 1). The ratio of females to males was about 2 : 1.

This ratio is remarkably consistent across cultures. There is a suggestion of decreasing sex differences among persons born over the past 30–40 years, although this finding is controversial and warrants further study.

Secular changes

The ECA data show an unexpected decrease in the cumulative rates of major depression with age. Cumulative lifetime rates should increase with age or flatten out if older age is protective. However, the data show that persons born

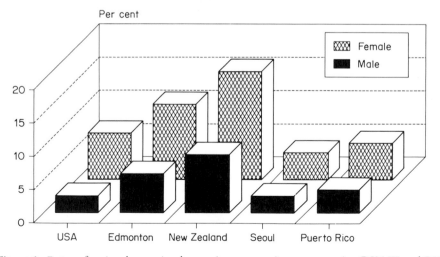

Figure 1. Rates of major depression by sex in community surveys using DSM-III and DIS diagnoses.

after the Second World War have a higher lifetime risk of major depression than those born before. This finding is remarkably consistent across cultures (Wickramaratne et al., 1989; Klerman and Weissman, 1989). The *drop* in lifetime risk with age is seen in studies from the USA (Klerman and Weissman, 1989), Germany (Wittchen, 1986), New Zealand (Joyce et al., 1990; Oakley-Brown et al., in press), Canada (Bland et al., 1988a; Newman et al., 1988) and perhaps urban Seoul (Lee et al., 1987).

There are arguments that these findings are due to an artefact, especially memory loss with age. However, several studies fail to report a diminishing recall hypothesis (Farrer et al., 1989; Lavori et al., 1987). This decreased rate with age is also not seen with dysthymic disorder, which should occur if a simple memory artefact was responsible.

Other possible explanations include selective mortality and/or institutionalization, selective migration, changing diagnostic criteria, threshold changes in reporting and bias of those interviewed. These and other questions of artefact are reviewed extensively elsewhere (Klerman and Weissman, 1980).

Two other possible reasons for these findings include a period effect and/or a birth cohort effect. A birth cohort effect refers to changing rates of an illness associated with when a person was born. A period effect refers to changing rates of an illness associated with when someone becomes ill. Ample evidence exists for *both* these effects, which are difficult to distinguish from each other.

Klerman and Weissman (1989) recognized a strong birth cohort effect and earlier age of onset of affective disorders in both cross-national community and large-scale family studies in the USA. Hagnell and coworkers (1986) conducted a 25-year longitudinal follow-up of 2500 inhabitants of Lundby, Sweden, between 1947 and 1975. They found an increased risk for depression in the cohorts born after 1937. Most pronounced, however, was a *ten*-fold increased risk for 20–39-year-old males during the period 1957–1972 compared with men of the same age in 1947–1957.

Lavori et al. (1987) reported evidence for both a post-1930 birth cohort effect and a powerful 1965–1975 period effect. Wickramaratne et al. (1989) closely analysed the ECA data and discovered a similar combination of birth cohort (especially 1935–1945) and period (1960–1975) effects. This latter period effect was most powerful in the 'at risk' birth cohort.

These findings are consistent with other widely recognized temporal trends associated with depression, such as increased alcoholism, drug abuse and suicide. All these have markedly increased, particularly among young males born since the mid-1950s.

Race/ethnicity
Overall, the similarities rather than differences among racial groups in rates of major depression in the ECA were most striking (Somervell et al., 1989). Puerto Rico did not significantly differ from the ECA, except for the absence of a birth

cohort effect (Canino *et al.*, 1987). On the other hand, the study in Taiwan (Hwu *et al.*, 1989) yielded a lower rate of major depression than in Western countries.

It is possible that this lower overall rate reflects a racial difference or that the Taiwanese selectively under-report some types of symptoms. The Taiwanese data do show lower overall rates of psychopathology than in the USA, but the most striking differences are between rates for specific diagnoses. Anxiety-related and psychophysiological disorders prevail in Taiwan, whereas substance abuse/dependence and major depression are the most common in the ECA study. This argues for a true racial differences in rates.

The Korean study found a total lifetime prevalence per hundred of 3.4. This is higher than Taiwan and comparable to the lower range of rates reported in the five-site ECA study. Like Taiwan, however, this rate was exceeded by anxiety-related disorders.

Socio-economic status (SES)
The ECA study found no association between SES and major depression. In contrast, the 1975 small community survey by Weissman and Myers (1978) found that current rates of major depression were higher among lower SES classes. Lifetime rates were higher among the upper classes. They hypothesized that this may have reflected greater persistence rather than frequency of depression among the presumably less well-treated lower classes. Although in the ECA study SES had little effect, the rates of major depression were lower among employed and/or financially independent persons. The unemployed and those on public assistance had a threefold increased risk of major depression. The causal direction is unclear, however, since those with major depression are less likely to be capable of obtaining or maintaining employment. Lack of employment, with or without public assistance, also poses psychological stress that could contribute to developing or maintaining major depression.

Urban/rural residents
The ECA study found significant but conflicting differences in urban versus rural rates of major depression. Durham (where rural areas were outlying and isolated from the urban centre) revealed more than twice the one-year prevalence in the urban compared to the rural areas. Puerto Rico also showed greater trends in six-month and lifetime rates among urbanites compared with rural dwellers.

The other ECA site that looked for this effect was St Louis, where the urban area is substantially larger than Durham and is connected via 'suburban sprawl' to the rural area. Here major depression was about 40% more prevalent in the rural area. Similarly, the Taiwanese 'small town' samples (compared to 'rural' or 'metropolitan') showed a trend toward higher rates of depression. This was markedly significant for females (Hwu *et al.*, 1989). Hwu hypothesized that small town residents in Taiwan experienced more instability, and therefore stress, because of a conflict in values between the industrialized metropolitan area and traditional rural areas.

Marital status

Marital status had a powerful effect on rates of major depression in the ECA study. Married and never-divorced persons had the lowest one-year prevalence; those divorced or, interestingly, 'cohabitating' had the highest rates. However, persons never married (or cohabitating) had rates of major depression relatively close to the low rates for the continuously married persons. People who were separated or divorced at the time of the study had two to three times the risk of current depression than those in any other status. Edmonton, Canada, reported similar findings. These data are also consistent with Brown and Harris's report (1978) that women with a close, confiding, reciprocal relationship are four times less likely to develop major depression under stress.

Family history

A possible genetic susceptibility to affective disorders has been suggested at least since the 1960s. Then the discovery of differential clustering for bipolar and unipolar illness prompted creation of these two categories. Studies in the following decade (Winokur and Morison, 1973; Winokur, 1979) showed a two to threefold increased risk of major depression among first-degree relatives of depressed probands compared to relatives of normal controls. Lifetime diagnosis of major depression is also more than twice as likely among first-degree relatives of bipolar probands compared with relatives of normal control (Freimer and Weissman, 1990; Gershon *et al.*, 1982). Twin studies using DSM-III or RDC criteria revealed 27% versus 12% concordance rates among monozygotic and dizygotic twins with major depression. Studies like these suggest genetic bases for major depression. They support some overlap as well as clear differentiation between major depression and bipolar disorder.

Dysthymia

Rates for dysthymia are limited to lifetime prevalence, since the disorder is chronic by definition (Table III). The ECA study's overall dysthymia rate was 3 per hundred. Almost half (42%) of those with dysthymia had also experienced an episode of major depression in their lifetime.

There exists considerable agreement among the limited studies of dysthymia on its prevalence. The overall prevalence in Edmonton, Canada, was 3.7 (Bland *et al.*, 1988c), which was much like the US rate. Korea reported a 2.2 rate per hundred, and Italy (Faravelli and Incerpi, 1985) a 2.3 rate per hundred (given as a one-year prevalence). Puerto Rico had the highest rate, 4.7, due to a very high prevalence among women. As with all the DSM-III disorders, Taiwan had the lowest rate per hundred.

Table III. Lifetime rates of dysthymic disorder.

	Rates per hundred
USA–ECA	3.0
New Haven	3.2
Baltimore	2.1
St Louis	3.8
Durham, NC	2.3
Los Angeles	4.2
Edmonton, Canada	3.7
Puerto Rico	4.7
Florence, Italy	2.3
Seoul, Korea	2.2
Taiwan	
Urban	0.9
Small towns	1.5
Rural villages	0.9

Risk factors

One might expect risk factors to be similar for dysthymia and major depression if the two disorders lie on a continuum of severity. In fact, there is evidence that some dysthymia may be incompletely resolved major depression or a prodromal state of major depression. However, in either of these cases there should be a higher prevalence of dysthymia than major depression, which is not so. Family studies support some overlap as well as distinction of these disorders. For more detail on the association between dysthymia and sociodemographic variables see Weissman *et al.* (1988a, 1988b).

Sex

The ECA study yielded about a 1.9 female to male ratio for dysthymia—slightly less than for major depression. As mentioned above, the female to male sex ratio was considerably higher in Puerto Rico, at 4.8.

Age

Unlike major depression, studies find that rates of dysthymia generally increase with age. This increased prevalence with age argues against a simple memory effect to explain the decreased rates of major depression with age, since one would expect the same effect for dysthymia.

Race

Race comparisons were made only in the ECA study where, as with major depression, there were no significant black/white differences. Hispanic rates exceeded whites and blacks, consistent with Puerto Rico's relatively high dysthymia rate. South Korea again reported rates roughly comparable to Western nations, whereas Taiwan had markedly lower figures.

SES
The ECA study found significantly higher dysthymia rates among 18–44-year-olds with less than $20 000 a year income, compared with those earning more. However, income had little effect in older groups (Weissman *et al.*, 1988b).

Marital status
The ECA study found that dysthymia was more prevalent among unmarried persons under age 65, with rates in the 45–65-year-old range double those of married persons. Edmonton also reported higher rates among the divorced or widowed, although by far the lowest rates were among those who never married.

Urban/rural
While the ECA has not examined data for differences in dysthymia in urban versus rural residents, Taiwan, Korea and Puerto Rico have. Urbanites in Puerto Rico had significantly higher rates of dysthymia compared with rural dwellers (5.5% versus 3.3%). City dwellers in Korea had a trend to higher rates (2.4% versus 1.9%). In Taiwan, on the other hand, urban and rural areas differed little.

Bipolar disorder

Table IV shows the published six-month annual and/or lifetime rates of bipolar disorder. The consistency is remarkable, especially since these rates are not adjusted for age or other demographic variables. The current and lifetime rates are close, which may reflect the chronic nature of bipolar disorder. The highest rates per hundred are found in Puerto Rico and the USA. Interestingly, this lifetime rate of about 1% is similar to the morbidity risk rates of 0.6 and 0.9% in industrialized nations previously extracted from studies using a variety of diagnostic methods (Boyd and Weissman, 1982).

Risk factors

Sex
No significant sex differences were found in studies reporting rate of bipolar disorder by sex (ECA, Puerto Rico, Edmonton, Taiwan). No mention is made of sex differences in the other published data.

Table IV. Rate per hundred of bipolar disorder.

	Six-month	One-year	Lifetime
USA–ECA	0.9	1.0	1.2
New Haven	1.1	1.3	1.6
Baltimore	0.9	0.9	1.2
St Louis	1.2	1.4	1.6
Durham, NC	0.6	0.6	0.7
Los Angeles	0.1	0.6	1.1
Edmonton, Canada	0.1	0.2	0.6
Puerto Rico	0.3	0	0.5
Florence, Italy	–	1.7	–
Seoul, Korea	–	–	0.4
Taiwan			
Urban	–	0.12	0.16
Small towns	–	0.03	0.07
Rural villages	–	0.1	0.1
New Zealand	–	–	–

Age of onset

Bipolar disorder has an earlier age of onset and narrower period of risk than the other depressive disorders. The ECA found a mean age of onset of 21 years. The Edmonton (Canada) study found a median age of onset in the late teens.

As with major depression there is evidence of significant birth cohort effects. The lifetime prevalence of bipolar disorder is apparently increasing in younger birth cohorts. Gershon *et al.* (1987) first observed increasing rates of mania as well as schizoaffective and unipolar illness among family members of affectively ill probands born after 1940. Lasch *et al.* (1990) recently reported an increasing prevalence of bipolar disorder in Caucasians born since 1935.

SES

Several earlier studies found an increased prevalence of bipolar disorder in the higher socio-economic groups (Farris and Dunham, 1967; Weissman and Myers, 1978; Krauthammer and Klerman, 1979). However, the recent community surveys do not support this. The ECA, which had a considerably larger and more diverse patient sample than these earlier studies, found no differential prevalence within occupation, income or education categories. Although the Puerto Rico study did not examine socio-economic class per se, it did include education level and found no significant differences for bipolar illness (Canino *et al.*, 1987).

Race

There is no evidence from the ECA study that the rates of bipolar disorder are different between whites and blacks. As with SES, previous studies had suggested such a difference might exist (Somervell *et al.*, 1989). Both the South Korean and Taiwanese community surveys reported the lowest prevalence rates for bipolar disorder.

Marital status
The ECA data clearly show that married persons have significantly lower rates of bipolar illness than people who are divorced or never married. There was also an increased rate of bipolar disorder among multiply divorced persons, which may represent a consequence of the illness.

Geographical area
Bipolar disorder appears to be more common in urban areas. The St Louis and Durham, NC, ECA sites sampled rural as well as urban areas and found significantly higher one-year rates of bipolar disorder in urban areas. A similar trend was found in Puerto Rico (Canino *et al.*, 1987) and Taiwan (Hwu *et al.*, 1989).

Family history
The familial nature of bipolar illness has been well established and should be included as an important risk factor. Bipolar disorder is consistently increased in first-degree relatives of bipolar patients compared with relatives of either patients with major depression or normal controls. Cyclothymia, hyperthymia and major depression are also significantly elevated in relatives of bipolar patients.

Future directions

Wing and a group of international investigators have developed a new diagnostic instrument known as Schedules for Clinical Assessment in Neuropsychiatry (SCAN) (Wing *et al.*, 1990). This system is being tested with the aim of developing a comprehensive procedure for clinical examination that can also generate many of the diagnoses in the *International Classification of Diseases* (10th edition) and DSM-III-R.

In a parallel development, Robins *et al.* (1988) have developed the Composite International Diagnostic Interview (CIDI). The CIDI is based on the National Institute of Mental Health Diagnostic Interview Schedule. The interview is modified for international use and has adopted certain features of the ninth edition of the Present State Examination (PSE-9).

The two instruments are complementary in that the CIDI is designed for use in large community surveys by lay interviewers, whereas SCAN can only be fully used by professionals. The availability of two such diagnostic tools that bridge the major classification system will facilitate cross-national studies.

Methods applicable to children are also being field tested in several US centres in preparation for a large epidemiological study. When the next revision of this volume occurs, the first high-quality data on the psychiatric epidemiology of children should be available.

References

Akiskal HS, Downs J, Jordan P *et al.* (1985) Affective disorders in referred children and younger siblings of manic depressives. *Arch Gen Psychiatry* **42**, 996–1003.

American Psychiatric Association (1987) *Diagnostic and Statistical Manual of Mental Disorders DSM-III* (3rd edn, revised). Washington, DC: American Psychiatric Association Press.

Bagley C (1973) Occupational status and symptoms of depression. *Soc Sci Med* **7**, 327–339.

Bland RC, Newman SC, Orn H (1988a) Period prevalence of psychiatric disorders in Edmonton. *Acta Psychiatr Scand* **77**, 33–42.

Bland RC, Newman SC, Orn H (1988b) Age of onset of psychiatric disorders. *Acta Psychiatr Scand* **77**, 43–49.

Bland RC, Orn H, Newman SC (1988c) Lifetime prevalence of psychiatric disorders in Edmonton. *Acta Psychiatr Scand* **77**, 24–32.

Blazer D, Williams CD (1980) Epidemiology of dysphoria and depression in an elderly population. *Am J Psychiatry* **137**, 439–444.

Boyd JH, Weissman MM (1982) Epidemiology. In: Paykel ES (ed.) *Handbook of Affective Disorders*, pp. 109–125. Edinburgh: Churchill Livingstone.

Brown GW, Harris TO (1978) *Social Origins of Depression: A Study of Psychiatric Disorder in Women.* London: Tavistock.

Burnam MA, Hough RL, Escobar JI, Karno M (1987) Six-month prevalence of specific psychiatric disorders among Mexican Americans and Non-hispanic whites in Los Angeles. *Arch Gen Psychiatry* **44**, 687–691.

Canino GJ, Bird HR, Shrout PE *et al.* (1987) The prevalence of specific psychiatric disorders in Puerto Rico. *Arch Gen Psychiatry* **44**, 727–735.

Charney EA, Weissman MM (1988) Epidemiology of depressive and manic syndromes. In: Georgotas A and Carcro R (eds) *Depression and Mania*, pp. 45–74. New York: Elsevier.

Clayton PJ (1981) The epidemiology of bipolar affective disorder. *Compr Psychiatry* **22**, 31–41.

Cooper JE, Kendell RE, Gurland BJ *et al.* (1972) *Psychiatric Diagnosis in New York and London: A Comparative Study of Mental Hospital Admissions* (Maudsley Monograph No. 22). London: Oxford University Press.

Dohrenwend BP, Dohrenwend BS (1982) Perspectives on the past and future of psychiatric epidemiology. *Am J Public Health* **72**, 1271–1277.

Eaton WW, Kramer M, Anthony JC *et al.* (1989) The incidence of specific DIS/DSM-III mental disorders. Data from the NIMH Epidemiologic Catchment Area Program. *Acta Psychiatr Scand* **79**, 163–178.

Faravelli C, Incerpi G (1985) Epidemiology of affective disorders in Florence. *Acta Psychiatr Scand* **72**, 331–333.

Faris REL, Dunham HW (1967) *Mental Disorders in Urban Areas: An Ecological Study of Schizophrenia and Other Psychoses.* Chicago: University of Chicago Press.

Farrer LA, Florio LP, Bruce ML *et al.* (1989) Reliability and consistency of self-reported age at onset of major depression. *J Psychiatr Res* **23**, 35–47.

Feighner JP, Robins E, Guze SB *et al.* (1972) Diagnostic criteria for use in psychiatric research. *Arch Gen Psychiatry* **26**, 57–63.

Freimer N, Weissman MM (1990) The genetics of affective disorder. In: Deutsch SI, Weizman A, Weizman R (eds) *Application of Basic Neuroscience to Child Psychiatry*, pp. 285–296. New York: Plenum.

Gammon GD, John K, Rothblum ED *et al.* (1983) Use of a structured diagnostic interview to identify bipolar disorder in adolescent inpatients: Frequency and manifestations of the disorder. *Am J Psychiatry* **140**, 543–547.

Gershon EC, Hamovit J, Guroff JJ *et al.* (1982) A family study of schizoaffective bipolar I, bipolar II, unipolar, and normal control probands. *Arch Gen Psychiatry* **39**, 1157–1167.

Gershon E, Hamovit J, Gurroff J *et al.* (1987) Birth-cohort changes in manic and depressive disorders in relatives of bipolar and schizoaffective patients. *Arch Gen Psychiatry* **44**, 314–319.

Hagnell O (1986) The 25-year follow-up of the Lundby study: Incidence and risk of alcoholism, depression, and disorders of the senium. In: Barret R (ed.) *Mental Disorders in the Community: Findings from Psychiatric Epidemiology.* New York/London: Guildford Press.

Hollingshead AB, Redlich FD (1958) *Social Class and Mental Illness.* New York: Wiley.

Hwu H-G, Yeh E-K, Chang L-Y (1989) Prevalence of psychiatric disorders in Taiwan defined by the Chinese Diagnostic Interview Schedule. *Acta Psychiatr Scand* **79**, 136–147.

Joyce PR, Oakley-Browne MA, Wells JE *et al.* (1990) Birth cohort trends in major depression: Increasing rates and earlier onset in New Zealand. *J Affect Disord* **18**, 83–90.

Karno M, Hough RL, Burnam MA *et al.* (1987) Lifetime prevalence of specific psychiatric disorders among Mexican Americans and non-Hispanic whites in Los Angeles. *Arch Gen Psychiatry* **44**, 695–701.

Karno M, Golding JM, Burnam MA *et al.* (1989) Anxiety disorders among Mexican Americans and non-Hispanic whites in Los Angeles. *J Nerv Ment Dis* **177**, 202–209.

Klerman GL (1980) Overview of affective disorders. In: Kaplan HJ, Freedman AM, Sadock BJ (eds) *Comprehensive Textbook of Psychiatry* (3rd edn). Baltimore: Williams & Wilkins.

Klerman GL, Weissman MM (1989) Increasing rates of depression. *JAMA* **261**, 2229–2235.

Kraepelin E (1921) *Manic Depressive Insanity and Paranoia.* Edinburgh: Livingstone.

Krauthammer C, Klerman GL (1979) The epidemiology of mania. In: Shopsin B (ed.) *Manic Illness*, pp. 11–28. New York: Raven Press.

Lasch K, Weissman MM, Wickramaratne PJ, Bruce ML (1990) Birth cohort changes in the rates of mania. *Psychiatry Res* **33**, 31-37.

Lavori PW, Klerman GL, Keller MB *et al.* (1987) Age–period–cohort analysis of secular trends in onset of major depression: Findings in siblings of patients with major affective disorder. *J Psychiatr Res* **21**, 23–36.

Lee C-K, Han J-H, Choi J-O (1987) The epidemiological study of mental disorders in Korea (IX): Alcoholism, anxiety and depression. *Seoul J Psychiatry* **12**, 183–191.

Leighton DC, Harding JS, Macklin DB *et al.* (1963) *The Character of Danger.* New York: Basic Books.

Loranger AW, Levine PM (1978) Age at onset of bipolar affective illness. *Arch Gen Psychiatry* **35**, 1345–1348.

Myers JK, Weissman MM (1980) Screening for depression in a community sample: The use of a self-report scale to detect the depressive syndrome. *Am J Psychiatry* **137**, 1081–1084.

Newman SC, Bland RC, Orn H (1988) Morbidity risk of psychiatric disorders. *Acta Psychiatr Scand* **77**, 50–56.

Oakley-Browne MA, Joyce PR, Wells JE *et al.* (1989) Christchurch Psychiatric Epidemiology Study Part II: Six-month and other period prevalences of specific psychiatric disorders. *Aust NZ J Psychiatry*, **23**, 327–340.

Orley J, Wing JK (1979) Psychiatric disorders in two African villages. *Arch Gen Psychiatry* **36**, 513–520.

Pasaminick B, Roberts DW, Lemkau PV, Krieger DE (1986) A survey of mental disease in an urban population. *Am J Public Health* **47**, 923–929.

Perris C (1966) A study of bipolar (manic-depressive) and unipolar recurrent depressive psychoses. *Acta Psychiatr Scand* (Suppl.), 194.

Regier DA, Myers JK, Kramer M (1984) The NIMH Epidemiologic Catchment Area Program: Historical context, major objectives, and study population characteristics. *Arch Gen Psychiatry* **41**, 934–941.

Robins LN, Helzer JE, Croughan J, Ratcliff KS (1981) National Institute of Mental Health Diagnostic Interview Schedule. *Arch Gen Psychiatry* **38**, 381–389.

Robins LN, Wing J, Wittchen HU *et al.* (1988) The composite international diagnostic interview: An epidemiologic instrument suitable for use in conjunction with different diagnostic systems and in different cultures. *Arch Gen Psychiatry* **45**, 1069–1077.

Somervell PD, Leaf PJ, Weissman MM *et al* (1989) The prevalence of major depression in black and white adults in five United States communities. *Am J Epidemiol* **130**, 725–735.

Spitzer RL, Endicott J, Robins E (1978) *Research Diagnostic Criteria*. New York: Biometrics Research Division, Evaluation Section, New York State Psychiatry Institute.

Srole L, Langner TS, Michael ST (1962) *Mental Health in the Metropolis*. New York: McGraw-Hill.

Torgersen S (1986) Genetic factors in moderately severe and mild affective disorders. *Arch Gen Psychiatry* **43**, 222–226.

Weissman MM, Klerman GL (1977) Sex differences in the epidemiology of depression. *Arch Gen Psychiatry* **34**, 98–111.

Weissman MM, Klerman GL (1978) Epidemiology of mental disorders: Emerging trends in the US. *Arch Gen Psychiatry* **35**, 705–712.

Weissman MM, Klerman GL (1985) Gender and depression. *Trends Neurosci* **8**, 416–420.

Weissman MM, Myers JK (1978) Affective disorders in a US urban community. *Arch Gen Psychiatry* **35**, 1304–1311.

Weissman MM, Leaf PJ, Tischler GL *et al.* (1988a) Affective disorders in five United States communities. *Psychol Med* **18**, 141–153.

Weissman MM, Leaf PJ, Bruce ML, Florio L (1988b) The epidemiology of dysthymia in five communities: Rates, risks, comorbidity, and treatment. *Am J Psychiatry* **145**, 815–819.

Weissman MM, Bruce ML, Leaf PJ (1991) Affective disorders: In: Robins L, Regier D (eds) *Affective Disorders*, pp. 53–80. New York: Free Press.

Welner A, Marten S, Wochnick E *et al.* (1979) Psychiatric disorders among professional women. *Arch Gen Psychiatry* **36**, 169–173.

Wickramaratne PJ, Weissman MM, Leaf PJ, Holford TR (1989) Age, period and cohort effects on the risk of major depression: Results from five United States communities. *J Clin Epidemiol* **42**, 333–343.

Williams DH (1986) The epidemiology of mental illness in Afro-Americans. *Hosp Community Psychiatry* **37**, 42–49.

Wing JK, Cooper JE, Sartorius N (1974) *Measurement and Classification of Psychiatric Symptoms: An Instructional Manual for the PSE and CATEGO Program.* New York: Cambridge University Press.

Wing JK, Mann SA, Leff JP, Nixon JM (1978) The concept of 'case' in psychiatric population surveys. *Psychol Med* **8**, 203–217.

Wing JK, Babor T, Brugha T *et al.* (1990) SCAN: Schedules for clinical assessment in neuropsychiatry. *Arch Gen Psychiatry* **47**, 589–592.

Winokur G (1979) Unipolar depression: Is it divisible into autonomous subtypes? *Arch Gen Psychiatry* **36**, 47–52.

Winokur G, Morrison J (1973) The Iowa 500: Follow-up of 225 depressives. *Br J Psychiatry* **123**, 543–548.

Winokur GW, Clayton PJ, Reich T (1969) *Manic Depressive Illness.* St Louis: Mosby.

Wittchen HU (1986) Contribution of epidemiological data to the classification of anxiety disorders. In: Hand I, Wittchen HU (eds) *Panic Phobias*, pp. 18–27. Berlin: Springer.

Woodruff RA, Robins LN, Winokur G, Reich T (1971) Manic depressive illness and social achievement. *Acta Psychiatr Scand* **47**, 237–249.

World Health Organization (1973) *Schizophrenia: Report of an International Pilot Study.* Geneva: WHO.

3

The classification of depressive disorders in the tenth revision of the International Classification of Diseases (ICD-10)

N. Sartorius

One of the constitutional functions of the World Health Organization (WHO) is 'to establish and revise as necessary international nomenclatures of diseases, of causes of death and of public health practices'. The organization has prepared proposals for the last five revisions of the International Classification of Diseases (ICD). The most recent revision, the tenth, was submitted to the World Health Assembly—the decision-making organ of the WHO composed of representatives from its 166 member states—and adopted in May 1990. It will, however, enter into use on the 1st January 1993. The two years will be used to translate texts, prepare training material, reprogramme statistical and allied systems, write instructions for medical records librarians, and similar tasks.

ICD-10 has 22 chapters, each dealing with a group of conditions which have to be classified and reported to public health authorities. The chapters provide a classificatory structure for groups of diseases or syndromes, causes of death, reasons for contact with health services and other health information. The chapter dealing with mental disorders is entitled 'Mental and Behavioural Disorders (including disorders of psychological development)'. It is the only one which has brief definitions for each of the categories of the classification.

This exception was made for the first time in the eighth revision of the ICD. It resulted from a recommendation by the international group of experts who

The Diagnosis of Depression. Edited by J.P. Feighner and W.F. Boyer
© 1991 John Wiley & Sons Ltd

participated in the WHO programme on standardization of psychiatric diagnosis, classification and statistics (Sartorius, 1976; Kramer *et al.*, 1979). This
programme was launched in the early 1960s. It became obvious then that
comparison of data and collaborative projects in psychiatry could not be done
because of significant differences in the classificatory systems in different countries and various interpretations of the same diagnostic labels (Stengel, 1959).
The programme brought together leading psychiatrists, public health experts
and statisticians in different countries and lasted for some nine years. A core
group of experts met each year to review the diagnosis and classification of a
group of diseases. Each time they met in a different part of the world, together
with a larger group of psychiatrists and other experts interested in classification
from the host and neighbouring countries whom WHO invited to join the core
group in discussions. The group as a whole reviewed available literature, conducted joint ratings of videotaped and audiotaped interviews with patients,
carried out diagnostic exercises using written case histories and made proposals
about the classification of a group of disorders. This material was used to
produce proposals for the classification of mental disorders which were to be
included in the eighth revision of the ICD.

The next few years witnessed a worldwide reawakening of interest in the
classification of mental disorders. This was stimulated to a large extent by an
upsurge of research, particularly on psychopharmacological treatment. This
interest was reflected in the production of operational research criteria
(Feighner *et al.*, 1972) and numerous national guidelines for classification (e.g.
in France, India and the USSR). The International Classification of Diseases
meanwhile passed through its ninth revision. This contained an almost un-
changed classification of mental disorders, thus following the recommendation
of several WHO advisory groups that major changes in the ICD should be
introduced only on the basis of significant new evidence about mental disorders. Such evidence was, however, not present when the ninth revision of the
ICD was being finalized.

After the ninth revision of the ICD came into force the American Psychiatric
Association (APA) developed operational criteria to accompany the third revision of its Diagnostic and Statistical Manual (DSM-III). The fact that specific
criteria were provided for each of the categories contributed to a significant
change of attitude towards diagnosis and classification. Also, it became obvious
that it is possible to have a useful debate about a diagnostic concept once it is
sufficiently clearly defined. The clear statements about the boundary of categories were not to everyone's liking. Unprecedented debates followed the publication of DSM-III, eventually leading to a better understanding of the
classification, its limitations and advantages.

The experience gained in the production of APA's DSM-III and in the production of other national classifications was valuable. It aided the consultations
which developed proposals for the classification of mental disorders in the

tenth revision of the ICD. These were developed in what is undoubtedly the largest international collaborative programme ever undertaken in psychiatry. More than 120 centres in some 40 countries participated in this work over the years.

The programme started by a systematic examination of the available evidence about classification and diagnosis by groups of experts from different countries. These groups produced specific recommendations which were brought to an international advisory group and subsequently presented to a conference (WHO/ADAMHA, 1985).

The conference reviewed the proposals and made specific recommendations about further work. These dealt with the production of instruments for the standardized assessment of mental states in epidemiological and clinical studies (Wing *et al.*, 1990; Robins *et al.*, 1988; Loranger *et al.*, in press) and the development of a lexicon of psychiatric terms, with priorities for further research, and with ways to improve training in the use of the classification.

This conference—and the meetings of the groups that preceded it—were organized within an international programme on diagnosis and classification carried out in collaboration with the US Alcohol, Drug Abuse and Mental Health Administration (Sartorius *et al.*, 1984).

The programme to produce the proposals for ICD-10 used a different strategy from those employed in the development of national classifications. This strategy had several main tenets:

1. The classification will be produced in several versions for different types of users. As a consequence the ICD proposals were produced in:
   (a) a version for use by clinicians, formulated in a language with which clinicians are familiar and allowing a flexibility of categorization likely to be useful in clinical work;
   (b) a version for researchers;
   (c) a version for use in primary health care, accompanied by guidelines for management;
   (d) a multi-axial presentation of the classification using axes of clinical syndrome, environmental factors and disability;
   (e) a version for inclusion into the main body of the ICD containing brief definitions for each of the categories of the classification.

These versions of the classification are fully compatible but differ in the amount of detail provided and in the style used in the description of the categories (see also Appendix 1).

2. The proposals for the classification will be produced in as many languages as possible *at the same time*. The previous method of developing a classification in a language and then translating it into others after it has been tested in the source language version led to considerable problems. Some of the

concepts and formulations did not have corresponding words in other languages and were so foreign to the users that they refused to use it. Worse still, translated versions were sometimes treated as if they were equivalent, thus producing misleading results.

3. The proposals for the classification will be field tested and discussed with as many experts as possible. These tests and discussions will involve both academic psychiatrists and practitioners in the field of psychiatry.

4. Close collaboration will be maintained with those producing national classifications (e.g. the committee involved in the production of DSM-IV) and experts with a special interest in the classification of a particular group of disorders (e.g. sleep disorders).

5. In order to ensure standardization of instruments and their agreement with the classification, work on the internationally applicable assessment instruments will be conducted in congruence with the development of the classification. The instruments will include items relevant for the classification, and the results of studies to test the instruments will be considered in the formulation of the diagnostic criteria.

6. The classification of the mental disorders will be carefully articulated with the other classifications in the ICD family of classifications—e.g. the classification of disability and the classification of reasons for contact with health services.

The strategy was so far successful. A set of brief definitions for use in conjunction with the main body of ICD-10 has been drafted and reviewed by experts in many countries. It was also debated and further improved after a series of discussions with various non-governmental organizations and professional associations (e.g. and in particular the World Psychiatric Association). This version was accepted by the World Health Assembly and will be used as part of the official reporting system in all the many WHO member states which use the ICD.

A set of clinical guidelines has also been produced for each of the categories in the classification. These guidelines briefly define the conditions, provide instructions for diagnosis and differential diagnosis, list synonyms and inclusion terms for each of the categories and advise users where to place different diagnoses. The clinical guidelines were produced in language-equivalent versions in more than 20 countries. They were then assessed in a series of trials, using case histories and joint rating exercises in live and videotaped interviews (Burke, 1988). In addition to assessing the reliability between raters these tests obtained the views of clinicians about the goodness of fit between the classification and the clinical material. The tests were carried out in field research centres coordinated by Field Trial Coordinating Centres. Each of these worked with a group of centres using the same language or sharing the same diagnostic tradition (Sartorius et al., 1988).

The results of the field tests were encouraging. The clinicians found the guidelines useful, applicable to their work and covering most of the diagnostic problems adequately. Satisfactory reliability of diagnostic assessment was achieved in all the groups of centres and for most groups of diseases. Numerous specific comments received in the field research were incorporated in the guidelines and were then further tested. This process is completed and the guidelines are in print.

The tests of the ICD Diagnostic Criteria for Research began in 1990 and will be completed late in 1991. The tests of the multi-axial version of ICD-10 and the primary health care version will be tested in 1991 and 1992. The diagnostic instruments that accompany the classification have also been developed sufficiently to be released in a 'frozen' version. These will be revised once results of further field tests and feedback from users are available.

All of the above comments are directly relevant to the classification of depressive illness in ICD-10. This group of disorders has been significantly recast from the ninth to the tenth revision so it was particularly important to carry out the tests just described. On the basis of the information obtained in the tests and in the many consultations described above the disorders in which the depressive syndrome is predominant in ICD-10 are classified as follows:

Chapter V—Mental and Behavioural Disorders

F06.3	*Organic mood (affective) disorders*
	.31 Organic bipolar disorder
	.32 Organic depressive disorder
	.33 Organic mixed affective disorder
F10-F19	*Mental and behavioural disorders due to psychoactive substance use*
	Flx.54 Psychotic disorder, predominantly depressive symptoms
	Flx.72 Residual affective disorder
F25.1	*Schizoaffective disorder, depressive type*
	.10 Moderate severity
	.11 Severe
F31	*Bipolar affective disorder*
F31.3	Current episode moderate or mild depression
	.30 without somatic symptoms
	.31 with somatic symptoms
F31.4	Current episode severe depression without psychotic symptoms
F31.5	Current episode severe depression with psychotic symptoms
F31.6	Current episode mixed
F31.7	Currently in remission
F31.8	Other, including recurrent manic episodes
F31.9	Bipolar affective disorder, unspecified

F32	*Depressive episodes*
F32.0	Mild depressive episode
	.00 without somatic symptoms
	.01 with somatic symptoms
F32.1	Moderate depressive episode
	.10 without somatic symptoms
	.11 with somatic symptoms
F32.2	Severe depressive episode without psychotic symptoms
F32.3	Severe depressive episode with psychotic symptoms
F32.8	Other
F32.9	Depressive episode, unspecified
F33	*Recurrent depressive disorder*
F33.0	Current episode mild
	.00 without somatic symptoms
	.01 with somatic symptoms
F33.1	Current episode moderate
	.10 without somatic symptoms
	.11 with somatic symptoms
F33.2	Current episode severe without psychotic symptoms
F33.3	Current episode severe with psychotic symptoms
F33.4	Currently in remission
F33.8	Other
F33.9	Recurrent depressive disorder, unspecified
F34	*Persistent mood (affective) disorders*
F34.0	Cyclothymia
F34.1	Dysthymia
F34.8	Other
F34.9	Persistent mood (affective) disorder, unspecified
F38	*Other mood (affective) disorders*
F38.0	Other single mood (affective) disorders
	.00 mixed affective episode
F38.1	Other recurrent mood (affective) disorders
	.10 recurrent brief depressive disorder
F38.8	Other specified
F39	*Unspecified mood (affective) disorder*
F41	*Other anxiety disorders*
F41.2	Mixed anxiety and depressive disorder
F43	*Reaction to severe stress, and adjustment disorders*
F43.2	Adjustment disorders
	.20 brief depressive reaction
	.21 prolonged depressive reaction
	.22 mixed anxiety and depressive reaction
F92	*Mixed disorders of conduct and emotions*
F92.0	Depressive conduct disorder

Several categories on this list deserve a brief comment. The affective disorders due to substance abuse are new in the classification. They were added so that the classification of drug abuse problems can give sufficient information about the type of drug abused *and* the clinical syndromes which resulted. The finer subdivisions of the depressive disorders, e.g. in F31 and F32, became possible because of a significant—threefold—increase of categories reserved for mental disorders from the ninth to the tenth revision. This increase was made possible by the introduction of alphanumeric codes in ICD-10.

The category of mixed anxiety and depression (F41.2) has been introduced—in spite of the rule to avoid double syndrome coding—because a significant number of studies (particularly from general health services surveys) showed that this combination category occurs frequently and needs to be classifiable on its own. Once sufficient data are available it may become possible to classify these conditions differently.

As mentioned earlier, each of the categories has a clinical description, a set of research criteria and a brief definition. Examples of these three types of descriptions are given in the Appendix.

The field tests of the diagnostic criteria for research, which have just begun, will help to answer a series of important questions. First, they will provide information about the inter-rater reliability of experts using the classification. Second, they will test the cross-cultural acceptability of the criteria. Third, they will help construct the assessment instruments necessary to acquire data about the symptoms relevant to the diagnosis. Fourth, they will help construct algorithms to convert symptoms into criteria and diagnoses and to classify diagnoses into categories. Fifth, they should help to resolve several epistemological questions which remain in spite of the mass of data about classification and diagnosis.

Three examples of such epistemological questions can be given. The first is that of ponderation (weighting) of criteria. At present most diagnostic categories assume that the various criteria are of similar diagnostic significance. Clinicians, however, know that this is not so and often find it difficult to accept the recommendations contained in the classification. At present there is no satisfactory and generally accepted method to help in the ponderation of criteria; nor is it clear what would be the best way to produce one.

The second epistemological question is the utilization of concepts and classificatory principles based on a particular theory in a classification that is based on a different theory. Classifications based on the similarity of syndromes are difficult to convert into classifications based on a particular, e.g. hierarchical, theory of mental functioning. At present a one-to-one correspondence of categories is possible and serves the immediate purpose of translating results from one system into another. It is, however, difficult to carry this correspondence to the finer subdivisions without contradictions.

The third important epistemological question is the weighting of criteria for different sociodemographic patient groups. The importance of individual criteria may be different, for example, in women and men. It is also possible to imagine that different clusters of criteria should be used to diagnose a mental disorder in different population groups.

Further research will provide data which may allow the formulation of more adequate classifications, but the process cannot end there. In the past WHO produced major revisions of the International Classification of Diseases at regular intervals. The tenth revision is the most recent. It is also probably the last major revision. Modern information technology may allow modification of the classification in less paroxysmal and drastic steps; it will make it possible to introduce changes reflecting the findings of good research as they become available without having to wait ten or more years for the next revision. This change of strategy is particularly important in the case of affective disorders because we are currently acquiring so much new and important information that it is very likely that changes of their classification will become scientifically justified in the near future.

APPENDIX*

F32 depressive episodes—clinical diagnostic guidelines

F3   Mood (affective) disorders: introduction
The relationship between the aetiology, symptoms, underlying biochemical processes, response to treatment and outcome of affective disorders are not yet sufficiently understood to allow their classification in a way which is likely to meet with universal approval. Nevertheless a classification must be attempted, and the one presented here is put forward in the hope that it will at least be acceptable, since it is the result of widespread consultation.

In these disorders, the fundamental disturbance is a change in mood or affect, usually to depression (with or without associated anxiety), or to elation. This mood change is usually accompanied by a change in the overall level of activity and most of the other symptoms are either secondary to, or easily understood in the context of these changes in mood and activity. Most of these disorders tend to be recurrent and the onset of individual episodes is often related to stressful events or situations. This section deals with mood disorders in all age groups; those arising in childhood and adolescence should therefore be coded here.

The main criteria by which the affective disorders have been divided have been chosen for practical reasons in that they allow common clinical disorders to be easily identified; single episodes have been distinguished from bipolar

---

* Copyright in these extracts, and the texts from which they are reproduced, is held by the World Health Organization.

and other multiple episode disorders because substantial proportions of patients have only one episode of illness, and severity is given prominence because of implications for treatment and different levels of service provision. It is acknowledged that the symptoms referred to here as 'somatic' could also have been called 'melancholic', 'vital', 'biological' or 'endogenomorphic', and that the scientific status of this syndrome is in any case somewhat questionable. Nevertheless, this syndrome has been included because of a widespread international clinical interest in its survival. It is hoped that the result will be a similarly widespread critical appraisal of its usefulness. The classification is arranged so that this somatic syndrome can be recorded by those who so wish, but can also be ignored without loss of any other information.

How to make distinctions between different grades of severity remains a problem; the three grades of mild, moderate and severe have been specified here because many clinicians wish to have them available.

F32   Depressive episodes

In typical episodes of all three varieties described below (mild (F32.0), moderate (F32.1) and severe (F32.2 and .3)), the subject usually suffers from depressed mood, los of interest and enjoyment, and reduction of energy leading to increased fatigability and diminished activity. Marked tiredness after only slight effort is common. Other common symptoms are (i) reduced concentration and attention; (ii) reduced self-esteem and self-confidence; (iii) ideas of guilt and unworthiness (even in a mild type of episode); (iv) bleak and pessimistic views of the future; (v) ideas of acts of self-harm or suicide; (vi) disturbed sleep; (vii) diminished appetite. The lowered mood varies little from day to day, and is often unresponsive to circumstances, but may yet show a characteristic diurnal variation as the day goes on.

As with manic episodes, the clinical presentation shows marked individual variations and atypical presentations are particularly common in adolescence. In some cases, anxiety, distress and motor agitation may be more prominent at times than the depression, and the mood change may also be masked by added features such as irritability, excessive consumption of alcohol, histrionic behaviour, exacerbation of pre-existing phobic or obsessional symptoms, or by hypochondriacal pre-occupations. For depressive episodes of all three grades of severity a duration of at least two weeks is usually required, but shorter periods may be reasonable if symptoms are unusually severe and of rapid onset.

Some of the above symptoms may be marked, and develop characteristic features that are widely regarded as having special clinical significance. The most typical examples of these 'somatic' symptoms are: (i) loss of interest or loss of pleasure in activities which are normally pleasant; (ii) lack of emotional reactivity to normally pleasurable surroundings and events' (iii) waking in the morning two hours or more before the usual time; (iv) depression worse in the morning; (v) objective evidence of definite psychomotor retardation or agitation (remarked on or reported by other persons); (vi) marked loss of appetite; (vii) weight loss (often defined as 5% or more of body weight in the last month); (viii) and marked loss of libido. Usually, this somatic syndrome is not regarded as present unless about four of the above are definitely present.

The categories of mild (F32.0), moderate (F32.1) and severe (F32.2 and .3) depressive episodes described in more detail below should only be used for a single (first) depressive episode. Further depressive episodes should be classified under one of the subdivisions of recurrent depressive disorder (F33).

These grades of severity are specified so that they cover a wide range of clinical states that are encountered in different types of psychiatric practice. Patients with mild depressive episodes are common in primary care and general medical settings, whereas psychiatric in-patient units will be dealing largely with patients suffering from the severe grades.

Acts of self-harm, most commonly self-poisoning by prescribed medication, that are associated with mood (affective) disorders, should be recorded by means of an additional code from Chapter XX, External Causes of Morbidity and Mortality, Section X. These codes do not involve judgements about the differentiation between attempted suicide and 'parasuicide', both being included in the general category of self-harm.

Differentiation between the mild, moderate and severe degrees recommended here rests upon a complicated clinical judgement that involves the number, type and severity of symptoms present. The degree of ordinary social and work activities is often a useful general guide to the likely degree of severity of the episode, but individual, social and cultural influences that disrupt a smooth relationship between severity of symptoms and social performance are sufficiently common and powerful to make it unwise to include social performance amongst the essential criteria of severity.

The presence of dementia (F00–F03) or mental retardation (F7) does not rule out the diagnosis of a treatable depressive episode, but communication difficulties are likely to make it necessary to rely more than usual for the diagnosis upon objectively observed somatic symptoms, such as psychomotor retardation, loss of appetite and weight, and sleep disturbance.

F32.0   Mild depressive episode

Depressed mood, loss of interest and enjoyment, and increased fatigability are usually regarded as the most typical symptom of depression, and at least two of these three, plus at least two of the other symptoms described for F32, should usually be present for a definite diagnosis. None of the symptoms should be present to an intense degree, and the minimal duration for the whole episode is about two weeks.

A subject with a mild depressive episode is usually distressed by the symptoms and has some difficulty in carrying on with ordinary work and social activities, but will probably not cease to function completely.

A fifth character may be used to specify the presence of the somatic syndrome:

F32.00   Depressive episode, mild severity, without somatic symptoms
 The criteria for depressive episode, mild severity are fulfilled, and there are few or none of the somatic symptoms present.
F32.01   Depressive episode, mild severity, with somatic symptoms
 The criteria for depressive episode, mild severity are fulfilled, and four or more of the somatic symptoms are also present (if only two or three are present but they are unusually severe, it may be justified to use this category).

F32.1   Moderate depressive episode

DIAGNOSTIC GUIDELINES
At least two of the three most typical symptoms noted for mild severity above (F32.0) should be present, plus at least three (and preferably four) of the other symptoms. Several symptoms are likely to be present to a marked degree, but if a particularly wide variety of symptoms is present overall this is not essential. The minimal duration for the whole episode is about two weeks.

A subject with a moderately severe depressive episode will usually have considerable difficulty in continuing with social, work or domestic activities.

A fifth character may be used to specify the occurrence of somatic symptoms:

F32.10   Depressive episode, moderate severity without somatic symptoms
 The criteria for depressive episode, moderate severity are fulfilled, and there are few or none of the somatic symptoms present.
F32.11   Depressive episode, moderate severity with somatic symptoms
 The criteria for depressive episode, moderate severity, are fulfilled, and four or more of the somatic symptoms are present (if only two or three are present but they are unusually severe, it may be justified to use this category).

F32.2   Severe depressive episode without psychotic symptoms
In a severe depressive episode, the subject usually shows considerable distress or agitation, unless retardation is a marked feature. Loss of self-esteem or feelings of usefulness or guilt are likely to be prominent, and suicide is a distinct danger in the particularly severe cases. It is presumed here that the somatic syndrome will virtually always be present in a severe depressive episode.

DIAGNOSTIC GUIDELINES
All three of the typical symptoms noted for mild and moderate severity should

be present, plus usually four or more other symptoms, some of which should be of severe intensity. However, if important symptoms such as agitation or retardation are marked, the patient may be unwilling or unable to describe many symptoms in detail. An overall grading of severe episode may still be justified in such instances. The depressive episode should usually last at least two weeks, but if the symptoms are particularly severe and of very rapid onset it may be justified to make diagnosis of after less than two weeks.

During a severe depressive episode it is very unlikely that the subject will be able to continue with social, work or domestic activities, except to a very partial or limited extent.

Use this category only for single episodes of severe depression without psychotic symptoms; for further episodes use a subcategory of recurrent depressive disorder (F33).

F32.3   Severe depressive episode with psychotic symptoms

DIAGNOSTIC GUIDELINES
A severe depressive episode which meets the criteria given for F32.2 above, and in which delusions, hallucinations or depressive stupor are present. The delusions usually involve ideas of sin, poverty, or imminent disasters, responsibility for which may be assumed by the subject. Auditory or olfactory hallucinations are usually of defamatory or accusatory voices or of rotting filth or decomposing flesh. Severe psychomotor retardation may progress to stupor. If required, delusions or hallucinations may be specified as mood congruent or incongruent.

Differential diagnosis: depressive stupor needs to be differentiated from catatonic schizophrenia (F20.2), from dissociative stupor (F44.2), and from organic forms of stupor. Use this category only for single episodes of severe depression with psychotic symptoms; for further episodes use a subcategory of recurrent depressive disorder (F33).

F32.8   Other depressive episodes
Include here episodes which do not fit the descriptions given for depressive episodes described in F32.0–F32.3, but for which the overall diagnostic impression is gained that they are depressive in nature; for instance, fluctuating mixtures of depressive symptoms (particularly the somatic variety) with non-diagnostic symptoms such as tension, worrying and distress; or mixtures of somatic depressive symptoms with persistent pain or fatigue not due to organic causes (as sometimes seen in general hospital liaison services).

F32.9   Depressive episode, unspecified

Diagnostic criteria for research

F32   Depressive episodes
The following general criteria apply to all subcategories of F32:

A.   The depressive episode should last for at least two weeks.
B.   The episode is not attributable to alcohol or drug abuse, endocrine disorder, drug treatment or any organic mental disorder.
C.   Absence of hypomanic or manic symptoms sufficient to meet the criteria for hypomanic or manic episode (F30.–) at any time in the subject's life.

F32.0   MILD DEPRESSIVE EPISODE
A.   The general criteria of F32 Depressive episodes are fulfilled.
B.   At least two of the following three symptoms:
   (1) Depressed mood to a degree that is definitely abnormal for the subject, present for most of the day and almost every day, largely uninfluenced by circumstances, and sustained for at least two weeks.
   (2) Marked loss of interest or pleasure in activities which are normally pleasurable.
   (3) Decreased energy or increased fatigability.
C.   An additional symptom or symptoms from the following to give a total of at least *four.*
   (4) Loss of confidence and self-esteem.
   (5) Unreasonable feelings of self-reproach or excessive and inappropriate guilt.
   (6) Recurrent thoughts of death or suicide, or any suicidal behaviour.
   (7) Complaints or evidence of diminished ability to think or concentrate, such as indecisiveness or vacillation.
   (8) Change in psychomotor activity, with agitation or retardation.
   (9) Sleep disturbance of any type.
   (10) Change in appetite (decrease or increase) with corresponding weight change.

A fifth character should be used to specify the presence of the 'somatic syndrome' as defined below:

F32.00   without somatic symptoms
F32.01   with somatic symptoms

F32.1   MODERATE DEPRESSIVE EPISODE
A.   The general criteria of F32 Depressive episodes are fulfilled.
B.   At least two of the three symptoms in B, F32.0.
C.   Additional symptoms from C, F32.0, to give a total of at least *six* symptoms.

A fifth character should be used to specify the presence of the 'somatic syndrome' as defined below:

F32.10   without somatic symptoms
F32.11   with somatic symptoms

F32.2   SEVERE DEPRESSIVE EPISODE WITHOUT PSYCHOTIC SYMPTOMS
A.   The general criteria of F32 Depressive episodes are fulfilled.
B.   All three of the symptoms in B, F32.0.
C.   Additional symptoms from C, F32.0, to give a total of at least *eight* symptoms.
D.   The absence of hallucinations, delusions or depressive stupor.

The warning in the diagnostic guidelines about the effect of severe retardation or agitation upon the reporting of symptoms should be taken into account.

F32.3   SEVERE DEPRESSIVE EPISODE WITH PSYCHOTIC SYMPTOMS
A.   The general criteria of F32 Depressive episodes are fulfilled.
B.   The criteria for severe depressive episode without psychotic symptoms (F32.2) are met with the exception of criterion D.
C.   The criteria for schizophrenia (F20) or schizoaffective disorder, depressive type, either severe or moderate (F25.10 and F25.11) are not met.
D.   *Either*
    (1)   Hallucinations or delusions are present which do not fulfil the criteria for any of the symptom groups A1(b), (c) or (d) or A2(e) in F20, Schizophrenia.*

    or
    (2)   Depressive stupor.

A fifth character should be used to specify whether the psychotic symptoms are congruent or incongruent with the mood:

F32.30   with mood-congruent psychotic symptoms (i.e. delusions of guilt, worthlessness, bodily disease or impending disaster, derisive or condemnatory auditory hallucinations)
F32.31   with mood-incongruent psychotic symptoms

Somatic syndrome
Some depressive symptoms are widely regarded as having special clinical significance, and are called here 'somatic' (terms such as biological, vital, melancholic or endogenomorphic are used for this syndrome in other classifications).
    A fifth character (as indicated in F31.3; F32.0 and .1; F33.0 and .1) may

---

* The most common qualifying symptoms here are delusions of persecution or reference.

be used to specify the presence or absence of the somatic syndrome. To qualify for the somatic syndrome, *four* of the following symptoms should be present:

(1) loss of interest or loss of pleasure in activities which are normally pleasurable;
(2) lack of reactivity to events or activities that normally produce a response;
(3) waking in the morning two hours or more before the usual time;
(4) depression worse in the morning;
(5) objective evidence of marked psychomotor retardation or agitation (remarked on or reported by other persons);
(6) marked loss of appetite;
(7) weight loss (5% or more of body weight in the last month);
(8) marked loss of libido.

NOTE: THE USE OF GRADINGS OF SEVERITY OF INDIVIDUAL SYMPTOMS
Comments are requested upon the usefulness of providing two options for defining the difference between mild, moderate and severe depressive episodes (please read also the points made about this in the 'Clinical Descriptions and Diagnostic Guidelines', April 1989 Draft, with respect to interference with activities). The simplest option is laid out above in the usual way, and uses only a simple count of the number of symptoms present, without reference to the severity of individual symptoms. A second option is outlined below for each grade of severity of episode, for consideration by research workers having available ratings which indicate the grade of severity of individual depressive symptoms (as when using some standardized interviews and rating procedures). This second option is given because it is not unusual to find patients with symptoms present at very different levels of severity: one or two may dominate the clinical picture and cause such distress that it is clear that the most reasonable description of the severity of the overall episode is at a higher level of severity than the simple count of presence or absence would indicate. It remains to be seen whether it is worthwhile making the extra effort to use the additional details about individual symptoms, if they are available. It is assumed here that any standardized ratings used will contain three degrees of severity, referred to here as mild, marked and severe; it is up to each research team to equate these with the rating grades in whatever standardized procedure they are using.

The following additional or alternative criteria are therefore suggested:

F32.0   DEPRESSIVE EPISODE, MILD SEVERITY
An additional criterion:

D   None of the symptoms are graded as severe.

F32.1   DEPRESSIVE EPISODE, MODERATE SEVERITY
To criterion C, add:

OR   Additional symptoms from C, F32.0, to give a total of at least *five* symptoms, of which at least three should be rated as *marked.*

F32.2   SEVERE DEPRESSIVE EPISODE WITHOUT PSYCHOTIC SYMPTOMS
To criterion C add:

OR   Additional symptoms from C, F32.0, to give a total of at least *seven* symptoms, of which at least two should be rated as *severe.*

Short glossary definitions, included in the ICD-10, Volume 1

F32   Depressive episodes
In typical mild, moderate or severe episodes described below, the subject suffers from lowering of mood, reduction of energy and decrease in activity. Capacity for enjoyment, interest, and concentration are reduced, and marked tiredness after even minimum effort is common. Sleep is usually disturbed and appetite diminished. Self-esteem and self-confidence are almost always reduced, and even in the mild form some ideas of guilt or worthlessness are often present. The lowered mood varies little from day to day, is unresponsive to circumstances and may be accompanied by so-called 'somatic' symptoms, such as loss of interest and pleasurable feelings, waking in the morning several hours before the usual time; depression worst in the morning, marked psychomotor retardation, agitation, loss of appetite, weight loss and loss of libido. Depending upon the number and severity of the symptoms, a depressive episode may be specified as mild, moderate or severe.

Includes single episodes of:
• depressive reaction
• episodic depressive disorder
• psychogenic depression
• reactive depression

Excludes:
• adjustment disorder (F43.2)
• recurrent depressive disorder (F33.–)
• when associated with conduct disorders in F91.– (F92.0)

F32.0   Mild depressive episode
      Usually at least two or three of the above symptoms are present. The subject is usually distressed by these but will probably be able to carry on with most activities.

F32.1   Moderate depressive episode
Usually four or more of the above symptoms are present and the subject is likely to have great difficulty in continuing with ordinary activities.

F32.2   Severe depressive episode without psychotic symptoms
An episode of depression in which several of the symptoms are marked and distressing, typically loss of self-esteem and ideas of worthlessness or guilt. Suicidal thoughts and acts are common and a number of 'somatic' symptoms are usually present.

Agitated depression
Major depression   ⎫
Vital depression   ⎬ single episode without psychotic symptoms
                            ⎭

F32.3   Severe depressive episode with psychotic symptoms
An episode of depression as described in F32.2 above, but with the presence of hallucinations, delusions, psychomotor retardation or stupor so severe that ordinary social activities are impossible; there may be danger to life from suicide, dehydration or starvation. The hallucinations and delusions may or may not be mood congruent.

Single episodes of:
● major depression with psychotic symptoms
● psychogenic depressive psychosis
● psychotic depression
● reactive depressive psychosis

F32.8   Other depressive episodes
Atypical depression
Single episodes of 'masked' depression NOS

F32.9   Depressive episode, unspecified
Depression NOS
Depressive disorder NOS

Acknowledgement

The author is very grateful to Dr Jenny van Drimmell for her help in assuring congruence with the ICD-10 materials.

References

Burke JD (1988) Field trials of the 1987 draft of Chapter V (F) of ICD-10. *Br J Psychiatry* **152**, 33–37 (Suppl. I).

Feighner JP, Robins E, Guze SB *et al.* (1972) Diagnostic criteria for use in psychiatric research. *Arch Gen Psychiatry* **26**, 57–63.

Kramer M, Sartorius N, Jablensky A and Gulbinat W (1979) The ICD-9 Classification of Mental Disorders: A review of its development and contents. *Acta Psychiatr Scand* **59**, 241–262.

Loranger A, Hirschfeld R, Sartorius N and Regier D (in press) The WHO/ADAMHA International Pilot Study of Personality Disorders: Background and purpose.

Robins LN, Wing J, Wittchen HU *et al.* (1988) The Composite International Diagnostic Interview. *Arch Gen Psychiatry* **45**, 1069–1077.

Sartorius N (1976) The Cross-National Standardization of Psychiatric Diagnosis and Classification. In Pflanz M and Schach E (eds) *Cross-National Sociomedical Research: Concepts, Methods, Practice*, pp. 73–81. Stuttgart: Thieme.

Sartorius N and Jablensky A (1984) Diagnostic et classification en psychiatrie: à propos notamment de certains problèmes qui ont surgi dans un projet conjoint OMS–ADAMHA. *Confrontations Psychiatr* **24**, 131–139.

Sartorius N, Jablensky A, Cooper JE and Burke JD (eds) (1988) Psychiatric classification in an international perspective. *Br J Psychiatry* **152** (Suppl. 1).

Stengel E (1959) Classification of mental disorders. *Bull WHO* **21**, 601–663.

Wing JE, Babor T, Brugha T *et al* (1990) SCAN: Schedule for Clinical Assessment in Neuropsychiatry. *Arch Gen Psychiatry* **47**, 589–593.

World Health Organization/Alcohol, Drug Abuse and Mental Health Administration (1985) Mental disorders, alcohol- and drug-related problems: International perspective on their diagnosis and classification. *International Congress Series, 669.* Amsterdam: Excerpta Medica.

4

Work in progress on the DSM-IV mood disorders

A. Frances and W. Hall

Introduction

Work on the mood disorders section of DSM-IV began in the summer of 1988 and is expected to culminate with publication in 1993. DSM-IV is being generated in an integrated three-stage process, intended to provide the fullest possible empirical documentation for the system of classification (Frances *et al.*, 1989b). The first stage was the identification of the major diagnostic issues for comprehensive literature review (Widiger *et al.*, in press). The literature reviews conducted with the DSM-IV Mood Disorders Work Group and its advisors include: schizoaffective disorder, post-schizophrenic depression, mood-congruent and incongruent psychotic features, psychotic depression, melancholia, 'bipolar II', the rapid cycling modifier for bipolar disorder, seasonal mood disorders, post-partum depression, minor depression, mixed anxiety depression, depressive personality, atypical depression and dysthymia. Modified versions of these literature reviews will appear in the first volume of a *DSM-IV Source Book* with expected publication in late 1991. This source book will help to document what is known about and what remains to be learned concerning the disorders in question.

The relative sparsity of data on some of the most crucial issues has led us to a

---

The opinions expressed herein are those of the authors and do not necessarily represent the position of the American Psychiatric Association and its Task Force on DSM-IV.

---

second plan of empirical review, supported by funds from the MacArthur Foundation. This consists of data reanalyses with several aims: to supplement the information available in the literature; to test proposals for changes in criteria sets suggested by the literature reviews; and to generate new, empirically derived criteria sets for field testing (Frances *et al.*, 1990). Reanalyses are being conducted on clinical databases from multiple sites and on the Epidemiological Catchment Area community population database. Thus far in the mood disorders section, such reanalyses have focused on the definition of minor depression. Additional reanalyses are contemplated on the definition of bipolar II and rapid cycling. The results of these reanalyses will be published in the second volume of the *DSM-IV Source Book* in 1993.

The third stage of work on DSM-IV consists of focused field trials. These are intended to determine the impact of suggested changes in DSM-IV definitions on the reliability, performance characteristics, identification of caseness, prevalence and validity of the diagnoses. Another major purpose of field trials is to compare DSM-III, DSM-III-R, DSM-IV proposals and ICD-10 draft criteria. This should help reconcile differences between DSM-IV and ICD-10 and to find how the various systems map against one another (Frances *et al.*, in press). The topics of the focused field trials that pertain to the Mood Disorders Work Group are mixed anxiety–depression, minor depression, the definition of dysthymic disorder and the reliability of the assessment of lifetime course features. These studies are supported by the National Institute of Mental Health (NIMH).

We also will conduct extensive videotape field test reliability studies using 50 tapes covering ten diagnoses (including several types of mood disorders) among many thousands of clinicians of all disciplines and experiences around the world. This will provide an opportunity to study reliability of diagnosis as a dependent variable to learn how it varies with patient prototypicality, clinician training and method of assessment. We are particularly interested to investigate how reliably mood disorders can be diagnosed when patients present at the boundary with various near-neighbour conditions. This work is also supported by the John D. and Catherine T. MacArthur Foundation.

The results of the field trials also will be published in the second volume of the *DSM-IV Source Book* in 1993. This second volume will contain an overview of the issues confronted for all the disorders and the interpretations of the literature reviews, data reanalyses and field trials that led to the decisions made in DSM-IV, plus an indication of how these relate to ICD-10. This systematic evaluation, review and interpretation of the available empirical data is likely to be a much more important innovation of DSM-IV than any of its specific changes. At the same time it ensures that the system will be as up to date as possible given the available data.

The major goal of DSM-IV is to establish a model of empirical review and documentation for changes in the classification. The effort is meant to be conservative to provide minimal disruption to clinical communication, training and research (Frances *et al.*, 1991). Changes from DSM-III-R will be made only to increase compatibility with ICD-10, to accommodate evidence from the literature, data reanalyses and/or field trials, and to increase clarity and user-friendliness. The DSM-IV Work Group has sought and received extensive help from a cohort of more than 100 advisors representing a wide diversity of theoretical orientations, clinical and research experience, and geographical settings. This wide input was necessary both to accomplish the vast amount of work required and to ensure that the definitions included in DSM-IV represent a widely accepted consensus of the field.

The purpose of this chapter is briefly to review several issues that are of most concern to the DSM-IV Mood Disorders Work Group. We have divided the body of the chapter into two parts. The first section will deal with the interesting and, to some degree currently insolvable, boundary disputes. These throw into question how best to distinguish mood disorders from their near neighbours and how to set the boundaries among the conditions within the mood disorders section. The second part will outline the pros and cons of some modifiers that might be included in the mood disorders section. Each issue has already been subjected to extensive literature review. Some of these are also being studied with data reanalyses and field trials. Eventually, the detailed summary of the findings of the Mood Disorders Work Group included in the *DSM-IV Source Book* will greatly expand the very brief summaries within this chapter. The *Source Book* will provide a detailed documentary archive of the evidence that justifies the decisions that will ultimately be made. Our intention in this chapter is no more than to stimulate continued comment and suggestions and to bring forth additional data that might pertain to our considerations.

Boundary disorders

Unfortunately, we do not have the benefit of clear boundaries to separate the mood disorders from near neighbours or even clearly to demarcate the categories within the mood disorders section. In fact, patients at the boundary between mood and other disorders appear with such frequency as to suggest the need for categories that straddle the boundaries (e.g., schizoaffective for the boundary with schizophrenia; mixed anxiety/depression for the boundary with anxiety disorders; depressive personality for the boundary with personality disorders; and minor depression for the boundary with normality). There is also considerable controversy concerning the boundary between unipolar and bipolar mood disorders. This has resulted in a proposal for a new category to describe patients who have been designated as bipolar II (Dunner, 1991a).

The difficulty in setting boundaries has led to interesting and heated discussions concerning the advantages and disadvantages of separate categorical distinctions versus regarding these syndromes along a dimensional, general neurotic continuum (Roth, 1990; Tyrer 1989; Andrews *et al.*, 1990) (see Chapter 5). The scope of this controversy, which obviously has great implications, is clearly beyond our purview here. It is almost certainly one of those issues in our field in which both sides are right. More definitive answers must await a much deeper understanding of the pathogenesis of the disorders than is now available.

We will now provide a brief summary of some of the DSM-IV reviews and deliberations on each of these issues as they stand now.

Schizoaffective disorders
One of the most consequential definitional decisions in DSM-III was to accord priority to the mood disorder whenever a patient presented with a mood disorder and psychotic features, despite the phenomenological nature of the psychosis (Lalive *et al.*, 1991). Because of this decision, many patients who were considered schizoaffective prior to DSM-III because of their mood-incongruent psychotic symptoms were now diagnosed in a new subtype called mood disorder with mood-incongruent psychotic features. This was in recognition of accumulating evidence that such individuals tend to have a greater resemblance in family history, course and treatment response to mood disorder patients than to schizophrenics. The important implication of this decision was to expand greatly the boundary of the mood disorders and, in the process, to narrow greatly the boundary of schizoaffective disorder (and indirectly also of schizophrenia) (Pope and Lipinski, 1978). Recent reviews of the current literature confirm that this was indeed a useful decision and that it should be maintained in DSM-IV (Kendler, 1991). Individuals whose psychotic symptoms occur in the context of a mood disorder do indeed sort better with mood disorders than with schizophrenia on all available validators.

What remains less clear is how to define the criteria for the now truncated schizoaffective disorder. This was the only category in DSM-III to have no diagnostic criteria. DSM-III-R attempted to provide criteria for schizoaffective disorder that included: (1) a major depressive or manic syndrome concurrent with active psychotic symptoms; (2) during an episode of the disturbance there have been delusions or hallucinations for at least two weeks but no prominent mood symptoms; (3) schizophrenia has been ruled out (i.e. duration of all depressive episodes has not been brief relative to the total duration of the psychotic episode; and (4) there are no established organic factors maintaining the disturbance.

There is little literature to suggest the DSM-III-R criteria are useful or optimal, but also no compelling reason on which to base changes. It seems likely that this is an inherently unclear boundary that will be clarified only with advances in understanding pathogenesis. There is some evidence that the schizoaffective-depressed patients resemble schizophrenics more than do schizoaffective-manics, and that course features (i.e. acute, chronic or episodic) may be especially important in an eventually improved definition of schizoaffective disorder. Nonetheless, it would be premature to revise criteria now based on these findings. Although it seems therefore likely that DSM-IV will maintain the DSM-III-R criteria, this should not be seen as an endorsement, since we know so little concerning their performance characteristics and validity.

Two other issues deserve some note. The ICD-10 (International Classification of Diseases) Research Diagnostic Criteria definition of schizoaffective disorder consists of the following: (1) the disorder meets criteria of one of the affective disorders—manic, depressive episode of moderate severity, or severe depressive episode; (2) active psychotic symptoms are present for most of the time during a period of at least two weeks; (3) symptoms of the affective disorder are concurrent with active psychotic symptoms; and (4) the disorder is not attributable to any organic factors. This definition is unfortunate. It is inconsistent not only with DSM-III-R, but also with the definitions in ICD-10 for mood disorders. The ICD-10 schizoaffective definition overlaps entirely with the definitions of mood-incongruent psychotic mood disorder included in ICD-10. This is likely to create confusion within ICD-10 and across ICD 10 and DSM-IV in distinguishing these disorders.

There is one other issue relating to the boundary of schizophrenia and mood disorder. ICD-10 has included a new category to describe post-schizophrenic depression. The utility of such a category also seems to be supported by a DSM-IV literature review (although this is still under discussion). Post-schizophrenic depression, as defined in ICD-10 research criteria, is characterized by the following: (1) the general criteria for schizophrenia must have been met within the past 12 months with some schizophrenia symptoms still present but insufficient for current diagnosis; and (2) depressive symptoms must meet criteria for at least mild depressive episode. The DSM-IV proposed criteria for post-schizophrenia depression are just now being drafted but will likely define a more or less equivalent construct. This disorder meets an important need and is likely to be included in DSM-IV. One problem, however, is to establish a definitional boundary between schizoaffective disorder and post-schizophrenic depression to distinguish the sequelae of illness from a boundary condition (Siris, 1991).

Mixed anxiety/depression

There is abundant evidence that mood disorders and anxiety disorders very frequently occur together. Patients often meet criteria for both types of disorder at the full syndromal level of severity. This can be (and was) interpreted in a variety of ways and may reflect: (1) similar underlying aetiology and pathogenesis of mood and anxiety disorders; (2) predisposition of one condition to the other (e.g., anxiety disorder may lead to secondary demoralization that is descriptively diagnosed as depression); (3) definitional artefact resulting from either the artificial splitting in DSM-III-R of more complex syndromes combining anxiety and other features (e.g., a more generic 'neurosis') or because similar items are included in the criteria sets of both disorders; or (4) chance co-occurrence of common conditions (Clark and Watson, 1991). It has also been noted (especially in primary care, out-patient psychiatric and cross-cultural settings) that a number of patients who fail to meet the full syndromal criteria for either a mood or an anxiety disorder may have both mood and anxiety symptoms that cause clinically significant impairment and deserve recognition as a mental disorder (Katon and Roy-Byrne, 1991). To provide coverage for such individuals (who would now in DSM-III-R be included only in either the Mood or Anxiety Disorders sections considered under the Not Otherwise Specified rubric), ICD-10 has introduced a new category for mixed anxiety depression.

The desirability of including such a category in DSM-IV is now under consideration (with extensive literature reviews completed and field trials underway). It is difficult to make decisions on the utility of this category because of the very limited data that are available. Any decision will need to balance the disadvantages of omitting the category (and thereby having, at least in some settings, patients who fail to receive adequate diagnosis and treatment) with the disadvantages of including it (e.g., patients who might receive inappropriate and excessive diagnosis and treatment). Including a category for mixed anxiety–depression also would cause a substantial increase in the prevalence of mood disorders that may or may not be warranted, especially given that the newly included individuals often have only relatively mild impairment and are on the boundary of normality.

It has also been argued that the reason mixed anxiety–depression is diagnosed in patients who seem subthreshold in primary care settings may have more to do with the inexperience of the assessors, or the brief nature of the assessment in such settings, than with actual differences from those patients who meet criteria for anxiety, depression or both. To study this question, a DSM-IV field trial will compare diagnostic assessments conducted by experienced psychiatrists and primary care physicians on persons with mixed anxiety–depression. This will detemine whether a syndrome of mixed anxiety–depression (without severity sufficient for an anxiety or depression diagnosis) retains its niche even when patients receive careful assessment.

Unfortunately, although several treatment studies are now underway, the only currently available validators of this syndrome are descriptive validity and impairment. DSM-IV decisions will likely have to be made before we know very much about course, family loading or treatment response of patients with milder forms of mixed anxiety and depression. If this category is insufficiently supported for official inclusion in DSM-IV, it may be included in a DSM-IV Appendix of suggested new diagnoses that do not yet have sufficient empirical support to be in the official nomenclature.

Minor depression

The threshold for severity and duration established in DSM-III and DSM-III-R was necessarily fairly arbitrary and not based on any very strong evidence. It is therefore not surprising that a number of studies, again particularly those performed in primary care and community settings, report that many patients who fall short of the DSM thresholds for mood disorder nonetheless exhibit clinically significant impairment, as measured by functional disability and health care utilization. In fact, two very different types of subthreshold depressions have been identified—one that is subthreshold to major depression in symptom severity (so-called 'minor depression') (Klerman, 1989; Wells *et al.*, 1989), the other that is subthreshold to major depression in duration (e.g., so-called 'brief recurrent depression' consisting of many episodes a year, each meeting the full symptom severity criteria of major depression but lasting for only two or three days) (Angst *et al.*, 1990) (see Chapter 8).

Suggestions for subthreshold categorization of mood disorders make it especially difficult to define the boundary between psychopathology and normality. This is as true for minor depression as it is for mixed anxiety–depression. There are several concerns: (1) the inclusion of minor depression and/or brief recurrent depression could make patients receive unnecessary treatment; (2) the category may trivialize the construct of mental disorder and artificially inflate prevalence rates; (3) the evidence suggesting that subthreshold depressions are associated with significant impairment may also be difficult to interpret because the patients have received inadequate assessments. At least some of them might have met criteria for major depression were they diagnosed more carefully. On the other hand, it must also be noted that the treatment implications of the proposed categories are unknown. We may be depriving patients of effective treatment by not recognizing this category and/or we may be protecting them from unnecessary and ineffective treatment. Only systematic treatment trials will answer this question. These are unlikely to be available in time for DSM-IV decisions. If the categories are deemed premature for separate status in DSM-IV, after further data reanalysis and field trails, they may be more clearly elaborated as specific examples in the Mood Disorders Not Otherwise Specified section. They also might receive further description in the DSM-IV Appendix of suggested new disorders that may deserve further study but are not sufficiently supported for inclusion in the official nomenclature.

Depressive personality disorder

By incorporating cyclothymic and dysthymic disorders as Axis I conditions, DSM-III expanded the boundaries of the Mood Disorders section not only into schizophrenia but also into the personality disorders. This led to an inconsistency in how the pervasive spectrum disorders in Axis I conditions are treated in DSM-III-R. The spectrum disorders in DSM-III-R that are related to the mood disorders are considered Axis I conditions. However, the spectrum disorders in DSM-III-R that are related to schizophrenia (schizotypal personality, and perhaps schizoid and paranoid disorders) remain on Axis II. The ICD-10 attempts to resolve this inconsistency by transforming schizotypal personality disorder to schizotypal disorder, and removing it from the personality disorder section. Unfortunately this creates other potential inconsistencies because a number of the remaining Axis II disorders (e.g., avoidant, paranoid, schizoid, obsessive compulsive and borderline) may have their spectrum relationships to Axis I conditions.

Possible solutions (none of which is satisfactory or is likely to achieve anything approaching consensus) to the problem of handling the boundary relationship between personality and other disorders include: (1) defining personality disorder sufficiently broadly as to include all the spectrum disorders; this implies that dysthymic and cyclothymic disorders should be returned to the personality disorders section because they have an early insidious onset, chronic course and pervasive impact on personality functioning; (2) removing all reasonably well-documented spectrum disorders from Axis II and placing them within their Axis I parent category (including perhaps schizotypal and avoidant given current levels of information); (3) eliminating Axis II altogether; or (4) cross-tabulating boundary spectrum disorders on both Axis I and Axis II.

What is most pertinent in this regard is one suggested solution to this problem—that DSM-IV include an Axis II category for depressive personality disorder (Hirshfield *et al.*, 1991). This has been conceived in two different ways. One notion is that there may be a constellation of depressive personality items (especially cognitive and interpersonal) that is sufficiently distinct from dysthymic disorder as to merit separate Axis II attention. Another notion is that all early-onset dysthymic disorders might be considered depressive personality. The two arguments for the inclusion of a depressive personality on Axis II are that this condition has a long historical tradition that spans the literatures of many different orientations (e.g., psychodynamic, descriptive, cognitive) and that dysthymic patients with early, insidious onset; chronic course; and pervasive impairment in all areas of personality functioning meet all the definitional features of personality disorder.

Those who are against the inclusion of this new diagnosis of depressive personality argue that it overlaps (perhaps completely) with currently existing disorders. There is also a frequently expressed (and we believe incorrect) opinion that the construct of personality disorder should be understood to connote an increased emphasis on psychosocial causality and that somatic treatments are not likely to be effective. This results in a concern that the inclusion of a depressive personality in DSM-IV might lead to less aggressive somatic treatment for chronic depressives when this might be helpful. The depressive personality proposal is being studied in a field trial that will compare it to chronic depressions. Given the limited available data, it seems more likely that depressive personality will be included in a new disorder appendix than to be included as an official diagnosis.

Bipolar II

It has been observed for almost twenty years that some patients present with descriptive features and a course that might be considered intermediary between unipolar and bipolar mood disorders (Dunner, 1991a). Such individuals have recurrent episodes of full syndromal depression and hypomanic episodes that suggest bipolar disorder but fail to meet the full criteria for mania. Some investigators and clinicians are convinced that the existing evidence suggests that these so-called 'Bipolar II' patients are more similar to bipolar than to unipolar patients in course, family loading and treatment response. Others remain unconvinced that the exisiting literature compels regarding these intermediate cases as bipolar disorders. They prefer the diagnosis of 'major depression, recurrent and with hypomanic episodes'.

However this issue is ultimately decided, the boundary between bipolar and unipolar presentations remains anything but clearly defined. Available definitions of bipolar II require only that the patients have had one (or possibly several) episodes of hypomania. These episodes usually require only relatively brief duration and mild symptom severity. It also must be noted that it is very difficult to assess hypomania, especially retrospectively in individuals with relatively long-standing depression for whom any temporary lifting of the cloud may be experienced incorrectly as a relative high (rather than as a rare moment of euthymia). The role of antidepressant medication in triggering temporary switches from depression to hypomanic is also controversial and difficult to assess.

This is another decision for DSM-IV with very profound potential implications that will likely have to be made on limited data. Any decisions to include a bipolar II diagnosis will likely have a dramatic impact on the prevalence ratio of unpiolar as compared to bipolar disorders. While this redefinition of caseness should not necessarily be overly influential in treatment, lacking as we do any clear treatment guidelines based on available evidence, there is little doubt that clinicians will respond strongly to the new diagnostic conventions. 'Bipolar II patients' as compared to 'Unipolar patients with hypomanic episodes'— although identical in defining features—would, merely because of the change in terminology, be more likely to receive lithium prophylaxes and more cautious antidepressant treatment of depressive episodes. This might be a treatment advance for at least some individuals, but it may also be an unfounded change in prescribing habits based on little supportive evidence.

One way of studying this conundrum is a data reanalysis including a variety of data sets to determine the reliability, caseness definition, thresholds, defining features and, whenever available, treatment implications of the different definitions. A possible compromise would be to set sufficiently high thresholds for the number, duration and severity of the hypomanic episodes in a bipolar II diagnosis to avoid unnecessarily high false-positive rates. A final, more trivial issue, is the lack of appeal of the term Bipolar II, but possible substitutes have also lacked clarity.

Subtypes and modifiers

Just as there are many questions regarding the boundaries of mood disorders, there are many issues concerning how best to subtype within the overall envelope of mood disorders. This creates difficulty especially because so many different subtyping schemata have been used and suggested, and because so few (beyond delusional/non-delusional and melancholia) have had a substantial literature documenting specific treatment implications. Moreover, the more subtypes offered within the system, the more cumbersome it becomes, particularly as many patients may qualify for a multiplicty of subtypes. Although this has the value of providing what may be additional useful information, the complexity of a system often results in its relative neglect. These issues must be balanced in considering suggestions for new subtypes and modifications for those already in DSM-III-R.

Melancholia
A thorough review of the extensive literature on melancholia suggests that it is useful in DSM-IV to continue to include this as a subtype of major depression (Rush *et al.*, 1991). The presence of melancholia helps to predict that the patient is especially likely to have a poor response to placebo, to have an especially good response to electroconvulsive therapy (ECT), and also may indicate an increased likelihood of positive results on a number of biological tests. Several issues remain controversial. Most interesting, it is not yet clear how the categorical subtype of melancholia relates to the dimensional rating of severity. Does the melancholic subtype denote a qualitatively distinct type of depression which can occur at different levels of severity, or is it merely an expression of the higher ranges of depression severity? In other words, does the categorical term melancholia capture more and different variance than would a dimensional rating of severity or is it more or less redundant with severity ratings? Furthermore, the method of defining melancholia in DSM-III-R is cumbersome and difficult to remember. It includes treatment response and course features that may be tautological and are not in keeping with the descriptive method used in defining criteria in the rest of the system.

The review of the literature on melancholia, comparing nine different systems for defining it, suggests great heterogeneity in the definition of this term. At least 15 different symptom features and nine different course features are included in at least one of the definitions of melancholia. Most of them are included in fewer than one half the systems. Factor analytic studies have produced inconsistent, but overlapping, definitional suggestions. Certain items recur as most characteristic of melancholia across many systems and studies. These include psychomotor retardation, anhedonia, early morning worsening, unreactive mood and distinct quality to the mood. A selection of these might constitute a simpler, more data-based criterion set than the one now available. The DSM-III-R definition is admittedly cumbersome and idiosyncratic compared to most other systems. On the other hand, there is considerable concern that the definition of melancholia has changed so frequently and disruptively across rating instruments, across the years and across diagnostic systems—all based on insufficient evidence. It might be best to leave the current very imperfect system alone in the interest of continuity and to await more definitive studies before making changes.

Mood-congruent versus mood-incongruent psychotic features

As indicated above, this distinction was included for the first time in DSM-III and had the effect of greatly broadening the construct of mood disorder. A second question is whether the distinction itself makes sense or whether all psychotic mood disorders should be grouped together. A thorough review of this distinction suggests that mood-incongruent, compared to mood-congruent, psychotic symptoms may predict somewhat greater severity, worse outcome and greater family history of schizophrenia. However, these differences are modest and inconsistent across studies (Kendler, 1991). The distinction has a long history and some empirical support. It deserves continued inclusion in DSM-IV to encourage further research and for the possible light it sheds on management.

Psychotic mood disorders

The question has also been reviewed whether psychotic mood disorders are so different from the non-psychotic type as to warrant separate categorization or clearer differentiation than is possible within DSM-III-R (Schatzberg and Rothschild, 1991). The review found that the presence of psychosis predicts high severity but is not synonymous with it. A number of studies have reported descriptive differences in depressive symptomatology between psychotic and non-psychotically depressed patients, but these have been modest and inconsistent. Family studies have also not been consistent but suggest that psychotically depressed patients have higher rates of mood disorders, specifically of psychotic and bipolar illness, than do non-psychotically depressed patients. A number of biological test result differences between psychotic and non-psychotic mood disorders have also been reported but these are preliminary, not fully consistent, and may be confounded with severity. Psychotic depression predicts a relatively poor prognosis compared with non-psychotic depression, including more chronicity, hospitalization, episodes, impairment and perhaps suicide risk.

The strongest arguments supporting the value of separate categorization for psychotic mood disorders relate to course and treatment reports. Patients who have had psychotic mood disorders are more likely to become psychotic during recurrences. They often maintain the content of their delusions across episodes. Most important, however, is the compelling evidence that psychotic mood disorders respond poorly to antidepressants or neurolopetics when given alone, but do respond to combinations of these medications or ECT. It seems clear that the psychotic distinction in mood disorders is a crucial prognostic and treatment guide and supports the emphasis placed on this phenomenology in DSM-III-R. The current system is probably adequate for highlighting this subtype. Any efforts to create a more prominent subcategorization for psychotic mood disorders is unnecessary and would be very difficult from the perspective of ICD-10 compatibility.

Atypical

There has been a twenty-year, but relatively limited, literature suggesting the importance of depression characterized (variously) by prominent anxiety, reversed vegetative syptoms, and/or rejection sensitivity and histrionic personality features. This syndrome is not called 'atypical' because it is infrequently encountered. In fact such patients are common especially in out-patient practice. The term 'atypical' was meant to contrast with the pattern of depression more commonly encountered in in-patient settings and in clinical drug trials. Several retrospective and prospective studies suggest that individuals presenting with 'atypical' features respond better to monoamine oxidase (MAO) inhibitors (about 70%) than to imipramine (about 50%) or placebo (about 30%) (Rabkin *et al.*, 1991).

The inclusion of a category to convey the construct of atypical depression remains controversial for a number of reasons. It is not yet clear how best to define the disorder. Very little has been reported on its reliability, prevalence, relationship to other subtypes of depression and the characteristics of possible defining items. Furthermore, the differential treatment response has been reported retrospectively only by one research centre. This may be shifting sand on which to build a diagnosis (especially since the available MAO inhibitors are already being superseded by some newer antidepressants as the first-line drug for such individuals).

Rapid cycling

There have been a number of studies suggesting the value of a subtype of rapid cycling for bipolar disorder (Bauer and Whybrew, 1991). Rapid cycling has generally been defined as four or more episodes occurring during a 12-month period. Risk factors for rapid cycling include female gender, use of antidepressants, hypothyroidism and positive family history. Frequent episodes have been associated with poor treatment response to lithium and the frequent need to consider the use of carbamezapine or high-dose thyroid hormone. It appears that rapid cycling is equally prevalent in bipolar I and bipolar II patients. There are no special phenomenological features, other than frequent episodes, which distinguish such patients. The major question is how best to define the number of required episodes and the duration required for each of these. Clinical researchers generally count relatively brief episodes toward a rapid cycling diagnosis, but the appropriate duration requirement is not clear. It is also not clear how many episodes should be required, especially since most rapid cycling patients have many more than four episodes per year. Setting a higher threshold for episode frequency would create a more homogeneous category and reduce false positives. These questions on definition are being studied in a multisite data reanalysis. The consensus is clear that the rapid cycling subtype will be a useful addition in DSM-IV.

Seasonal

DSM-III-R introduced a seasonal modifier for mood disorder. This was done mostly because of treatment studies suggesting that patients with winter depression may be responsive to the use of bright light therapy. The major problem in this literature is that there are very few studies on the psychometric properties of the possible definitions for seasonal mood disorder. The DSM-III-R definition of the seasonal subtype includes the following items: (1) a regular temporal relationship between the onset of an episode of Bipolar Disorder or Recurrent Major Depression and a particular 60-day period of the year (disregarding psychosocial stressors); (2) full remissions (or a change from depression to mania or hypomania) also occurring within a particular 60-day period of the year; (3) at least three episodes of mood disturbances in three separate years that demonstrated the temporal seasonal relationship defined above, with two consecutive years; (4) seasonal episodes of mood disturbances outnumber any non-seasonal episodes that may have occurred by more than three to one.

Researchers in the field have generally not adopted the DSM-III-R criteria, finding them too narrow. It is also not clear that such a definition is useful in general clinical practice. Other ways of defining the temporal relationship between the onset and time of year are being considered and shared with the field. Unfortunately there are very little data on which to base decisions. It is also not clear if the light treatment response is specific to seasonal mood disorder since there are few data on the drug responsivity of such patients or the efficacy of light therapy in non-seasonals (Dunner, 1991a).

Course modifiers

There is a widespread concern that the diagnostic system in general pays too much attention to cross-sectional descriptive features at the expense of longitudinal course features. This has resulted at least in part because there is no widely accepted method for classifying course. It is probably inherently easier to achieve reliability in the assessment of cross-sectional symptoms than for their patterns of onset and evolution. There is a particular reason for addressing course in the consideration of the mood disorders section. DSM-III distinguished between major depression and dysthymic disorder, but defined the latter as a mild, chronic form of mood disorder. To meet criteria for dysthymic disorder, patients had to differ from those with major depression both by having a milder condition and one that was more or less chronic rather than episodic. This led to a heterogeneous category of dysthymic disorder that included: (1) some patients with early onset and lifelong course and others with a late onset and course of only two years; (2) some patients with dysthymia alone or preceding other conditions; and (3) others whose dysthymia seemed secondary to another psychiatric or medical disorder or psychosocial stress. It was also noted that most chronic depressives, at least those seen in clinical settings, have at some point met criteria for major depression. This suggests either the necessity for some construct of 'double depression', or that DSM had erred in confounding both course and severity features in the definition of dysthymic disorder.

DSM-III-R introduced several changes that were meant to reduce the heterogeneity in the dysthymic disorder section. It became possible to classify onsets as early or late, and primary or secondary. A subtype of chronic major depression was recognized to distinguish patients whose chronicity followed an episode of major depression, instead of arising insidiously. These would be distinguished from patients (double depressives) who presented with dysthymia first and only later went on to develop major depression. They therefore would receive both diagnoses. It has been noted that there is nothing really very double about double depression, since it probably describes the evolution and shifting severities of a unitary condition. In fact, in DSM-III the severity thresholds of dysthymic disorder and major depression had been set so close to one another that a dysthymic patient who gained one symptom might qualify for the diagnosis of major depression. It has also been pointed out that the particular items chosen to define dysthymic disorder do not stand on any extensive literature. There is no reason to suppose that they represent an optimal set (Kocsis and Frances, 1987; Frances *et al.*, 1989a).

The changes made between DSM-III and DSM-III-R in the definition of dysthymic disorder have some face validity but are unsupported by data (Keller, 1991). The particular item set chosen for dysthymia is particularly inadequate. We are therefore conducting a DSM-IV field trial to determine the optimal definitive features and to find ways of describing the onset and relationship of dysthymic disorder to other psychiatric and medical conditions. This field test also will determine whether clinicians can reliably assess the lifetime trajectory of depressive illness. We have developed a number of prototypical course evolutions in both picture and language form. If these course assessments can be made reliably by clinicians, it may be useful to introduce course modifiers into the mood disorders section, especially since prior course may be one of the best predictors of future prognosis and patterns of illness evolution.

Conclusion

Each issue described above might lend itself to multiple plausible solutions. None has sufficient available evidence (especially validity) to make the optimal choice obvious. In many ways, the efforts to provide empirical documentation and to identify areas in which more empirical evidence is necessary may be the most important innovation in DSM-IV. The DSM-IV Mood Disorders Work Group is taking an especially conservative and careful approach to suggested changes. This is in keeping with the overall spirit of DSM-IV. It is appropriate in an area of investigation that has extensive ongoing research that is likely to be disrupted by unnecessary change. It is hoped that the three-step DSM-IV process of literature reviews, data reanalysis and field trials will culminate in a clinically useful DSM-IV; one that is as compatible as possible with both DSM-III-R and ICD-10, and which will encourage and facilitate research for the basic understanding of pathogenesis that will hopefully inform DSM-V.

References

Andrews G, Stewart G, Morris-Yates A *et al.* (1990) Evidence for a general neurotic syndrome. *Br J Psychiatry* **157**, 6–12.

Angst J, Merikangas K, Scheidegger P and Wicki W (1990) Recurrent brief depression: A new subtype of affective disorder. *J Affective Disord* **19**, 87–98.

Bauer M and Whybrew P (1991) Rapid cycling. In: *DSM-IV Sourcebook.* Washington, DC: American Psychiatric Press.

Dunner DL (1991a) A review of the diagnostic status of Bipolar II. In: *DSM-IV Sourcebook.* Washington, DC: American Psychiatric Press.

Dunner DL (1991b) Seasonal pattern for DSM-IV. In: *DSM-IV Sourcebook.* Washington, DC: American Psychiatric Press.

Frances A, Kocsis J, Marin D *et al.* (1989a) Diagnostic Criteria for dysthymia disorder. *Psychopharmacol Bull* **25**, 325–329.

Frances A, Widiger TA and Pincus HA (1989b) The development of DSM-IV. *Arch Gen Psychiatry* **46**, 373–375.

Frances A, Pincus HA, Widiger TA (1990) DSM-IV: Work in progress. *Am J Psychiatry* **147**, 1439–1448.

Frances A, First M, Pincus HA, *et al.* (1991) Toward a more empirical diagnostic system. *Can Psychol* **32**, 174–176.

Frances A, Pincus HA, Widiger TA *et al.* (in press) DSM-IV and international communication in psychiatric diagnosis. In: *DSM-IV Sourcebook.* Washington, DC: American Psychiatric Press.

Hirshfield R, Shea T, Gunderson J and Phillips K (1991) Proposal for a depressive personality disorder. In: *DSM-IV Sourcebook*. Washington, DC: American Psychiatric Press.
Katon W and Roy-Byrne P (1991) Mixed anxiety and depression. In: *DSM-IV Sourcebook*. Washington, DC: American Psychiatric Press.
Keller MB (1991) DSM-IV literature review of dysthymia. In: *DSM-IV Sourcebook*. Washington, DC: American Psychiatric Press.
Kendler K (1991) Mood incongruent psychotic affective illness: An historical and empirical review. In: *DSM-IV Sourcebook*. Washington, DC: American Psychiatric Press.
Klerman GL (1989) Depressive disorders: Further evidence for increased medical morbidity and impairment of social functioning. *Arch Gen Psychiatry* **46**, 856–858.
Kocsis J and Frances A (1987) DSM-III dysthymic disorder: An overview. *Am J Psychiatry* **144**, 1537–1542.
Lalive J, Rush AJ and Kendler KS (1991) DSM-IV schizoaffective disorder. In: *DSM-IV Sourcebook*. Washington, DC: American Psychiatric Press.
Pope HG and Lipinski JF (1978) Diagnosis in schizophrenia and manic-depressive illness: A reassessment of the specificity of 'schizophrenic' symptoms in light of current research. *Arch Gen Psychiatry* **35**, 811–828.
Rabkin J, Stewart J, Quitkin F *et al.* (1991) Should atypical depression be included as a separate entity in DSM-IV? A review of the research evidence. In: *DSM-IV Sourcebook*. Washington, DC: American Psychiatric Press.
Roth M (1990) Categorical and unitary classifications of neurotic disorder. *J R Soc Med* **83**.
Rush AJ, Hay BJ and Weissenburger JE (1991) Melancholic symptom features: A review and commentary for DSM-IV. In: *DSM-IV Sourcebook*. Washington, DC: American Psychiatric Press.
Schatzberg AF and Rothschild AJ (1991) Psychotic major depression: Evidence in support of its inclusion as a distinct syndrome in DSM-IV. In: *DSM-IV Sourcebook*. Washington, DC: American Psychiatric Press.
Siris S (1991) Secondary depression in schizophrenia. In: *DSM-IV Sourcebook*. Washington, DC: American Psychiatric Press.
Tyrer PJ (1989) *Classification of Neurosis*. Chichester: Wiley.
Wells KB, Stewart A, Hays RD *et al.* (1989) The functioning and well-being of depressed patients: Results from the medical outcomes study. *JAMA* **262**, 914–919.
Widiger TA, Frances A, Pincus HA and Davis W (in press) DSM-IV literature reviews: Rationale process, and limitations. *J Psychopathol Behav Assessment*.

5

Diagnosing depression: a two-tier approach

S. Wetzler, H.M. van Praag and M.M. Katz

The nosological approach to diagnosis

The medical model has cast its spell over diagnostic thinking in psychiatry ever since Kraepelin classified mental disorders in the late nineteenth century. Influenced by Virchov's attempt to tie medical diseases to their underlying pathological roots, Kraepelin's intention was to tie mental diseases to their underlying neuropathological roots. Kraepelin imagined that, in the future, psychiatry and pathology would be co-equal scientific partners. Classification was the first step in his grand plan to identify biological markers of mental illnesses, and thus ultimately to determine their biological causes. It was at this time that the medical model became associated with a nosological or categorical approach to psychiatric diagnosis, from which it has been unable to extricate itself.

Unfortunately, Kraepelin's hope of finding biological markers of mental disorders has not been realized during the last one hundred years. Despite only partial success, the medical model remains the modus operandi of biological psychiatry, and psychiatrists stubbornly cling to the traditional nosology. Contemporary psychiatric diagnosis, as exemplified by DSM-III-R, is essentially a categorical approach, resembling the one constructed by Kraepelin. Not to detract from Kraepelin's great accomplishments, we contend that it is only by adding a complementary dimensional evaluation to our nosological diagnosis that researchers will be able to determine the underlying biological bases of behaviour.

The nosological model assumes that psychiatric illnesses are discrete entities

The Diagnosis of Depression. Edited by J.P. Feighner and W.F. Boyer
© 1991 John Wiley & Sons Ltd

with distinct configurations of characteristics, qualitatively different from each other, which appear and disappear as whole entities. The unit of measurement, therefore, is the disorder itself, and researchers try to establish links between the entire disorder and neurobiological systems. In our view, this holistic way of thinking has tended to impede rather than advance research (Katz and Wetzler, 1991).

According to the nosological model in psychiatry, classification is the process of grouping illnesses with similar configurations, thereby separating them from illnesses with different configurations. It is a categorical or typological process. Patients are segregated, separated and differentiated. To do this, the clinician must draw black/white, all-or-nothing distinctions. Patients fit within one or another category of psychiatric disorder. For example, a patient either has a major depression or they have a generalized anxiety disorder, not something in between. In some exceptional cases, patients are diagnosed with multiple psychiatric disorders (called 'comorbidity'); that is, they fit into both categories. To escape the problems presented by a categorical diagnostic approach, the DSM-III introduced a hierarchical system with its own arbitrary rules (e.g. see van Praag, 1990).

In summary, the nosological approach stipulates the existence of whole disorders which fit neatly into one or another clearly defined, homogeneous diagnostic category. These disorders come and go as whole entities, as does a disease entity invading and then leaving an otherwise normal and healthy body. The explicit assumption is that a particular psychiatric disorder is linked to a particular pathophysiological substrate. The validation of a diagnostic disorder evolves from research on course, treatment response and long-term outcome. When a diagnostic label is able to predict these features, then it is considered a valid diagnostic entity.

We believe that the capacity to do this for most disorders is wishful thinking on the part of nosologists. While some categories are more reliable than others and better approximate these requirements, many do not. In actual practice, many psychiatric disorders are not best described as entities, and they hold little predictive validity. They are quite heterogeneous in character, composed of many disparate components and psychological dysfunctions, not homogeneous or whole entities unto themselves. An either/or, all-or-nothing approach fails to appreciate the degree of overlap between disorders as well as the grey areas and partial syndromes which characterize most psychopathology. Patients rarely fit neatly into one or another category. While some clearly meet the criteria, many meet criteria for multiple categories, and others fall between the cracks. In most instances, the nosological approach is not a useful way of thinking.

For example, one depressed patient has fully depressed and non-reactive mood, all neurovegetative signs and relatively intact personality functioning, whereas another depressed patient may present with only partially and inconsistently depressed mood and ruminations about life circumstances indicative of significant obsessionality and personality dysfunction. The former patient is the prototypic major depression. However, the latter case is a partial instance bearing only a faint resemblance to the prototype. Should these two patients be grouped under the same rubric? In addition, if the former patient with prototypic major depression meets criteria for schizophrenia as well, then the diagnostician confronts the dilemma of deciding into which category to place the patient. And the latter patient may not be classifiable because they exhibit parts of several syndromes simultaneously. All too often, according to DSM-III-R, patients fit into too many places or they fit nowhere at all.

The prodromal period of psychiatric disorders is often extended, such that illnesses develop gradually. They do not appear fully formed. Then, during the course of treatment, illnesses typically recede in an incremental, cascading fashion. Many patients partially recover and are left with residual deficits. A distinction between normality and pathology is not as clear-cut as assumed by the medical, nosological model. They merge, and pathological dysfunctions appear to evolve out of normal psychological functioning. The nosological approach fails to appreciate this continuity.

As long as we seek to identify single biological markers of fundamentally heterogeneous and variable illnesses, Kraepelin's aim will be difficult to achieve. Similarly, we are unlikely to find biological treatments which are uniquely appropriate for particular psychiatric disorders. The evidence supports this generalization. Tricyclic antidepressants have been found to be effective in the treatment of many disorders: major depression, dysthymia, and panic disorder; clomipramine and selective serotonin uptake inhibitors are effective in depression and obsessive compulsive disorder; anxiolytics appear to have some efficacy in depressive disorders as well as anxiety states; and lithium may be useful in treating aggressive in addition to bipolar patients. A uniform correspondence between disorders and treatments does not exist.

Given the early stage of development of the science of psychopathology, all nosological systems are by definition problematic, yet the DSM-III and DSM-III-R diagnostic systems pose additional difficulties. If the aim of a nosological system is to segregate homogeneous patient populations, then the DSM systems fall short of this goal. The use of a 'choice principle' (x symptoms out of y criteria to qualify for a diagnosis) generates unnecessarily heterogeneous categories. For example, two patients may both be diagnosed with major depression, and yet share few symptoms in common, whereas they each may share important characteristics with patients in other diagnostic categories. Secondly, the employment of hierarchical decision rules mandates that important features of a patient's illness may not be diagnosed (or are considered to be subsumed under the diagnostic hegemony of a more important diagnostic category).

Finally, the DSM systems ignore the 'goodness of fit' of a patient into a given diagnostic category. Is this patient a prototypical example of a particular disorder or are they a poor example? The introduction of residual diagnostic categories for patients who do not fit within the rubric of standard criteria is a by-product of difficulties of using a categorical system: everybody must fit somewhere.

Thus, categorical diagnostic systems in general and the DSM-III-R diagnostic system in particular exemplify the problems of a nosological classification of psychopathology. The categorical approach is necessary, but it is only a partial solution to the problem of classification. Diagnostic labels are approximations at best. Only by expanding our thinking will we be able adequately to describe psychopathology and to make further progress in biological psychiatry.

The dimensional approach to diagnosis

A complement to the categorical approach to diagnosis is the dimensional or componential approach (Katz and Wetzler, 1991; van Praag, 1989; van Praag *et al.*, 1975, 1987; van Praag and Leijnse, 1965). In this way of thinking, all human psychological states, pathological as well as normal, are conceived of as patterns of perception, thinking, emotion and behaviour. For the purposes of scientific investigation, however, the components that comprise this complex psychological structure are better viewed or seen as independent, or partially so, to be measured as separate functions in themselves. The units in this approach are, therefore, components—the various aspects of the disordered state. This framework permits quantification of these components, resulting in articulated measurement. It is more suited to the problem of uncovering relationships between biological and psychological factors.

The dimensional approach stipulates that basic components of psychological (dys)functioning are present to some degree in many psycho(patho)logical states, although they may be more or less prominent in certain psychiatric disorders. For example, anxiety is an emotion which is ubiquitous, found in psychologically healthy individuals as well as in psychiatric and physically ill patient populations (Wetzler and Katz, 1989). It may be measured on a continuum from minimal and rare to extreme and pervasive. Thus, we speak of the dimension of anxiety.

To continue with the illustration, anxiety is not specific to any particular psychiatric disorder. High levels of anxiety are exhibited by many different types of patients. It is most obviously seen in anxiety disorder patients, but is equally prominent in depressive disorders, mania and in acute psychosis (Katz *et al.*, 1989). Patients with personality and substance abuse disorders also suffer from poor anxiety regulation (Sanderson and Wetzler, 1991).

Using a dimensional approach, each patient may be evaluated from high to low on the various components of emotion, cognition and perception, e.g. high anxiety, moderately depressed mood, intact perceptual function, poor concentration, highly agitated, adequate social relationships, etc. Any clinical state may be described within this framework. Although the components are universal, a dimensional evaluation captures the complexity and uniqueness of each patient. This contrasts with the categorical approach to diagnosis which offers prototypical descriptors that may not apply to a particular patient. The dimensional approach describes the particular patient in full detail. While the dimensional approach appreciates the importance of individual differences, it also provides a framework for detecting important similarities between patients—groupings which may be determined empirically through various mathematical procedures.

For practical purposes, the success of the dimensional approach is contingent upon the quality of methods applied to the problem. Patients may be measured on each of the basic psychological dimensions. These measures then generate profiles which describe a given patient in highly specific ways. This permits the easy determination of the relative prominence of one or another component (i.e., 'this man is more anxious than depressed'), a comparison of profiles of different patients (i.e., 'this woman is more depressed than that man'), or a comparison of a given patient's profile at different points in time (i.e., 'this patient's anxiety has significantly diminished during the past two weeks').

Many psychological tests, such as the Minnesota Multiphasic Personality Inventory (MMPI) or the Symptom Checklist–90R (SCL-90), are constructed for such a dimensional approach and are readily interpreted by trained clinical psychologists. These tests generate multidimensional profiles which quantify the patient's clinical presentation on a number of important psychological (either symptomatic or personality) dimensions. For example, the Millon Clinical Multiaxial Inventory-II is sensitive to personality differences of patients diagnosed with major depression. Some depressed patients score high on scales indicative of conflicts over attachment, whereas others score high on scales reflecting greater comfort in dependent relationships (Wetzler *et al.*, 1989). The test's multidimensional approach is able to capture this variability, and to depict the relative prominence of one or another personality trait. Over the years, substantial literature has accumulated on the clinical significance and implications for treatment of these different test profiles. Despite these accomplishments, the science of psychopathological measurement remains in its infancy.

The dimensional approach recognizes the fundamental difficulties in separating discrete diagnostic entities. The presentation of a particular type of depression, for example, can be quite varied. Some depressions are characterized by high levels of agitation and others by retardation; some depressions have significant lowering of mood, whereas others are described by anhedonia. The intensity and duration of the depression may vary greatly. These factors exert an important influence on prognosis, treatment and, by inference, on the psychobiological causes of the depression. Similarly, the patient's personality structure is usually independent of the particular depressive syndrome, and yet, it too

must be incorporated into treatment decisions. The dimensional approach offers the opportunity to consider these manifold diagnostic issues.

As we will argue, the dimensional approach is more suited to research investigations than the categorical approach. Even when an association between a
biological variable and a psychiatric disorder is discovered, there is still great
difficulty in determining which of the many aspects that comprise the complex
disorder are responsible for the relationship. For example, is the disturbance in
noradrenergic (NA) functioning often found in depressed patients a manifestation of the depression per se, or of depressed mood, anxiety, hostility, agitation,
retardation, or any other component of the depressed state? By the same token,
the NA dysfunction could be associated with the underlying personality disorder typically found in these depressed patients.

It is not surprising that most biological markers so far have proven to have low
specificity for psychiatric disorders. Biological variables may, however, prove to
be specific for particular components or dimensions of the psychiatric disorder
that might or might not be present in a given case (van Praag et al., 1990). But it is
only by applying a dimensional approach that researchers will have the opportunity to uncover these, as yet undetected, brain–behaviour relationships.

For example, an NA dysfunction has now been associated with the anxiety
and agitation components of major depression (Redmond et al., 1986). Therefore, we may expect to find NA dysfunctions associated with the anxiety component of generalized anxiety disorder, the anticipatory anxiety often found in
panic disorder, as well as the anxiety and agitation of manic and schizophrenic
patients. The next step would be to examine whether these associations also
apply to normal individuals in anxiety-provoking situations (e.g. prior to taking
tests, going on job interviews, etc.).

Since each dimension is considered separately, the dimensional approach
lets us determine what are the effects of a given treatment on each component.
For example, there is ample evidence that tricyclic antidepressants do not work
on the entire entity called 'Major Depression' (Katz et al., 1987). Rather, these
medications initially have effects on certain components (i.e. disturbed affects
such as anxiety and hostility) and later have effects on others (i.e. social functioning and activity level). By using a dimensional approach to detect these
relationships, we may begin to infer the mechanism of action of the tricyclics.
Their direct effects may be on anxiety and hostility, whereas other effects may
be considered indirect or epiphenomenal.

Thus, a narrow categorical approach may ignore important indications for
certain medications, which can be detected using a dimensional approach. For
example, many schizophrenic patients have significant depressive affect leading to suicidality. In such instances, it may be appropriate to treat the patient
with a tricyclic antidepressant, despite his or her diagnosis, in addition to neuroleptic medication. What the dimensional approach aims for is a more rational
clinical psychopharmacology.

As compounds with specific biological mechanisms of action are developed, they are likely to be less and less specific for a nosological entity. They may, however, be indicated for specific psychopathological dimensions which cut across diagnoses. Thus, the development of biochemically specific drugs will probably decrease their range of action and enable the clinician to compose a therapeutic regimen which is tied to particular psychopathological dysfunctions (van Praag *et al.* 1987, 1990; van Praag, 1989, 1990).

Goal-directed, component-oriented psychopharmacology is more than a chimera. Cardiology provides a useful analogy. Once a myocardial infarction has been diagnosed and the cardiac condition has been functionally analysed, drugs are administered to regulate discrete disturbances in, for instance, rhythm, conduction, frequency and output. These drugs are often prescribed simultaneously, and thus provide a model for goal-directed, dysfunction-oriented psychiatric pharmacology. Needless to say, the practicality of this inviting prospect will depend on the compatibility of the different drugs and their propensity to induce side effects.

The dimensional approach also permits the development of goal-directed, component-oriented focal psychotherapies comparable to the clinical psycho-pharmacology outlined above (Frances *et al.*, 1984; van Praag, 1990). As psychological states are dissected into those components which are dysfunctional and those which remain intact, it is possible to define treatment goals precisely and to rationally choose an appropriate treatment method. Certain psychotherapies may prove particularly effective with certain components of an illness. For example, in the treatment of alcohol abuse, it may be necessary to offer a therapy which focuses on the patient's ability to tolerate anxiety. Or, in the treatment of depression, it may be necessary to address the patient's sensitivity to rejection. All too often, psychotherapy based on a categorical approach pays little attention to these semi-independent components. Yet, it is only by evaluating these important issues that appropriate treatment planning may be initiated.

An example of the dimensional approach in biological research

An example will serve to illustrate how the dimensional approach has advantages over the categorical approach for biological research in psychiatry. In particular, the dimensional approach permits the interpretation of data which are poorly understood within traditional nosology, and thereby generate new predictions to be tested experimentally.

The role of serotonin (5-hydroxytryptamine, 5-HT) in depression is a case in point. Initially, van Praag *et al.* (1970) observed lowered levels of post-probenecid 5-hydroxyindoleacetic acid (5-HIAA, the major degradation product of 5-HT) in the cerebrospinal fluid (CSF) of a subgroup of depressed individuals, indicating diminished 5-HT metabolism. This finding led to the introduction of the concept of a '5-HT depression', a type of depression supposedly specifically linked to a central 5-HT disorder, although the unique clinical characteristics of this subgroup were never identified (van Praag and Korf, 1971). Still, a biological disturbance was tied to a nosological entity. This hypothesis, however, proved untenable after a series of studies with 5-HT precursors showed that increasing 5-HT availability alone did not have an antidepressant effect (van Praag, 1984; van Praag and Lemus, 1986). In contrast, combined augmentation of 5-HT and catecholamines using 5-hydroxytryptophan (5-HTP) or tryptophan plus tyrosine was beneficial.

If 5-HT disturbances were not linked to a particular syndromal subtype of depression then, one may ask, could they relate to particular psychopathological dimensions that may or may not occur in depression? This would explain why 5-HT disturbances occur in some, but not other, depressions and have been found in other diagnostic categories as well. Further research has supported this conclusion. 5-HT dysfunction appears to be associated with a dysregulation of aggression.

Asberg *et al.* (1976) determined that the lowered CSF 5-HIAA found in depressed patients was mostly limited to those individuals who had made suicide attempts. Subsequent studies revealed that low CSF 5-HIAA was observed in non-depressed suicide attempters with personality disorders as well as in schizophrenic patients who had made suicide attempts because 'voices' had ordered them to do so (van Praag, 1986). Thus, 5-HT dysfunction was related to the dimension of suicidality which spans many diagnostic categories.

Subsequent research has further refined our understanding of this 5-HT dysfunction. Individuals with increased outwardly directed aggression also showed lowered CSF 5-HIAA, no matter which diagnostic category they fell into (Brown *et al.*, 1982; Linnoila *et al.*, 1983; Virkkunen *et al.*, 1987). In linking the research on suicidality and outwardly directed aggression, van Praag *et al.* (1986) hypothesized that diminished 5-HT metabolism in the CNS was related to dysregulated aggression, irrespective of the direction it took (inwardly or outwardly) or the nosological context in which it occurred.

In addition to explaining existing data, the dimensional approach generates predictions about the role of 5-HT in dysregulated aggression in normal individuals, a process which would have been inappropriate using a categorical approach. For example, one may expect that psychologically healthy individuals during times of combat may exhibit lowered CSF 5-HIAA. We have been impressed with the usefulness of the dimensional approach for interpreting data regarding the 5-HT system. In addition, it seems to be equally valuable for understanding dysfunctions of other neurotransmitter systems (van Praag *et al.*, 1990).

A dimensional approach to depression

Psychological or psychopathological dimensions are constructs, which is to say they are abstractions. Based on our interpretation of available data, we infer that they exist, although they may not be directly observable. Most importantly these basic dimensions are not observable in splendid isolation from other dimensions of psychopathology. In order to understand how these dimensions work, we must disentangle them from one another. This is an artificial psychometric feat, not a fact of nature, and may require sophisticated multivariate statistical analysis.* Thus we speak of constructs. What is remarkable is that we seem to be able to tie these high-level abstractions or constructs to their biological underpinnings.

The problem of identifying and disentangling psychological dimensions which are intermingled is illustrated by the relationship of anxiety and depressed mood (Wetzler and Katz, 1989). These two components of psychopathology are omnipresent, and they are said to 'merge insensibly' (Lewis, 1934). It is almost impossible to find someone with depressed mood who does not also manifest prominent anxious mood. Self-report tests of depression correlate at $r = 0.70$ with self-report tests of anxiety, which is a level comparable to the correlation of different self-report tests of depression with each other, and of different self-report tests of anxiety with each other (Wetzler, 1986). To speak of a dimension of anxiety separate from that of depressed mood is to make an abstract distinction. However abstract this distinction may be, it is useful since it has real psychobiological consequences.

Even in a population of severely depressed patients where anxiety and depression are thoroughly intermingled, it is possible to disentangle separable 'pure' dimensions of anxiety and depression using refined psychometric methodology (see Mullaney, 1984, for a review of 40 studies). For example, in the NIMH Collaborative Project for the Psychobiological Study of Depression using 132 in-patients with major depression, the components of anxiety and depressed mood were both quite prominent (Katz *et al.*, 1989). This study used a multi-vantaged approach which combined data from the patient's self-report, doctor's interview, nurse's observational rating and direct performance measures. The combination of data from several vantages compensated for the weaknesses of any single method.

In the Collaborative Project sample, the components of anxiety and depressed mood correlated at $r = 0.71$; thus, they were considered to be

---

* The difference between the categorical approach and the dimensional approach is reflected by the kinds of multivariate statistical procedures used. The categorical approach uses discriminant function analysis to differentiate groups (or subgroups) and subsequently to characterize the qualities of classes of patients. The dimensional approach uses factor analysis to uncover independent dimensions.

substantially intermingled. However, using principal components factor analysis, the investigators were able to find orthogonal depression and anxiety dimensions (Katz *et al.*, 1984; Wetzler and Katz, 1989). These dimensions were separated when agitation and retardation (clearly related to anxiety and depressed mood) were incorporated. Based on this separation, it was possible to link these orthogonal dimensions to different underlying biological variables (e.g. the anxiety/agitation dimension correlated with CSF 3-methoxy-4-hydroxyphenylglycol (MHPG) at $r = 0.43$) (Redmond *et al.*, 1986). Such linkages were not fruitful using a categorical approach. Further analysis using the componential approach revealed gender differences in the non-verbal expression of anxiety and depressed mood (i.e. body posture and facial expression) with implications for the study of gender and depression (Katz *et al.*, unpublished data). Depressed women manifested a kind of 'constricted agitation' when they became anxious, whereas depressed men became hostile. Finally, anxiety and depressed mood components appeared to be differentially sensitive to early signs of therapeutic change, and offered significant information about the recovery process (Katz *et al.*, 1987).

In summary, although it is a difficult process to differentiate components of psychopathology, such as anxiety and depressed mood in depressive states, it is useful to think of them as (partially) independent, and as such to be studied in terms of underlying neuronal (dys)function. The delineation of these basic dimensions or components offers important advantages over the categorical approach.

The core problem for the dimensional approach, however, is determining the basic dimensions and then measuring them. What psycho(patho)logical (dys)functions are the appropriate building blocks? What are the fundamental components of psychopathological states, especially depression? How may they be differentiated from one another? Finally, we may ask the practical question: out of the large, although not infinite, number of psychological components, which ones are relevant to a particular study and should therefore be selected for inclusion? This clearly depends on the study and problem definition. No selective list of clinical dimensions will invariably be appropriate for all studies.

The 5-HT and depression discussion provides an illustration of the complexity of identifying and delineating a psychopathological dimension. Focusing solely on the association between violent suicidality and 5-HT disturbance would be to miss the fundamental psychological dysfunction, which probably is dysregulation of aggression or impulsivity. Only by connecting violent suicidality with outwardly directed aggression was this basic dimension delineated at an appropriate level of abstraction.

Bearing in mind that no list of psychological components is complete, we may identify certain ones which seem relevant to us for any study of depression: the disturbed affects of depressed mood, anxiety and hostility: poor hedonic tone; motor behaviours of agitation and retardation; and reality-testing capacity.

The dimensional approach is also particularly suitable for the evaluation of personality traits associated with depression, which are all too often ignored by both clinicians and researchers (Wetzler *et al.*, 1990). During the depressed state, normal and healthy personality traits are submerged, only to return gradually during the process of recovery.

It is beyond the scope of this chapter to discuss the assessment of personality, but suffice it to say that one may take a narrow or broad approach. A single, non-specific dimension of personality, named 'neuroticism', has been identified. It may have some aetiological significance for depression, appears to hinder treatment and bodes poorly for prognosis (Kerr *et al.*, 1970). Alternatively, three basic dimensions of personality which may have psychobiological significance, named 'novelty seeking', 'harm avoidance' and 'reward dependence', have also been identified (Cloninger, 1987). If, as postulated, these dimensions may be linked to specific neurotransmitter dysfunctions, they would be useful in determining appropriate pharmacological treatments. Finally, the field of personality assessment itself has generated a multitude of dimensional systems covering dozens of normal and pathological traits (e.g. Millon's (1987) or Jackson's (1976) systems; see Wetzler (1989) for a list of inventories). The choice of personality dimensions depends on the aims of the study.

In addition to the psychopathological components listed above, there are several other features of depression which are clearly relevant: course of illness (i.e. bipolar or unipolar), severity, duration of illness (i.e. acute or chronic) and age of onset. We may not speak of these characteristics of depression as components. However, they are dimensions which describe the quality of the patient's depression. They too should be evaluated on independent axes.

In summary, the dimensional approach identifies important components of depression (equally relevant to other psychopathological states) which, although highly intermingled, may be considered to function independently, and have psychobiological consequences.

A recommendation

While we advocate the introduction of a dimensional approach to classification, we are by no means suggesting that the traditional, Kraepelian nosological approach be discarded. The dimensional approach is not a replacement for nosological diagnosis, but its complement. We therefore recommend a two-tier approach to classification (van Praag, 1990).

Patients first receive a traditional nosological diagnosis, based on criteria from DSM-III or its latest revision. Such a categorical approach serves a number of useful purposes, not the least of which is providing a shorthand means of communication. For example, we use the categorical label 'Major Depression' to connote an aggregate of psychopathological symptoms and components, rather than go into excruciating detail about each component. However imprecise, this label is a telegraphic language used by professionals to communicate necessary information about the patient. The nosological approach represents the first tier of diagnosis, placing the patient in a broad, general diagnostic framework.

But this first-tier nosological diagnosis is not sufficient in and of itself. We must also evaluate important psychological (dys)functions. The dimensional approach represents the second tier of diagnosis in which these components and (dys)functions are depicted in detail. For example, in addition to assigning the label 'Major Depression', we characterize the patient's affective functioning, hedonic tone, goal-directed behaviour, reality testing and personality traits. Using a two-tier approach, we get the benefits of both applications.

As we have discussed, the dimensional approach generates unexpected associations between biological variables and psychopathological dimensions. It can function as a catalyst for psychiatry's ongoing scientific orientation and development. In particular, the second-tier diagnosis improves on the clinician's usual measurement of behaviour. Therefore, it should have an impact on decisions about specific pharmacological and psychotherapeutic treatments.

As long as clinicians and researchers rely on the nosological approach alone, psychiatry's growth will be stunted. The traditional nosological approach, used alone, has taken us as far as it can. We now need to expand our diagnostic concepts in both research and clinical work along the lines described by the dimensional approach. Unfortunately, putting aside the nosological viewpoint is easier said than done. This way of thinking has become ingrained. The two-tier approach affords us the opportunity to keep the best of the old and to incorporate the best of the new.

References

Asberg M, Traskman L and Thoren P (1976) 5-HIAA in the cerebrospinal fluid: A biochemical suicide predictor? *Arch Gen Psychiatry* **33**, 1193–1197.

Brown G, Ebert M, Goyer P *et al.* (1982) Aggression, suicide and serotonin: Relationships to CSF amine metabolites. *Am J Psychiatry* **139**, 741–746.

Cloninger C (1987) A systematic method for clinical description and classification of personality variants. *Arch Gen Psychiatry* **44**, 573–588.

Frances A, Clarkin J and Perry S (1984) *Differential Therapeutics in Psychiatry: The Art and Science of Treatment Selection.* New York: Brunner Mazel.

Jackson D (1976) *Jackson Personality Inventory.* Port Huron, MI: Research Psychologist's Press.

Katz M, Koslow S, Berman N *et al.* (1984) A multi-vantaged approach to measurement of behavioral and affect states for clinical and psychobiological research. *Psychol Reports* **55**, 619–671, mono. suppl. 1.

Katz M and Wetzler S (1991) Behavior measurement in psychobiological research. In: *Encyclopedia of Human Biology*, Vol. 1, pp. 607–614. San Diego: Academic Press.

Katz M, Koslow S, Maas J *et al.* (1987) The timing, specificity and clinical prediction of tricyclic drug effects in depression. *Psychol Med* **17**, 297–309.

Katz M, Wetzler S, Koslow S and Secunda S (1989) Video methodology in the study of the psychopathology and treatment of depression. *Psychiatr Ann* **19**, 372–381.

Katz M, Cloitre M, Wetzler S *et al.* (unpublished data) Expressive characteristics of anxiety in depressed men and women.

Kerr T, Schapira K, Roth M and Garside R (1970) The relationship between the Maudsley Personality Inventory and the course of affective disorders. *Br J Psychiatry* **116**, 11–19.

Lewis A (1934) Melancholia: A clinical survey of depressive states. *J Ment Sci* **80**, 1–42; 277–378; 488–558.

Linnoila M, Virkhunen M, Scheinin M *et al.* (1983) Low cerebrospinal fluid 5-hydroxyindoleacetic acid concentration differentiates impulsive from nonimpulsive violent behaviour. *Life Sci* **33**, 2609–2614.

Millon T (1987) *Manual for the MCMI-II* (2nd edn). Minneapolis: National Computer Systems.

Mullaney J (1984) The relationship between anxiety and depression: A review of some principal components analytic studies. *J Affect Dis* **7**, 139–148.

Redmond D, Katz M, Maas J *et al.* (1986) Cerebrospinal fluid amine metabolites. *Arch Gen Psychiatry* **43**, 938–947.

Sanderson W and Wetzler S (1991) Chronic anxiety and Generalized Anxiety Disorder: Issues in comorbidity. In: Rapee R and Barlow D (eds) *Chronic Anxiety and Generalized Anxiety Disorder*, pp. 119–135. New York: Guilford Press.

van Praag HM (1984) Studies in the mechanism of action of serotonin precursors in depression. *Psychopharmacol Bull* **20**, 599–602.

van Praag HM (1986) Biological suicide research: Outcome and limitations. *Biol Psychiatry* **21**, 1305–1323.

van Praag HM (1989) Diagnosing depression: Looking backward into the future. *Devel Psychiatry* **4**, 375–397.

van Praag HM (1990) The DSM-IV (depression) classification: To be or not to be? *J Nerv Ment Dis* **178**, 147–149.

van Praag HM (1990) Two-tier diagnosing in psychiatry. *Psychiatr Res* **34**, 1–11.

van Praag HM and Korf J (1971) Endogenous depressions with and without disturbances in the 5-hydroxytryptamine metabolism: A biochemical classification? *Psychopharmacology* **19**, 148–152.

van Praag HM and Leijnse B (1965) Neubewertung des syndroms. Skizze einer funktionellen pathologie. *Psychiatr Neurol Neurochir* **68**, 50–66.

van Praag HM and Lemus C (1986) Monoamine precursors in the treatment of psychiatric disorders. In: Wurtman R and Wurtman J (eds) *Nutrition and the Brain.* New York: Raven Press.

van Praag HM, Korf J and Puite J (1970) 5-Hydroxyindoleacetic acid levels in the cerebrospinal fluid of depressive patients treated with probenecid. *Nature* **225**, 1259–1260.

van Praag HM, Korf J, Lakke J and Schut T (1975) Dopamine metabolism in depression, psychoses and Parkinson's disease: The problem of the specificity of biological variables in behavior disorders. *Psychol Med* **5**, 138–146.

van Praag HM, Plutchik R and Conte H (1986) The serotonin hypothesis of (auto)aggression: Critical appraisal of the evidence. *Ann NY Acad Sci* **487**, 150–167.

van Praag HM, Kahn R, Asnis G *et al.* (1987) Denosologization of biological psychiatry: On the specificity of 5-HT disturbances in psychiatric disorders. *J Affect Dis* **13**, 1–8.

van Praag HM, Asnis G, Kahn R *et al.* (1990) Monoamines and abnormal behavior: A multiaminergic perspective. *Br J Psychiatry* **157**, 723–734.

Virkkunen M, Nuutila A, Goodwin F and Linnoila M (1987) Cerebrospinal fluid mono-amine metabolite levels in male arsonists. *Arch Gen Psychiatry* **44**, 241–247.

Wetzler S (1986) Methodological issues for the differentiation of anxiety and depression. *Clin Neuropharmacol* **9** (Suppl 4), 248–250.

Wetzler S (1989) *Measuring Mental Illness: Psychometric Assessment for Clinicians.* Washington, DC: American Psychiatric Press.

Wetzler S and Katz M (1989) Problems with the differentiation of anxiety and depression. *J Psychiatr Res* **23**, 1–12.

Wetzler S, Kahn R, Strauman T and Dubro A (1989) The diagnosis of major depression by self-report. *J Pers Assess* **53**, 22–30.

Wetzler S, Kahn R, Cahn W *et al.* (1990) Psychological test characteristics of depressed and panic patients. *Psychiatry Res* **31**, 179–192.

6

Biological markers of depression

D.J. Kupfer

Introduction

The concept of biological 'markers' has become increasingly important in our attempts to elucidate the pathophysiology of psychiatric disorders. The actual term 'biological marker', however, is not well defined and is frequently abused. Relatively little attention is given to determining the criteria for a valid biological marker. Prior to any discussion of any specific putative biological 'markers' or correlates or psychiatric illness, we should delineate several conceptual and methodological issues in the application of such laboratory methods. Second, we ought to highlight several points which address the state/trait controversy or the issue of persistent versus episodic biological alterations. Third, we should review critically our current state of knowledge with respect to biological markers in several selected domains directly relevant to depression.

Conceptual issues*

As we have discussed (Kupfer and Thase, 1989) recently, laboratory methods usually serve three major purposes in psychiatric diagnosis: (1) to rule out or to confirm a primary medical pathogenesis for a psychiatric syndrome; (2) as a specific laboratory test to confirm a psychiatric diagnosis; and (3) to gain a

---

* This section is adapted from Kupfer, D.J. and Thase, M.E. (1989). Laboratory studies and validity of psychiatric diagnosis: Has there been progress? In *The Validity of Psychiatric Diagnosis* (eds L.N. Robins and J.E. Barrett), Raven Press, New York, 1989 (pp. 179–181).

The Diagnosis of Depression. Edited by J.P. Feighner and W.F. Boyer
© 1991 John Wiley & Sons Ltd

better understanding of the underlying biological processes. In our contemporary medical practice the first purpose is useful, is well established, and should be a part of every patient's initial assessment and differential diagnosis. We can cite many relevant examples: assessment of thyroid function in a patient with depression; cardiovascular evaluation in a patient suffering from severe panic and anxiety; or screening for unreported illicit drug use in a patient with a recent onset of psychosis. While such evaluations may often be negative in patients with a psychiatric disorder, failure to perform such relevant medical evaluations can easily lead to incorrect diagnosis. This is particularly true since approximately 15% of new admissions to a tertiary care clinical research inpatient unit have a significant unrecognized medical syndrome underlying the presenting diagnosis of affective disorder (Kupfer and Spiker, 1981).

The development of reasonably accurate laboratory tests to rule out and/or confirm diagnoses of the major psychiatric syndromes represents a second major role for laboratory methods. Enthusiasm for biological 'markers' in clinical psychiatry has been fuelled by the desire for an accurate and sensitive laboratory test. The introduction of such tests is usually considered a goal of applied research on the biological disturbances of psychiatric disorders. While such reliable and valid tests could be used for: (1) screening of new cases; (2) differential diagnosis; or (3) confirmation of presumed clinical diagnosis, it is our opinion that no such standard laboratory tests for routine screening or differential diagnosis are yet available for the affective disorders. However, a research strategy similar or identical to the one described below suggests a number of steps necessary to develop such laboratory 'markers' which, when proven reliable and valid, could be evaluated as tests for clinical diagnostic purposes in psychiatric settings. Once the accuracy of a laboratory parameter is established in research settings, then its value as a diagnostic indicator must be further examined, both in terms of generalizability and cost effectiveness. It is important to recognize differences in terms of strategy and underlying goals depending on whether the investigator is interested in developing a laboratory test for diagnosis or elucidating biological factors in the pathogenesis of the disorder (Buysse and Kupfer, 1990).

We propose that the biological variable being measured must meet at least two criteria for its potential use as a clinical 'marker': (1) it must clearly differentiate the criterion psychopathological group from a matched healthy control group; and (2) it must distinguish the criterion group from other unrelated psychopathological conditions. For example, the chosen variable not only should be able to distinguish individuals with a diagnosis of depression from age- and sex-matched normal controls, it must also differentiate patients with depression from individuals with other disorders such as panic and anxiety states. Since most current psychopathological classifications are based on description of clinical syndromes, not distinct and fully articulated disease states, studies of biological factors in various diagnostic groupings should be conducted with an eye open to the possibility that smaller subsets of patients within a clinical diagnostic condition may manifest an abnormality not present in the majority of cases. Thus, evaluation of sampling distributions for subgroups of outliers may be quite useful, even though the group mean for the criterion condition may not differ significantly from that of the relevant control groups (Buchsbaum and Rieder, 1979). A further refinement of this approach involves the assessment of comorbid conditions in understanding the relative sensitivity and specificity of such findings.

The third purpose of research on biological processes related to the major psychiatric syndromes is most pertinent to the current status of the field of laboratory studies and the development of potential biological correlates and markers. While the first two purposes for laboratory methods are important, we believe that emphasis on the biological underpinnings in the pathophysiology of affective disorders will yield the most valuable information. In turn, they will be very helpful in achieving the first two purposes.

It cannot be emphasized strongly enough (Thase *et al.*, 1985) that a number of factors may compromise the reliable and valid assessment of biological parameters in psychiatric disorders. Such factors include unreliable clinical diagnosis, the contribution of extraneous variables (age, sex, weight loss, menstrual status or time of day), the non-specific effects of stress or hospitalization, the direct biological effects of medication, treatment or withdrawal from drugs or alcohol, the confounding effects of intercurrent medical illness, and inaccuracy or unreliability of the biological test parameters being utilized. This wide array of factors which may adversely affect the results of biological research have facilitated the publication of many false leads and unreplicated findings in our field. Suggested solutions to these problems include emphasizing research on conditions for which operationalized, descriptive diagnostic criteria (based on standardized interviews and collateral sources of information) are available, study of matched patient and normal control groups, provision of relatively long medication-free washout periods, precise and definitive medical and neurological evaluations and exclusion of cases with potentially confounding medical conditions prior to research participation, documentation of intra- and inter-assay reliability of the biological parameter being studied, and inter-laboratory collaboration and comparisons of laboratory methods whenever possible (Thase *et al.*, 1985). Increased emphasis on diurnal or circadian factors should be included in the evaluation of certain specific parameters known to be affected by circadian phase. Furthermore, the list of more general recommendations developed several years ago for research in affective disorders (Kupfer and Rush, 1983) should be applied to the study of biological markers. These include methodological issues concerning sample reporting, patient recruitment, diagnostic questions similar to the ones listed previously and a series of additional patient variables such as severity, psychosis and degree of chronicity.

At the very minimum, we should consider the probability that there are two types of markers (Table I). The first is the episodic (so-called state) marker, present during an episode of the illness, but not present when the episode has ended and the patient is in a remitted or recovered state. We would also assume that such a marker was not present prior to the onset of the episode. Finally, it would be assumed that the marker would reappear if the individual suffered another episode. The second type of marker is considered to be a trait or persistent marker. This marker might be present in several different combinations. For example, it could be present non-episodically, i.e. between episodes, as well as present prior to the onset of the first episode (pre-morbid state). Such a marker might occur during individual episodes as well as between episodes and pre-morbidity. A third variation of trait marker would be present only after a first episode had occurred. It is important to understand the differences between these types of persistent markers before proceeding to describe what is currently known and what types of biological studies still need to be undertaken. Additionally, we also need to realize that the same biological variable might be involved in both types of markers.

Recently, Kraemer (personal communication, H.C. Kraemer) has reviewed 'state–trait basics' and highlighted the following issues. Trait and state could refer to contrasting aspects of an individual characteristic that may coexist. One ought to define the following parameters with respect to these aspects: (1) What is the characteristic? (2) How will it be measured? (3) In which subjects will it be measured? (4) What will be the population sampling issues? (5) Over what span of time will the characteristic be measured? Kraemer further suggests that trait refers to stable individual differences among subjects in the population, and that state refers to within-subject variation association with a criterion that defines the type of state of interest, e.g. clinical status, related states or physical health-related states.

A somewhat similar strategy to identify trait biological abnormalities has been undertaken by Rush and colleagues (1990). The identification of trait-like abnormalities does require investigation in patients when in a depressed state and again when not depressed. Therefore, it is important to define the clinical state at each point of measurement. Rush *et al.* have suggested that a biological

Table I. Characteristics of biological markers.

	Pre-morbid state	Episode	Remission	New episode
State (episodic)	−	+	−	+
Trait (persistent)				
1.	+	−	+	−
2.	+	+	+	+
3.	−	−	+	−

abnormality found both during and following remission from the depressed state may represent (see Table I): (1) a simple consequence of a prior episode; (2) a concomitant and longer-standing consequence of the state; (3) a true antecedent of the first episode of illness that is present before, during and after all episodes; or (4) a scar of more than one episode. Under ideal circumstances, a hierarchical series of research investigations to disentangle state versus trait might be useful. Rush *et al.* would expect that such research studies would determine whether the abnormality: (1) distinguishes symptomatic depressed patients from normals; (2) persists following partial remission (a residual dysthymic level of symptoms); (3) is present with complete, recent or more long-standing remission; (4) is exhibited by patients in their first episode; (5) is found in some never affected, but at-risk individuals (e.g. family members); and (6) predicts the development of the disorder in the never ill. This strategy as proposed by Rush and colleagues could further substantiate our understanding of biological correlates regardless of the domain chosen for measurement.

The next key issue is involved with the actual choice of biological correlates in depression. Over the last twenty years, a variety of biological investigations has yielded an array of biological changes which may serve as a potential episode or more persistent trait markers of a depressive illness. Our own pragmatic view is that episode correlates are worth studying even if they are state dependent and reversible. They appear to be easier to identify and quantitate as indicators of an episode than are clinical changes in symptoms or social/work impairments either of the index episode or the onset of the new episode. Furthermore, alterations that may persist beyond the episode could serve as important residual or trait markers during the phase of clinical remission. On the other hand, the persistence of biological abnormalities associated with no clinical symptoms may still represent state correlates of the depressive episode, since a significant degree of psychosocial impairment may be present at the end of an episode. Perhaps this represents circular reasoning since, traditionally, the termination of an episode is determined by clinical measurements. However, one underlying aim in biological psychiatry has been the hope that biological indicators may ultimately represent the gold standard to delineate the boundaries (onset and termination) of an episode.

The choice of which biological correlates to study is not easy, but it is now widely recognized that depression is associated with definite biological changes. Moreover, since the major affective disorders are characterized by a variety of disturbances in physiological functioning (including sleep, motor activity, appetite and libido), the pursuit of studies in potential biological mechanisms is conceptually appealing. Finally, evidence of the efficacy of various forms of somatic treatment for the major affective disorders strengthens the intuitive and conceptual appeal of the role of biological factors in these conditions.

Rather than attempt to review in a systematic fashion all the proposed biological 'markers' suggested for depression, the intent of this selective review is to demonstrate current research efforts (in a few specific domains) that appear most promising. Specifically, therefore, we will review some of the most recent work in the following domains: neuroendocrine/neoropeptide studies; neurochemistry of depression; aspects of neurophysiology/electrophysiology; and selected imaging studies in depression. A review in these areas should convey exciting developments and strategies which may ultimately lead us to a better understanding of acute biological changes and biological vulnerability factors in depressive illness.

Biological correlates

Neuroendocrine and neuropeptide studies

Over the past two decades, there has been intensive study of a variety of neuroendocrine and neuropeptide parameters in affective disorders. These research efforts have been of major interest, especially because of the close relationship between the limbic system and mechanisms of neuroendocrine regulation involving the hypothalamus and pituitary gland.

The hypothalamic–pituitary–adrenal cortex (HPA) axis has certainly been the best-studied neuroendocrine axis. Even the most critical reading of the scientific data on this axis would lead one to conclude that a significant subset of severely depressed patients show one or more abnormalities of the HPA axis. Investigative efforts of this area were stimulated by initial observations of hypercortisolaemia in depressed patients. Abnormalities in depressed patients usually include hypercortisolaemia and/or failure to suppress cortisol levels following administration of 1–2 mg dexamethasone (Carroll, 1982). The rates of test abnormality in depression are substantially higher (especially in hospitalized patients) than those seen in normal controls and generally higher than rates seen in other psychopathological populations (APA Task Force on Laboratory Tests in Psychiatry, 1987; Arana *et al.*, 1985; Carroll, 1982). However, attempts to develop routine clinical diagnostic tests based on these findings, such as the dexamethasone suppression test (DST), have not proved of immediate practical benefit (APA Task Force on Laboratory Tests in Psychiatry, 1987).

Four hypotheses have been proposed to explain why non-suppression on the DST occurs in patients with major depression (Kathol *et al.*, 1989). These have included increased dexamethasone metabolism, increased sensitivity of pituitary glucocorticoid receptors to dexamethasone, adrenal hyper-response, particularly to adrenocorticotrophic hormone (ACTH) stimulation, and increased central drive of pituitary from hypothalamic/limbic structures that may override the action of the dexamethasone. In a critical review of these four hypotheses, Kathol and colleagues (1989) concluded that the suprahypophyseal overactivity explanation was most closely supported by the available data (see below, Nemeroff, 1990).

Although the authors also suggested that the aetiology of the HPA axis changes might very well represent epiphenomena related to stress, they and others have argued that these abnormalities could represent central hypothalamic/limbic defects which may relate to the core set of pathophysiological changes in affective states. Indeed, the strategy of using DST and other challenges to measure HPA activity during depression has usually indicated a resolution of such abnormalities when re-evaluated at a time associated with clinical recovery. Preliminary evidence has suggested that when recovery following treatment occurs without normalization of these HPA parameters, there may be a high risk of clinical relapse (Braddock, 1986; Joyce and Paykel, 1989).

It has also been suggested that the behavioural dimensions of depression associated with dexamethasone non-suppression or hypercortisolaemia may relate to a more global severity construct or more general central nervous system arousal. Finally, harsh dieting with significant (5–10 kg) weight loss or alcoholic withdrawal states may induce a transient mimicking of this phenomenon (APA Task Force on Laboratory Tests in Psychiatry, 1987).

Regulation of the hypothalamic–thyroid (HPT) axis is a second area which has received extensive study in affective disorders (Nemeroff, 1989). Initially, clinical evidence of a high incidence of depression in individuals with thyroid disease sparked curiosity about this relationship. No specific alteration in the amount of thyroid hormone is usually reported in individuals with depression, but depressive states are associated with a transient increase in thyroid hormone levels which does not exceed the normal range (Prange *et al.*, 1984).

One dynamic test of thyroid function is the thyroid-releasing hormone (TRH) stimulation test (Kirkegaard, 1981; Prange *et al.*, 1984), which has been shown to be abnormally blunted in a sizeable minority (20–40%) of depressed individuals. Such blunting is not related to thyroid pathology and often does not normalize immediately following acute treatment. Unfortunately, blunted TRH stimulation test responses are not specific to depression, but are also observed in relatively high frequency in schizophrenia (Langer *et al.*, 1983) and in alcoholism (Loosen *et al.*, 1983). This set of observations suggests a commonality of biological processes in several psychopathological states, with perhaps an increased liability for this abnormality in depression. Studies following somatic treatment have provided some preliminary evidence of high risk for relapse in individuals with blunted TRH stimulation test results, both in depression and schizophrenia (Krog-Meyer *et al.*, 1984).

Other neuroendocrine parameters which have received less extensive study, of either basal levels or following specific probes, include regulation of growth hormone secretion (Jarrett *et al.*, 1990a), prolactin regulation (Jarrett *et al.*, 1987) and study of the pineal hormone, melatonin (Lewy, 1984; Thase *et al.*, 1985). While some evidence of disturbances in each of these systems in depression has been reported, none of these findings has been consistently replicated or is robust enough to meet the criteria for either a state or trait marker.

Recently, Jarrett *et al.* (1990b) reported systemic reduction in sleep-related growth hormone (GH) secretion in major depression. Since the reduction in sleep-related GH secretion found in depressed patients persisted during treatment and was also present in a period of drug-free clinical remission, the authors tentatively concluded that this abnormality in GH secretion is unrelated to the pathological changes described in the sleep EEG of depressed patients. Instead, they suggest the possibility of an irreversible disturbance in the regulation of GH secretion at the time of sleep onset. Furthermore, they argue that recurrent depression could represent a type of behavioural sensitization process which, with repeated episodes, established a physiological instability that manifests as a disturbance in sleep-related GH secretion. Such instability could predispose the susceptible individual to the disorder at times of increased risk or stress.

In summary, the widely replicated alterations in the HPA axis, as well as the data on the HPT axis and GH secretion, has accelerated the search for the central nervous system mechanisms that underlie these abnormalities. Furthermore, the elucidation of the actual structure of various neuropeptides has stimulated their study in depression. For example, two current strategies include: (1) measurement of neuropeptide concentrations and neuropeptide receptors in cerebrospinal fluid (CSF) and brain tissue, respectively; and (2) neuroendocrine challenge tests. Nemeroff and Bissette (1990) concluded that such approaches have revealed hypersecretion of corticotrophin-releasing factor (CRF) in the HPA axis as evidenced by increased CSF CRF concentrations, decreased CRF receptor number in frontal cortex of suicide victims and a blunted ACTH response to CRF. Considerable evidence exists that this CRF hypersecretion, like the associated hypercortisolaemia, is state dependent; as suggested earlier, a blunted TSH response to TRH is found in depression, often associated with hypersecretion of TRH (increased CSF TRH concentrations). Finally, reduced CSF concentrations of somatostatin (SRIF) have been found in depressed individuals. While the reduction in CSF SRIF levels in depression appears to be state dependent, it is unclear whether the alterations in HPT function are state or trait markers.

Neurochemical studies

Investigations of proposed neurochemical abnormalities in affective disorders have been of special appeal to researchers. Some of this attraction is due to the early role of catacholamines and serotonin (5-hydroxytryptamine, 5-HT) metabolites as the first biological parameters to be studied systematically in depression. The original catecholamine hypothesis was that diminished levels of norepinephrine (noradrenaline) or 5-HT in the brain were central to the pathogenesis of depression (Bunney and Davis, 1965; Murphy *et al.*, 1978; Schildkraut, 1965). Two effective treatments for depression (tricyclic antidepressants and monoamine oxidase inhibitors) had significant effects on these systems while agents which depleted monoaminergic activity, such as reserpine, could induce depression. These findings strengthened the intuitive appeal of studying these monoamines.

In time, it has become clear that the initial hypotheses concerning the role of amines in the development of depression were too simplistic. These hypotheses have nonetheless stimulated considerable human and animal research in attempts to understand the role of pharmacological agents acting as antidepressants. For example, both in vitro and in vivo experiments have demonstrated conclusively that tricyclic antidepressants increase the amount of norepinephrine available at the synapse by inhibiting the reuptake of norepinephrine. However, many of the second-generation antidepressants with novel biochemical structures have not demonstrated a primary effect on any specific system. As Goodwin and Jamison (1990) point out, the chronic application of a wide variety of antidepressant treatments demonstrates receptor effects that by and large are consistent across these treatments. Essentially, they all down-regulate (i.e. decrease the number of) postsynaptic β-adrenergic receptors while enhancing response to serotonergic and α-adrenergic stimulation. Further examination of neurochemical changes in depression have developed from the use of post-mortem brain tissue of depressed patients. To date, they have suggested a pattern of decreased 5-HT and its metabolite (5-HIAA) in depressed patients, particularly in those individals prone to impulsivity and suicidal behaviour (Träskman *et al.*, 1981).

Other neurochemical studies have focused on the relationship between two additional brain neurotransmitters, dopamine and acetylcholine (see Goodwin and Jamison, 1990; Kupfer and Thase, 1989). The significance to the mood disorders of dopamine, which historically had been linked more closely to the pathophysiology of schizophrenia, is slowly being appreciated. Indeed, the relationship of dopamine to psychomotor activity in depression and mania has already been studied (Linnoila *et al.*, 1983; Redmond *et al.*, 1986). While investigation of acetylcholine has been hampered by the ubiquitous nature of this tiny molecule, new methods employing various probes and challenges have shown promise; for example, the use of muscarinic agonists and antagonists to probe or challenge physiological systems (Carroll *et al.*, 1980; Sitaram *et al.*, 1979, 1982, 1987).

Neurophysiological studies
Among potential neurophysiological correlates of mood disorder, waking electroencephalograms (EEG) have received extensive study for several decades. Routine waking EEG studies are useful to rule out cerebral pathology which may cause an organic affective syndrome. More advanced technology permits studies employing spectral analysis, evoked potential and, more recently, brain electrical activity mapping (BEAM) methods (Kupfer and Reynolds, 1983). Some topographical studies have shown abnormal lateralization of waking EEG

rhythms in depression (Schaeffer *et al.*, 1983; Flor-Henry and Koles, 1980). Although these findings have not been consistently replicated (Kupfer and Reynolds, 1983), they are consonant with the preliminary evidence from sub-groups of depressed patients studied with positron-emission tomography (PET) scans and are pertinent to theories of non-dominant hemispheric lateralization in depression (Flor-Henry, 1979). Research employing computer-assisted methods to determine average EEG response amplitude suggests an approximately 25% reduction in average amplitude in depression (reviewed in Kupfer and Reynolds, 1983).

Routine day-time EEG studies have not proven of significant value as biological markers for depressive illness, except in the cases where coexistent medical disorders, specifically a neurological disorder, has been present. However, recently more sophisticated quantitative EEG and EP (evoked potential) analyses have been applied to neuropsychiatric states including affective disorders. While these investigations have been reviewed extensively elsewhere (Nuwer, 1988), it is worthwhile to point out that the application of BEAM technology has been suggested by several investigators (Schatzberg *et al.*, 1986; John *et al.*, 1988) to be of use in the differential diagnosis of depression. For example, Schatzberg and colleagues (1986) found that depressed patients differ from normals with a greater degree of right posterior temporal slowing and increased beta, especially on the left frontal side. However, most scientists have concluded that prior to the introduction of BEAM as a routine clinical tool in affective disorders a significantly greater number of well-controlled studies must be carried out before conclusions can be drawn from the available database. Such investigations would need to apply similar methodology across centres (Lopes da Silva, 1990).

All-night electroencephalographic sleep investigations have received considerable attention as possible biological 'markers' for depressive states. Such studies initially were utilized to document the characteristic sleep disturbances of depressed individuals (Kupfer and Thase, 1987). Despite the proliferation of studies in this area, there is still controversy about the sensitivity and specificity of the rapid eye movement (REM) and non-REM sleep changes observed in the state of depression (Buysse and Kupfer, 1990). It is still not understood why some patients do not display the 'classic' sleep stigmata during depression or, conversely, why some patients with other psychiatric or medical disorders display some of the sleep features associated with depression (Reynolds and Kupfer, 1987). Hudson *et al.* (1988) have also reported shortened REM sleep latency during the manic phase of bipolar illness, while Thase *et al.* (1989) reported normal REM sleep latency during the depressive phase of bipolar illness.

As stated previously, but germane to the issue of specificity, the traditional approach has been to focus on sleep features observed during an affective episode rather than before the illness begins or during a remission period.

However, for example, it is now believed that shortened REM latency during an episode is difficult to interpret unless one knows the patient's familial risk for depression (for a review of shortened REM latency, see Kupfer and Ehlers, 1989). For instance, Giles *et al.* (1987a) have shown that first-degree relatives of depressed probands are concordant for REM latency (i.e. reduced, non-reduced). Recently, Cartwright and colleagues (1988) suggested that a higher frequency of family history for depression is associated with short REM latency among divorcees with depression. Thus, under these conditions, one might view reduced REM latency as a vulnerability marker for affective illness.

This approach has also been applied to the study of schizophrenia patients who have been shown to display shortened REM latency in some studies (Zar-cone *et al.*, 1987; Hiatt *et al.*, 1985; Ganguli *et al.*, 1987). In a recent pilot study, Keshavan *et al.* (1990) reported a significant difference in REM latency between schizophrenics and controls. However, when they examined the family history of the schizophrenic patients, those patients with the affective family history had an REM latency which was significantly shorter than that of the other patients. In sum, family history represents an important new feature that needs to be included when examining the specificity of biological variables in affective disorder.

One set of data supporting the specificity of REM latency in depression has explored the relationships among REM latency, prognosis and treatment response in depressed patients. Several studies now suggest that pretreatment REM latency has predictive value in terms of clinical outcome. Giles *et al.* (1987b) have demonstrated that those individuals with a shortened REM latency have a poorer prognosis in terms of rapidity of relapse following remission than those individual with a more normal REM latency. Similarly, in a group of geriatric depressives, Reynolds *et al.* (1989) demonstrated that the patients who suffered a recurrence within 18 months of treatment had a significantly shorter baseline REM latency than those patients who did not. Finally, our data from a longitudinal study of recurrent depressives indicate that specific sleep features, including REM latency, are significantly associated with shorter time to recurrence (Kupfer and Frank, 1989). Another body of data, using sleep measurements early in the course of tricyclic antidepressant treatment, has also indicated that REM sleep measures, particularly REM latency, may be useful in predicting clinical response (Kupfer *et al.*, 1976, 1980, 1981, 1983; Gillin *et al.*, 1978; Höchli *et al.*, 1986).

Focus in recent years on the sleep abnormalities in depression has led to a number of observations including the fact that at least some of the sleep abnormalities once thought to be 'markers' of the episode (e.g. shortened REM latency) appear to persist not just early in remission but long into recovery (Cartwright, 1983; Giles *et al.*, 1987b; Reimann and Berger, 1989; Rush *et al.*, 1986; Steiger *et al.*, 1989) and that some of the abnormalities seen in depressed patients are also found in their never-ill first-degree relatives (Giles *et al.*, 1989).

These observations, in turn, point to new questions. With respect to the persistence of some EEG sleep abnormalities, it is imperative that we examine data on the same patient from the onset of the episode, through remission, throughout recovery and in recurrence. Such long-term longitudinal data can only be interpreted, however, against a background of similarly collected longitudinal data on normal controls. In addition, the findings demonstrating that never-ill first-degree relatives may have somewhat shortened REM latency calls into question the value of all normative data gathered to date. It is now clear that truly 'normal' EEG sleep data can be obtained with confidence only in a population screened for psychiatric disorder in first-degree relatives. Finally, the nature of the EEG sleep abnormalities observed in the relatives of depressed probands must be better understood.

A guiding factor is the hypothesis that the mechanisms which regulate REM and slow-wave sleep (SWS) are specifically modulated in depression by certain biological (probably genetic) variables which ultimately lead to disturbed sleep physiology such as reduced REM latency. This hypothesis represents one of several hypothesized models which could explain the alterations in sleep physiology associated with depression. In one current working model, disturbances in the mechanisms which regulate SWS and REM sleep are postulated to act through at least two 'paths' to produce such symptoms as a shortening of REM latency in depressives. In one path, REM latency is postulated to be reduced because of a 'weakening' of non-REM sleep, particularly SWS, which causes the first non-REM period of the night to end more quickly. In the other path, REM sleep occurs earlier in the night because of so-called increased 'REM pressure', i.e. REM sleep emerges earlier in the night due to an 'active dominance' of REM-related mechanisms. This distinction is important since it suggests that two separate factors may be responsible for the phenomenon of short REM latency, an SWS-related phenomenon and an REM sleep-related phenomenon. However, two intriguing problems that need to be addressed are the fact that the constellation of these sleep changes does not always appear in the same manner and that the clinical state may affect the manifestation of persistent or episode-related sleep disturbances. Indeed, a patient may demonstrate both persistent and episode-related sleep abnormalities during the clinical episode of depression.

Imaging studies
Over the last decade, great interest has been shown in the application of various imaging techniques as applied to neuropsychiatric states, including depression. While there exists considerable excitement about the potential application of magnetic resonance imaging (MRI) for possible structural localization of CNS abnormalities in neuropsychiatric states, more recent attention has been devoted to the potential application of *functional* imaging studies in the affective states. Such investigations have included the application of various cerebral

brain flow techniques including PET and single-photon emission computed tomography (SPECT) scans. While space does not permit us to review all these technological advances extensively, it is useful to outline some of the major approaches currently being applied to affective disorders.

The examination of regional blood flow in depressives and mania has been conducted by a number of investigators over the last five years. The findings to date are not consistent, and most investigators have tentatively concluded that no difference in global brain metabolic rates exist between depressed patients and controls, except in the presence of organic depressive disorder. Silfverskiöld and Risberg (1989) recently demonstrated that patients with depression and mania have a normal cerebral brain flow level and distribution. Nevertheless, a positive relationship was found between certain symptom clusters of depression and cognitive dysfunction and the CBF level.

In contrast to these findings using PET, Baxter and colleagues (1989) have reported a reduction in prefrontal cortex glucose metabolism in depressives. Specifically, they concluded that abnormal glucose metabolism function in the ALPFC (anterolaterial prefrontal cortex) is a common feature in various groups of major depression. They further believe that these findings are supported by neurobiological correlates of left ALPFC injury or dysfunction with depressive symptoms.

Since PET investigations are limited to few medical centres and are extremely expensive, there has been interest in using SPECT techniques to investigate similar types of questions. At the present time, four sets of studies have pointed to a lack of agreement about any potential CBF abnormality in depression using SPECT (Devous, 1989; Guenther *et al.*, 1986; Reischies *et al.*, 1989; Rush *et al.*, 1982). The availability of newer radioactive ligands and better resolution in the new SPECT cameras may provide a better opportunity for determining the existence of possible CBF abnormalities utilizing SPECT.

Finally, the application of nuclear magnetic resonance (NMR) spectroscopy as a novel non-invasive technique to measure metabolism in vivo could potentially provide important information on brain phospholipid and energy metabolism in major neuropsychiatric disorders including depression (Keshavan *et al.*, in press). Current limitations of this technology lie with respect to localization, use of spectroscopy contrast agents and higher-strength magnets preclude the routine clinical application of such techniques.

Conclusions and tentative model

As we have indicated in our selective review, this chapter does not represent an attempt to review systematically and comprehensively every putative marker that has been suggested from various domains of study. Indeed, we have not included important investigations that have earlier examined systematic

day-time electroencephalographic function including evoked potential record-
ings, motor activity measures, nor have we reviewed all the studies on other
neuropeptides or neurochemical substances potentially involved in the pathophysiology of depression. We have also not reviewed the exciting data relating
to specific alterations in biological rhythms such as temperature, motor activity
or newly elucidated neuropeptides. We have sought instead to communicate
several basic principles. First, there appears to be a growing consensus that in
order to investigate and identify the most appropriate biological markers for
laboratory analysis and eventually for clinical application, we need to study the
same individual over extended periods of time. Examining individuals both in
an episode and through recovery phases should facilitate a better discrimination
between state and trait variables. Second, the current neuroendocrine/
neuropeptide and sleep literature would appear to point to a set of relationships
which seem to cluster as either trait variables or episode variables. Recently, we
have suggested a particular strategy for examining sleep abnormalities which
divide the sleep abnormalities into state and trait-like abnormalities (Table II).
In addition to the sleep physiological changes, we can now include various
changes in the neuroendocrine/neuropeptide domains. While the majority of
investigators believe that abnormalities in the HPA axis are more state related
than trait related, it would appear that changes in growth-releasing factor (GRF)
and GH may represent more persistent abnormalities. While it is unclear
whether all proposed neurochemical changes such as alterations in available
neurotransmitter levels or receptors (e.g. 5-HT, norepinephrine) are related to
episode phenomena, it is hoped that a profile could be developed to separate
out trait-like phenomena from state-like phenomena. Furthermore, it is expected that our understanding of trait would lead to a better differentiation
between 'vulnerability' and 'scar', i.e. what are the characteristics that are

Table II. Two types of biological alterations in depression.

	Type 1 persistent	Type 2 episode
Genetic familial transmission	+++	+
Slow-wave sleep	+++	+
REM sleep dysregulation	+	+++
Episode	±	+++
Aging-related	+++	+
Stress and severity-related	+	+++
Antidepressant effects	+	+++
Neuroendocrine relationship	GRF	CRF (HPA axis)

  + A moderate level of possible relationship.
  ± An equivocal relationship.
+++ A strong relationship.

present before the first episode of a depressive illness versus what aspects persist after the end of the first episode. Most recently, Post and colleagues (1986) have suggested that behavioural sensitization and electrophysiological kindling provide models for the progressive evolution of recurrent depressive episode. Only further investigations will shed light on such models.

Although there is increasing evidence that ultimately genetic markers may represent the most important trait-like characteristics in the diagnosis of major depression, particularly for bipolar disorder, the evidence to date is somewhat controversial. Given the heterogeneity of unipolar depressive illness, it is unlikely that a single-gene locus will be elucidated for this disorder. More likely, over the next decade, several specific genes will be identified which are associated with subgroups of the overall category known as major depression. Several years ago it appeared that the Amish studies led by Egeland and colleagues (1987) had helped identify a specific marker for bipolar disorder on chromosome 11. More recently, analysis of this finding has raised questions concerning not only the specificity of the finding on chromosome 11, but the specificity with respect to any genetic marker for affective disorder (Kelsoe *et al.*, 1989). Given the current advances in molecular genetics and biology, it is nevertheless intriguing to speculate that a most promising candidate for a trait-like marker may very well be a genetic one. Space considerations have not permitted us to indicate relationships between proposed neuropeptide or neurotransmitter markers for depression and their proposed genetic linkage. It would still be expected that as we identify the trait-like characteristics of affective disorder, the association between these markers and their genetic component will also be elucidated.

It would have been expected in 1991 that research investigators would be able to routinely apply biological markers for clinical studies and for improved diagnostic differentiation. It would have been hoped that operational criteria for the DSM-IV nosology of affective disorders would have included specific laboratory methodology as part of the diagnostic criteria. Unfortunately, we have not yet achieved a sufficient level of sophistication with respect to the application of newer technology. More importantly, we have not been able to conduct a sufficient number of studies that apply techniques that derive from more than one domain at a time. Over the next decade the combined application of neurochemical, neuroendocrine, neurophysiology and imaging techniques should provide the necessary studies to lead to a more routine application of such tools as markers.

We hope that the reader will view our scepticism concerning our current state of affairs from the correct perspective. The future is particularly promising in the search for biological markers, both episodic and persistent. New technology coupled with more precise operational diagnostic criteria are likely to provide the necessary breakthroughs. Our major caveat concerning such investigative activities focuses on the need to employ rigorous criteria in establishing the evidence for biological 'markers'. We need to couple our enthusiasm with systematic verification by multiple settings prior to concluding that we have succeeded in doing for affective disorders what is being done in other medical disorders. Finally, we need to realize that it is very unlikely that one marker will emerge; more probably we can expect a profile of biological and clinical correlates from diverse domains to provide the markers of depressive illness.

Acknowledgement

This study was supported in part by National Institute of Mental Health grants MH–24652 and MH–30915.

References

APA Task Force on Laboratory Tests in Psychiatry (1987) The dexamethasone suppression test: An overview of its current status in psychiatry. *Am J Psychiatry* **144**, 1253–1262.

Arana GW, Baldessarini RJ and Ornsteen M (1985) The dexamethasone suppression test for diagnosis and prognosis in psychiatry. *Arch Gen Psychiatry* **42**, 1193–1204.

Baxter LR, Schwartz JM, Phelps ME *et al.* (1989) Reduction of prefrontal cortex glucose metabolism common to three types of depression. *Arch Gen Psychiatry* **46**, 243–250.

Braddock L (1986) The dexamethasone suppression test: Fact and artifact. *Br J Psychiatry* **148**, 363–374.

Buchsbaum MS and Rieder RO (1979) Biological heterogeneity and psychiatric research. *Arch Gen Psychiatry* **36**, 1163–1169.

Bunney WE Jr and Davis JM (1965) Norepinephrine and depressive reactions: A review. *Arch Gen Psychiatry* **13**, 483–494.

Buysse DJ and Kupfer DJ (1990) Diagnostic and research applications of electro-encephalographic sleep studies in depression: Conceptual and methodological issues. *J Nerv Ment Dis* **178**, 405–414.

Carroll BJ (1982) The dexamethasone suppression test for melancholia. *Br J Psychiatry* **140**, 292–304.

Carroll BJ, Greden JF, Haskett R *et al.* (1980) Neurotransmitter studies of neuroendocrine pathology in depression. *Acta Psychiatr Scand* **61** (Suppl. 280), 183–199.

Cartwright RD (1983) Rapid eye movement sleep characteristics during and after mood disturbing events. *Arch Gen Psychiatry* **40**, 197–201.

Cartwright RD, Stephenson K, Kravitz H and Eastman C (1988) REM latency stability and family history of depression. *Sleep Res* **17**, 119.

Devous MD Sr (1989) Imaging brain function by a single-photon emission computer tomography. In: Andreasen NC (ed.) *Brain Imaging Applications in Psychiatry*, pp. 147–234. Washington, DC: American Psychiatric Press.

Egeland JA, Gerhard DS, Pauls DL *et al.* (1987) Bipolar affective disorders linked to DNA markers on chromosome 11. *Nature* **325**, 783–787.

Flor-Henry P (1979) On certain aspects of the localization of the cerebral systems regulating and determining emotion. *Biol. Psychiatry* **14**, 677–698.

Flor-Henry P and Koles ZJ (1980) EEG studies in depression, mania and normals: Evidence for partial shifts of laterality in the affective psychoses. *Biol Psychiatry* **4**, 21–43.

Ganguli R, Reynolds CF and Kupfer DJ (1987) Electroencephalographic sleep in young, never medicated schizophrenics. *Arch Gen Psychiatry* **44**, 36–44.

Giles DE, Biggs MM, Rush AJ and Roffwarg HP (1987a) Risk factors in families of unipolar depression. I. Psychiatric illness and reduced REM latency. *J Affect Dis* **14**, 51–59.

Giles DE, Jarrett RB, Roffwarg HP and Rush AJ (1987b) Reduced rapid eye movement latency: A predictor of recurrence in depression. *Neuropsychopharmacology* **1**, 33–49.

Giles DE, Kupfer DJ, Roffwarg HP *et al.* (1989) Polysomnographic parameters in first-degree relatives of unipolar probands. *Psychiatry Res* **27**, 127–136.

Gillin JC, Wyatt RJ, Fram D and Snyder F (1978) The relationship between changes in REM sleep and clinical improvement in depressed patients treated with amitriptyline. *Psychopharmacology* **59**, 267–272.

Goodwin FK and Jamison KR (1990) Biochemical and pharmacological studies. *Manic-Depressive Illness*, pp. 416–502. New York: Oxford University Press.

Guenther W, Moser E, Mueller-Spahn F *et al.* (1986) Pathological cerebral blood flow during motor function in schizophrenic and endogenous depressed patients. *Biol Psychiatry* **21**, 889–899.

Hiatt JF, Floyd TC, Katz PH and Feinberg I (1985) Further evidence of abnormal non-rapid-eye-movement sleep in schizophrenia. *Arch Gen Psychiatry* **42**, 797–802.

Höchli D, Reimann D, Zulley J and Berger M (1986) Initial REM sleep suppression by clomipramine: A prognostic tool for treatment response in patients with a major depressive disorder. *Biol Psychiatry* **21**, 1217–1220.

Hudson JI, Lipinski JF, Frankenburg FR *et al.* (1988) Electroencephalographic sleep in mania. *Arch Gen Psychiatry* **45**, 267–273.

Jarrett DB, Miewald JM, Fedorka IB *et al.* (1987) Prolactin secretion during sleep: A comparison between depressed patients and healthy control subjects. *Biol Psychiatry* **22**, 1216–1226.

Jarrett DB, Greenhouse JB, Miewald *et al.* (1990a) A reexamination of the relationship between growth hormone secretion and slow wave sleep using delta wave analysis. *Biol Psychiatry* **27**, 497–509.

Jarrett DB, Miewald JM and Kupfer DJ (1990b) Recurrent depression is associated with a persistent reduction in sleep-related growth hormone secretion. *Arch Gen Psychiatry* **47**, 113–118.

John ER, Prichep LS, Friedman J and Easton P (1988) Neurometrics: Computer-assisted differential diagnosis of brain dysfunctions. *Science* **239**, 162–169.

Joyce PR and Paykel ES (1989) Predictors of drug response in depression. *Arch Gen Psychiatry* **46**, 89–99.

Kathol RG, Jaeckle RS, Lopez JF and Meller WH (1989) Pathophysiology of HPA axis abnormalities in patients with major depression: An update. *Am J Psychiatry* **146**, 311–317.

Kelsoe JR, Ginns EI, Egeland JA *et al.* (1989) Re-evaluation of the linkage relationship between chromosome 11p loci and the gene for bipolar affective disorders in the Old Order Amish. *Nature* **342**, 238–243.

Keshavan MS, Reynolds CF, Ganguli R *et al.* (1990) EEG sleep in familial subgroups of schizophrenia. *Sleep Res* **19**, 330.

Keshavan MS, Kapur S and Pettegrew JW (in press) Magnetic resonance spectroscopy in psychiatry: Potential, pitfalls and promise. *Am J Psychiatry*.

Kirkegaard C (1981) The thyrotropin response to thyrotropin-releasing hormone in endogenous depression. *Psychoneuroendocrinology* **6**, 189–212.

Krog-Meyer I, Kirkegaard C, Kijne B *et al.* (1984) Prediction of relapse with the TRH test and prophylactic amitriptyline in 39 patients with endogenous depression. *Am J Psychiatry* **141**, 945–948.

Kupfer DJ and Ehlers CL (1989) Two roads to rapid eye movement latency. *Arch Gen Psychiatry* **46**, 945–948.

Kupfer DJ and Frank E (1989) EEG sleep changes in recurrent depression. In: Lerer B and Gershon S (eds) *New Directions in Affective Disorders*, pp. 225–228. New York: Springer.

Kupfer DJ and Reynolds CF (1983) Neurophysiologic studies of depression: State of the art. In: Angst J (ed.) *The Origins of Depression: Current Concepts and Approaches*, pp. 235–252. New York: Springer.

Kupfer DJ and Rush AJ (1983) Recommendations for depression publications. *Psychopharmacol Bull* **19**, 162–164.

Kupfer DJ and Spiker DG (1981) Refractory depression: Prediction of nonresponse by clinical indicators. *J Clin Psychiatry* **42**, 307–312.

Kupfer DJ and Thase ME (1987) Validity of major depression: A psychobiological perspective. In: Tischler GL (ed.) *Diagnosis and Classification in Psychiatry: A Critical Appraisal of DSM-III*, pp. 32–60. New York: Cambridge University Press.

Kupfer DJ and Thase ME (1989) Laboratory studies and validity of psychiatric diagnosis: Has there been progress? In: Robins LN and Barrett JE (eds) *The Validity of Psychiatric Diagnosis*, pp. 177–201. New York: Raven Press.

Kupfer DJ, Foster FG, Reich L *et al.* (1976) EEG sleep changes as predictors in depression. *Am J Psychiatry* **133**, 622–626.

Kupfer DJ, Spiker DG, Coble PA *et al.* (1980) Depression, EEG sleep and clinical response. *Compr Psychiatry* **21**, 212–220.

Kupfer DJ, Spiker DG, Coble PA *et al.* (1981) Sleep and treatment prediction in endogenous depression. *Am J Psychiatry* **138**, 429–434.

Kupfer DJ, Spiker DG, Rossi A *et al.* (1983) Recent diagnostic and treatment advances in REM sleep and depression. In: Clayton P and Barrett J (eds) *Treatment of Depression: Old Controversies and New Approaches*, pp. 31–52. New York: Raven Press.

Langer G, Aschauer H, Koinig G *et al.* (1983) The TSH response to TRH: A possible predictor of outcome to antidepressant and neuroleptic treatment. *Prog Neuropsychopharmacol Biol Psychiatry* **7**, 335–342.

Lewy AJ (1984) Human melatonin secretion (II): A marker for the circadian system and the effects of light. In: Post RM and Ballenger JC (eds) *Neurobiology of Mood Disorders*, pp.215–226. Baltimore: Williams & Wilkins.

Linnoila M, Karoum F and Potter WZ (1983) Effects of antidepressant treatments on dopamine turnover in depressed patients. *Arch Gen Psychiatry* **40**, 1015–1017.

Loosen PT, Wilson IC, Dew B and Tipermas A (1983) Thyrotropin-releasing hormone (TRH) in abstinent alcoholic men. *Am J Psychiatry* **140**, 1145–1149.

Lopes da Silva FH (1990) A critical review of clinical applications of topographic mapping of brain potentials. *J Clin Neurophysiol* **7**, 535–551.

Murphy DL, Campbell I and Costa JL (1978) Current status of the indoleamine hypothesis of the affective disorders. In: Lipton MA, DiMascio A and Killam KF (eds) *Psychopharmacology: A Generation of Progress*, pp. 1235–1247. New York: Raven Press.

Nemeroff CB (1989) Clinical significance of psychoneuroendocrinology in psychiatry: Focus on the thyroid and adrenal. *J Clin Psychiatry* (Suppl.) **50**, 13–20.

Nemeroff CB (1990) Neuropeptide involvement in affective disorders. *Curr Opinion Psychiatry* **3**, 108–112.

Nemeroff CB and Bissette G (1990) Neuropeptide alterations in major depression: State or trait markers? Presented at the 1990 Annual ACNP Meeting, San Juan, Puerto Rico.

Nuwer MR (1988) Quantitative EEG: II. Frequency analysis and topographic mapping in clinical settings. *J Clin Neurophysiol* **5**, 45–85.

Post RM, Rubinow DR and Ballenger JC (1986) Conditioning and sensitization in the longitudinal course of affective illness. *Br J Psychiatry* **149**, 191–201.

Prange AJ, Loosen PT, Wilson IC and Lipton MA (1984) The therapeutic use of hormones of the thyroid axis in depression. In: Post RM and Ballenger JC (eds) *Neurobiology of Mood Disorders*, pp. 311–322. Baltimore: Williams & Wilkins.

Redmond DE, Katz MM, Maas JW *et al.* (1986) Cerebrospinal fluid amine metabolites: Relationships with behavioral measurements in depressed, manic, and healthy control subjects. *Arch Gen Psychiatry* **43**, 938–947.

Reischies FM, Hedde JP and Drochner R (1989) Clinical correlates of cerebral blood flow in depression. *Psychiatry Res* **29**, 323–326.

Reynolds CF and Kupfer DJ (1987) Sleep research in affective illness: State of the art circa 1987 (State-of-the-art review). *Sleep* **10**, 199–215.

Reynolds CF, Perel JM, Frank E *et al.* (1989) Open-trial maintenance nortriptyline in late-life depression: Survival analysis and preliminary data on the use of REM latency as a predictor of recurrence. *Psychopharmacology Bull* **25**, 129–132.

Riemann D and Berger M (1989) EEG sleep in depression and in remission and the REM sleep response to the cholinergic agonist RS 86. *Neuropsychopharmacology* **2**, 145–152.

Rush AJ, Schlesser MA, Stokely E *et al.* (1982) Cerebral blood flow in depression and mania. *Psychopharmacol Bull* **18**, 6–8.

Rush AJ, Erman MK, Giles DE *et al.* (1986) Polysomnographic findings in recently drug-free and clinically remitted depressed patients. *Arch Gen Psychiatry* **43**, 878–884.

Rush AJ, Guillion CM and Roffwarg HP (1990) Research strategies to identify trait-like biological abnormalities in major depression. Presented at the 1990 Annual ACNP Meeting, San Juan, Puerto Rico.

Schaeffer CE, Davidson RJ and Saron C (1983) Frontal and parietal electroencephalogram asymmetry in depressed and nondepressed subjects. *Biol Psychiatry* **18**, 753–762.

Schatzberg AF, Elliot GR, Lerbinger JE *et al.* (1986) Topographic mapping in depressed patients. In: Duffy FH (ed.) *Topographic Mapping of Brain Electrical Activity*, pp.389–391. Boston: Butterworths.

Schildkraut JJ (1965) The catecholamine hypothesis of affective disorder: A review of supporting evidence. *Am J Psychiatry* **122**, 509–522.

Silfverskiöld P and Risberg J (1989) Regional cerebral blood flow in depression and mania. *Arch Gen Psychiatry* **46**, 253–259.

Sitaram M, Moore AM and Gillin JC (1979) Scopolamine-induced muscarinic supersensitivity in normal man. *Psychiatry Res* **1**, 9–16.

Sitaram N, Nurnberger JI, Gershon ES and Gillin JC (1982) Cholinergic regulation of mood and REM sleep: Potential model and marker of vulnerability to affective disorders. *Am J Psychiatry* **139**, 571–576.

Sitaram N, Dube S, Keshavan M *et al.* (1987) The association of supersensitive cholinergic REM-induction and affective illness with pedigrees. *J Psychiatr Res* **21**, 487–497.

Steiger A, von Bardeleben U, Herth T and Holsboer F (1989) Sleep EEG and nocturnal secretion of cortisol and growth hormone in male patients with endogenous depression before treatment and after recovery. *J Affect Dis* **16**, 189–195.

Thase ME, Frank E and Kupfer DJ (1985) Biological processes in major depression. In: Beckham EE and Leber WR (eds) *Handbook of Depression: Treatment, Assessment, and Research*, pp. 816–913. Homewood, IL: Dorsey Press.

Thase ME, Himmelhoch JM, Mallinger AG *et al.* (1989) Sleep EEG and DST findings in anergic bipolar depression. *Am J Psychiatry* **146**, 329–333.

Träskman L, Asberg M, Bertilsson L and Sjöstrand L (1981) Monoamine metabolites in CSF and suicidal behavior. *Arch Gen Psychiatry* **38**, 631–636.

Zarcone VP, Benson KL and Berger PA (1987) Abnormal rapid eye movement latencies in schizophrenia. *Arch Gen Psychiatry* **44**, 45–48.

7

The masking and unmasking of depression

J.J. López-Ibor Jr

Introduction

Masked depression is a notion as old as it is controversial. According to Lange (1928) its fate is that of being rediscovered every decade. The term became quite popular in the 1960s and 1970s, because it was realized then that even in most developed countries, relatively abundant in psychiatric resources, a significant proportion of depressed patients never contacted psychiatrists. They were an important part of the everyday practice of many specialists, mainly general practitioners. This so-called 'iceberg phenomenon' (Watts, 1966) obliged physicians to be aware of the symptoms of depression, mainly the somatic ones, which led patients to contact them. Masked depression is a common problem in consultation–liaison psychiatry (Stoudemire *et al.*, 1985) and in psychosomatic medicine (Labhardt, 1986). Furthermore, psychotropic drugs, especially antidepressants, gave physicians training in psychiatry the opportunity of treating depressed patients, provided of course that a proper diagnosis was made. Therefore, the principal interest in masked depression was the diagnosis in non-psychiatric medical care. Unfortunately, the concept of masked depression was never clearly defined or fully understood. Therefore it opened the door to some abuses, such as becoming a last-resort diagnosis or the occasion to prescribe antidepressants when other therapeutic alternatives had failed or could not be considered. But as many antidepressants, mainly the

The Diagnosis of Depression. Edited by J.P. Feighner and W.F. Boyer
© 1991 John Wiley & Sons Ltd

tricyclics, are drugs with multiple pharmacological activities, the disappearance of a sympton under antidepressant treatment cannot be accepted as a 'post hoc, propter hoc' argument. An example is the notion that enuresis nocturna is a symptom of depression (depressive equivalent) due to the favourable response to imipramine. Although enuresis nocturna can be a manifestation of depression in childhood, a favourable response to a drug with anticholinergic activity may only be due, in many cases, to its effect on the bladder movements.

Murphy *et al.* (1985) have discussed the therapeutic response to tricyclic antidepressants in non-affective disorders, sometimes related to the improvement of secondary depressive symptoms, but also in the absence of secondary depression. Furthermore, many patients responding to tricyclic antidepressants display psychobiological abnormalities that show many similarities, but also some differences, compared to those observed in patients with mood disorders. A hypothesis is that of subclinical or masked depression, linking tricyclic responsiveness and shared biological abnormalities in a diverse group of diagnostic entities. An alternative hypothesis (the 'one disorder' hypothesis) put forward by Murphy *et al.* (1985) suggests the possibility that antidepressant responding patients have a core disorder with common psychobiological abnormalities but multiple clinical and diagnostic presentations. An alternative hypothesis (the 'shotgun' hypothesis) suggests that the multiple actions of tricyclic antidepressants (i.e. on adrenergic receptors versus muscarinic receptors versus serotonin system changes) may each be differentially important in the therapeutic outcome in patients with specific or predominant problems in one or another of these areas.

The concept of masked depression also has other implications, beyond the diagnostic interest in everyday clinical practice. Unfortunately, most of them have been overlooked in recent years. A reason why masked depression became popular in the 1960s was the crisis in the psychoanalytic foundations of psychosomatic medicine. This led to ways of investigating the origin of somatic symptoms from different perspectives. Already in the late 1940s López-Ibor (1950, 1972) had claimed that neurotic anxiety could not be considered of psychodynamic origin. He coined the expression 'vital anxiety' to describe this kind of mood, which was as endogenous as K. Schneider's (1962) vital sadness, the characteristic mood of endogenous depression. This approach was not describing a so-called pseudoneurotic depression (Kessel, 1968), but implying that every neurosis was a mood disorder (López-Ibor, 1966). The notion of vital anxiety paved the way to the notion of somatic equivalents of anxiety, i.e. vegetative correlates of mood disorders. In a sense, both vital anxiety and vital depression could manifest themselves as somatic equivalents (López-Ibor Jr, 1972, 1973). The distinction of anxiety equivalents from depressive equivalents is not always an easy task. It may be that less severe forms of anxiety and depressive disorders can have the same symptoms and they are not easily differentiated. That is why the tenth edition of the International Classification of Diseases (ICD-10) includes a category of mixed anxiety–depressive disorder (WHO, 1990).

Nevertheless, vital anxiety and vital sadness are not specific symptoms of specific disorders. They cannot always be precisely defined in clinical terms but sometimes only apprehended. A 'melancholisches Gefuehl' or empathic apprehension of the vital depressive character of a patient's clinical manifestations has been described by López-Ibor Jr (1972).

The nosological status of masked depression

Modern nosology as initiated by DSM-III has no clear place for masked depression. It is included in a waste-basket category (Atypical Depression), but even there it is probably misplaced. Pichot (1985) identified four main perspectives for psychiatric diagnosis according to which criteria are used to define it: the symptoms, the syndrome (in its evolution) the pathogenesis and the neuropathology. DSM-III chose symptoms as the main principle of classification. In this sense, when a physician is able to evaluate depressive symptoms accompanying various somatic complaints of a patient suffering a masked depression, he is not making the diagnosis of masked depression. He is simply unmasking a depressive disorder which should be included in one of the appropriate categories of depressive disorders. Masked depression is not a disorder. It is essentially a way to call attention to the need of a proper diagnostic process (the unmasking of the depression). In other words, the concept of masked depression has no place in a symptomatic classification. It would have one in a pathogenic classification (i.e. following the notions of vital anxiety and vital sadness). Furthermore, it should be kept in mind that if the definition of the mood disorders is difficult in modern nosology (ICD-10 is a good example of the difficulties; Sartorius, 1985; WHO, 1990), it is today impossible to designate a single clinical finding relevant to the pathogenesis (i.e. an abnormal neurochemical test) to be used for diagnosis. Therefore, the isolation of the symptoms from the pathogenesis of the disorder in order to select criteria for diagnosis is bound to confuse the field even more, especially in the realm of what was formerly described as psychosomatic pathology. Today this is covered by different, and not always clearly defined, disorders such as somatization disorders, conversion disorders, hypochondria, neurasthenia and others.

The concept of masked depression implies at least three different meanings for the word depression: a symptom, a syndrome and a nosological entity. Masked depression has been referred to as 'depressio sine depressione' (depressive disease without depressive symptoms; Priori, 1962), an expression which can only have a meaning if the same term is used for two different concepts (Glatzel, 1967). It is then necessary to distinguish between depression as an illness and depression as a syndrome, because it is possible to suffer from a depressio (disease) sine depressione (syndrome). According to Lange (1928), the pathogenics and the pathoplastics of a depressive disorder have to be distinguished. When both of them are present, the clinical picture corresponds to an endogenous depression; when only the pathoplastic is present the case would be one of symptomatic depression; and when only the pathogenic factors are present, masked depression would be the diagnosis.

But, as mentioned before, the diagnosis of depression according to present-day criteria is based on symptoms. There is a need for a better understanding of the natural history of depressive disorders to clarify this problem.

Transcultural aspects: the setting in which depression appears

Transcultural research does not give the expected answers. On the one side, there has been a clear trend towards a better recognition of depressive disorders in non-Western cultures. Depression is a word which has been considered typical of the Western Jewish–Christian culture and for the cultural atmosphere prevailing in developed countries after the Industrial Revolution. In several languages there is no word for being depressed, and in others, for example in Japanese, the same term 'depressive' simultaneously means 'nice' (Angst, 1973).* In the past the prevalence of depressive disorders was claimed to be almost nil in Africa or China. Nevertheless, in both parts of the world depression is now widely recognized. (Chen, 1986; Makanjuola and Olaifa, 1987). Looking at the different manifestations of depressions in different cultures, the mood alteration seems to be more common in Western countries, while disorders of circadian and other rhythms as well as somatic symptoms are more relevant in other cultures (Pfeiffer, 1971). Nevertheless, more recent studies have de-emphasized rhythm disorders, leaving somatic symptoms as the most characteristic of depression on a worldwide basis. The mood alterations are very difficult to characterize. Maybe the word 'depressive' is not precise enough as the mood alterations, which are the essence of the mood (affective) disorders but are not always that easy to demonstrate (López-Ibor Jr, 1990).

Transcultural psychopathology has examined what is typical and atypical in depressions and what is constant and fundamental in mood disorders. The contents of depressive delusions change through the decades in the same culture (Kranz, 1955; Orelli, 1954). The manifestations of depression change according to the age of the patient. Our own investigations (López-Ibor Jr, 1972, 1973) suggest that age is a decisive factor in the genesis of masked depressions. Depressions in childhood are very often masked (Table I) and the genuine (i.e. the typical) in children is exceptional in adults (Nissen, 1973).

---

* Chapter 11 makes the point that Japanese social norms foster depressive or pre-depressive personality characteristics (*Editor*).

Table I. Depression (masked) in childhood.

Age	Psychiatric symptoms	Vegetative symptoms
5–15 years	Apathy	Sleep disorders
	Lack of interest for playing	Appetite disorders
	Isolation	Weeping crisis
	Agitation	Jactitatio capitis
	Despair	Sleep terrors
	Hypersensibility	Encopresis
	Insecurity	Abdominal pains
	Boredom	Asthenia
	Temper tantrums	Alopecia areata
	Concentration difficulties	Tics
	Learning difficulties	Eczema
	School phobia	Allergies
	Dyslexia	Anorexia
	Fugues	Bulimia
	Feelings of inferiority	Asthma
	Nihilistic thoughts	Allergies
	Suicidal impulses	
	Obsessive thoughts	
	Depressive mood	
	Feelings of emptiness	
	Feelings of guilt	
	Feelings of depersonalization	
	Substance abuse	
	Offences	
	Accident proneness	
	Phobias, obsessions, hypochondria	
	Neurasthenia	
	Dysmorphophobia	

It should be taken into account that the symptoms of patients may be different in different settings. Ierodiakonov and Iacovides (1987) in Greece compared the manifestation of depression in an in-patient, an out-patient and in a mobile unit population. Although headache was the most prominent symptom it had its highest incidence in the mobile unit cases (62.6%). Ayuso and Saiz (1981) studied the symptoms of depression of patients admitted to a psychiatric unit in a general hospital in comparison with depressed patients seen in psychiatry consultation in the same hospital. The former showed more suicidal gestures and more severe behavioural symptoms; they also had a higher proportion of previous psychiatric episodes. Goldberg and Bridges (1987) differentiated two kinds of individuals according to their reaction to stress: the 'somatizers' and the 'psychologizers;. The former have some initial advantages as their symptoms are not burdened with stigmata, and they get better attention from the health care system. But, in the long run, this leads to a more chronic evolution than the psychological symptoms, more rejected by society.

It is not possible to confirm if the number of masked depressions is rising in the population. Kielholz (1973, 1974) claims that there is a tendency to somatization, based on materialism and the greater social tolerance for medical symptoms than for psychological manifestations. If masked depressions and depressive equivalents were included, the genetics of mood disorders would take a different shape. However, as pointed out by Walcher (1970), the methodological problem is enormous. The same can be said about epidemiology, biochemistry and other areas of research. In any case, the concept of masked depressions changes the psychopathology of the depressive disorders, in the sense of conceiving them as conditionas that transcend dualistic notions about human nature and not as purely psychological states of mind. This does not mean that the 'somatic symptoms' of depression have passed by unnoticed, but that they were considered as accessory or concomitant manifestations of the disorder.

Definitions

Masked depression includes those manifestations of depressive disorder of any kind where the somatic symptoms are in the foreground and the psychological ones in the background (Kielholz, 1973). A broader concept includes also those psychopathological and behavioural manifestations which do not correspond to the common description of depressive disorders, such as the behavioural masks (Lesse, 1974). In a sense, the so-called pseudodementia is also a form of masked depression.

The expression 'affective equivalents' has been used to describe psychosomatic disorders free of any mood symptomatology which, theoretically, are considered as manifestations of a depressive disorder. The diagnosis of these conditions is always difficult, and the concept should still be considered as hypothetical. Reasons for accepting these conditions rely on the course or on genetic data. For instance, Fernandes Da Fonseca (1973) described a higher proportion of specific psychosomatic disorders in monozygotic than in dizygotic twins of patients with manic-depressive disease. The term affective equivalents is also used for isolated symptoms in the context of a broader symptomatology of masked depression. Masked depression and depressive equivalents have received many other names in the literature: affective equivalents, vegetative equivalents (Cimbal, 1929), thymopathic equivalents (López-Ibor, 1966), vegetative-dystonic depression (Hempel, 1937), vegetative depression (Lemke, 1949), masked, unrecognized depression (Kielholz, 1973), 'depressio sine depressione' (Priori, 1962), incomplete depression (Glatzel, 1967), blurred depression, cryptic depressive states (Chamberlain, 1949), mild manic-depressive psychosis (Campbell, 1950) and monosymptomatic depression.

Differentiating masked depressions from other somatizing disorders

The differential diagnosis of masked depression and other somatization disorders may be difficult. In hypochondria, the important trait is the attitude of the patient towards the symptoms, and in conversion disorders it is the attitude of the patients towards himself and others. Nevertheless, probably a high proportion of patients with psychophysiological disorders and somatization disorders could be diagnosed as suffering from masked depression and benefit from proper treatment. A good example is chronic pain. On the one side, chronic pain can lead to complex psychopathology (algogenic psychosyndrome, López-Ibor Jr and Lozano, 1987) loaded with depressive symptoms. On the other side, a high proportion of patients with chronic non-neoplastic pain in pain clinics suffer from pain of psychological origin, very often of a depressive nature (Lozano, 1989, Table II).

DSM-III has established diagnostic criteria that separate somatization disorder from other overlapping symptom configurations. Terms such as 'masked depression' or 'alexithymia' imply that a disturbance of mood is a nuclear but hidden issue for at least some somatization patients. Through content analysis of speech, Oxman *et al.* (1985) investigated the self-experience of somatization disorder in relation to affective disorders. Rather than depression, a distinctive characteristic found in the language of patients with somatization disorder reflects a confused, negative self-identity. Again, this raises the problem of what is a mood disorder because the overlap of depression and somatization may change in different cultures, as can be deduced from the Kohn *et al.* (1989) study on older Soviet immigrants to the USA.

Neurasthenia is a diagnosis not accepted in DSM-III and later versions of the American Psychiatric Association classification, but it is quite a common diagnosis in many parts of the world. Nevertheless, there is a trend in many non-Western countries away from the diagnosis of neurasthenia to one of depression, and a considerable overlap may be present. Transcultural aspects are therefore essential to the notion of neurasthenia. The diagnosis became popular in European countries during the Industrial Revolution, reflecting a notion of a failure in the human machine. Nervous breakdown is still a popular expression today in many countries. It has been claimed that in the nineteenth century the concepts of neurasthenia and of pre-menstrual syndromes were medicalized (King, 1989). This implies that negative views of a woman's

Table II. Pain of psychological origin in a pain clinic (Lozano, 1989).

Algogenic psychosyndrome in pain of organic origin	11.5%
Pain of psychological origin	54.1%
Conversion	32.5%
Depressive	41.9%

condition may have created a clinical diagnosis where only negative attitudes towards human nature were present. To suffer from 'nerves' was related in the nineteenth century to social roles and class ideologies (Davis *et al.*, 1989).

The psychoanalytic and psychodynamic approach to psychiatric disorders was responsible for the substitution of the word neurasthenia for neurosis in Western countries. Freud himself was very critical of the notion of neurasthenia (Solms, 1989). Such theories did not have the same impact in other cultures where psychodynamics would, in any case, be quite different. Therefore the notion of a nervous exhaustion survived better. In Japan, Morita described in the early 1920s a specific type of neurotic disorder, the shinkeishitsu ('constitutional neurasthenia'), and a famous therapy which was very different from the psychodynamic Western approach (Munakata, 1989; Russell, 1989) (see Chapter 11). Morita therapy and Naikan therapy have deep-seated roots in Buddhist tradition (Suzuki, 1989).

Today, neurasthenia is a frequent diagnosis in countries going through an industrial revolution (e.g. China). According to Peng (1990), even nowadays neurasthenia is the most common neurosis in China, reaching 50% of all the diagnoses of neuroses. This implies that DSM-III and similar criteria could only be applied in China after an important educational process. Recent changes in that country will not automatically go in the direction of reducing the diagnosis of neurasthenia as it is related to the process of industrialization and is very common in workers with occupational hazards (up to 27–35%; Wang, 1989). In modern Hong Kong, neurasthenia serves the important function of destigmatizing psychiatric disorders (Cheung, 1989). In Taiwan, a younger generation of physicians within both general and neuropsychiatric practice on the whole reject neurasthenia as a diagnosis. However, one-third of neuropsychiatrists and 40% of general practitioners use this term in their practice in order to improve treatment and to establish good rapport with the patients they treat. Most of them, however, do not use the term in their formal diagnosis (Rin and Huang, 1989).

Few studies have focused on the transcultural diagnosis of neurotic disorders. In the one carried out by Tseng *et al.* (1986) videotapes and short case summaries of six Chinese patients were shown to psychiatrists in Beijing, Tokyo and Honolulu. Diagnostic disagreements occurred in cases with symptoms of decline in mental function, which were overwhelmingly diagnosed as neurasthenia by Chinese clinicians, and cases of situational stress, which were diagnosed as adjustment reaction by US clinicians. More recently, Zhang (1989) selected 40 patients diagnosed as suffering from neurasthenia by two Chinese psychiatrists to be rediagnosed using ICD-9 (using the CATEGO computerized system based on PSE findings) and DSM-III (based on findings of the Diagnostic Interview Schedule) criteria. He found that the distribution of rediagnoses ranged from mild character disorders to severe affective disorder. Most of the patients were rediagnosed as having an anxiety or depressive disorder. The majority of rediagnoses belonged to the field of neurosis, except for the DIS/DSM-III approach. There was also a group of patients not able to be rediagnosed; in other words, they could be considered as primary neurasthenia. Furthermore, the patients tended to over-report their suffering or symptoms, which produced a discrepancy between objective assessment and self-report.

Other authors have focused on the different kinds of asthenic disorders. According to Sokoslovskaia (1989), two types of the syndrome of asthenia can be distinguished: one of a conversion nature, and another one of psychovegetative nature. The latter one, consisting of pain, sleep disturbances and other somatic symptoms, may correspond to some form of depressive disorders.

Neurasthenia is accepted to be a symptom of chronic intoxications, often linked to occupational hazards and stressful working conditions. As such, it has received great attention in Scandinavian and other countries (Lang, 1986; Stornstein and Stabell, 1986; Flodin *et al.*, 1989; Van Vliet *et al.*, 1989; Orbaek and Nise, 1989). Often it is linked to the stress of occupation, e.g. in sailors (Nitka, 1986; Voloshina, 1989), to the need to process high amounts of information ('information neurosis'; Chkivishvili and Somundzian, 1987), to a post-traumatic stress disorder (Jakubik, 1988) or to the effects of migration (Kohn *et al.*, 1989).

Fatigue and neurasthenia are also symptoms of brain disorders such as cerebrovascular disease (Burtsev and Molokov, 1986). It has also been associated with pernicious anaemia (Magiera, 1986), exposure to high altitudes (Ryn, 1988) and brain injuries (Morozov, 1987). In Eastern European countries, the term pseudoneurasthenia is used for those cases secondary to cerebrovascular disorders, but a primary autonomous neurasthenia is accepted too (Gorchakova, 1988; Grassler, 1989). Fatigue is the core symptom of neurasthenia—it is a symptom ill defined and studied (Berrios, 1990). But to try to reduce the problem of neurasthenia to the diagnosis of the symptom is in error, because the symptom itself has different origins. The creation of 'fatigue clinics', following the model of pain, sleep and other 'clinics', to cover a social need or to have a market share is certainly not welcome.

Neurasthenia is a common symptom of influenza and other viral disorders. Recently, a 'new disease' associated with the 'virus of the year' (Holland, 1988) has gained great attention. Namely, a chronic mononucleosis infection has been blamed for a syndrome present mainly in middle-aged executives in the USA. The presenting symptoms are fatigue, muscle aches and other ill-defined symptoms (Straus, 1988) attributed to chronic mononucleosis or Epstein–Barr virus infection, also called myalgic encephalomyelitis (Richmond, 1989). The stigma of psychiatric disorders is the ground for the proliferation of novel, fashionable disorders, such as food allergies that cause psychological symptoms, post-infectious neuromyasthenia, candidiasis hypersensitivity, severe pre-menstrual syndrome (Stewart, 1990) and others. Recently, the supposed chronic fatigue syndrome related to chronic viral infection has been considered an affective disorder (Greenberg, 1990), although the problem is still unclear. Abbey and Garfinkel (1990) described an integrated behavioural and biological approach to the chronic fatigue syndrome, but they also stressed that the high prevalence of major depressive episodes stands out among many inconsistencies in the description of the syndrome. The same applies to so-called myalgic encephalomyelitis (Wessely, 1990).

The real question is whether after considering alternative diagnoses all of the neurasthenic patients could be placed in other diagnostic categories, as DSM-III forces one to do, or if there is a remaining group of patients with 'idiopathic chronic fatigue' (Van Amberg, 1990), perhaps of a primary nature. Several factors make this dilemma difficult, among them some of a cultural nature.

In any case, the notion of neurasthenia is as confusing today as it was a century ago. Some cases could be rediagnosed as masked depression and benefit from proper treatment. In some of them, the presence of alexithymic features, or of cultural factors in which the level of depression–anxiety–guilt feelings is different from what is common in Western countries, may be the reason for the 'masking' of the disorder. Other cases, belonging to the pseudoneurasthenia category, are clearly secondary to other disorders, mainly brain affections. But it is also possible that primary cases of neurasthenia do exist, in which the symptoms of fatigue are not secondary to any disorder. Nevertheless, the lack of a proper measuring instrument (Berrios, 1990) makes the answer to this question almost impossible today. To make things even more complicated, the term psychasthenia is still widely used in France, but with a precise meaning, namely the character traits of the obsessive personality according to Janet (1903), which has some concordance with sensitive personality of Kretschner (Loas and Samuel-Lajeunesse, 1989).

Masked depression and the impulse control disorders

In recent years there has been an increasing number of research reports about dysfunctions of serotonin (5-hydroxytryptamine, 5-HT), systems in a wide variety of psychiatric conditions and even in behaviour patterns which are not by themselves disorders. Among those the following are the more important (López-Ibor Jr, 1988): mood disorders, alcoholism, bulimia, pathological gambling, suicidal (specially violent) behaviour, aggressivity and hostility as measured with psychological instruments, violent offences and arson. Obsessive-compulsive disorder is related to this group, either because the high control over their own behaviour that those patients show is the expression of a poor modulation of impulse control, e.g. some of those patients may lose control and present severe and abrupt self- or heteroaggressivity (López-Ibor Jr, 1989), or because the serotonergic dysfunction is different, e.g. an increase in post-synaptic 5-HT receptors able to be reduced by serotonergic antidepressants (Insel *et al.*, 1985; Zohar *et al.*, 1988).

The recent description of brief recurrent depressive episodes by Angst and Dobler-Mikola (1985) and by Montgomery and Montgomery (1982), characterized by symptoms fulfilling all the criteria for depressive episodes except duration, which is much shorter, suggests that this area may be looked at from a different perspective. This new group of mood disorders has been described in research done in quite special conditions, beyond the scope of everyday practice. The question is if some of the disorders and behaviour patterns mentioned above, which do not fulfil diagnostic criteria for depressive disorders, may be related to brief recurrent depression. In other words, present diagnostic criteria may not be appropriate in this field.

There are reasons to believe that this might be the case. The disorders mentioned were described by Lesse (1974) as behavioural masks of depressions. We had included them among the depressive equivalents (López-Ibor Jr, 1972, 1973). The reasons for this had to do with the psychopathology and relied on the presence of underlying depressive and anxious moods which could be subclinical forms of mood disorders.

The relationship of mood and impulse has often been discussed and the relative importance and predominance of one over the other is linked to one's perspective on human nature. For Freud in his early years the libido impulse was emphasized. The anxiety mood was a consequence of repression of the libido. Nevertheless, after 1922 his views changed radically. Anxiety was to be considered primary, and repression became one of several defence mechanisms against anxiety. The whole discussion of what is mood and its relations could lead us too far away (for a summary see López-Ibor Jr, 1990). For the moment let it be enough to consider the possibility that at least some of the impulse control disorders can be related to masked depressions.

Clinical manifestations

The list of depressive equivalents which have been mentioned in the literature is endless and embraces almost the totality of the symptomatology. Therefore, their enumeration is not enough. The existence of disease with such diverse manifestations as depression has been known for centuries (Burton, 1977). The principal symptoms of masked depression in a series of 317 patients studied by ourselves (López-Ibor Jr, 1972) show some preferred forms:

(a) Aches and pain (melancholia algica: Petrilowitsch, 1961; melancholia neuralgica: Priori, 1962). Pain in these cases has more the character of a feeling than a sensation. It is usually diffuse and of a global character. It does not have a radicular or truncal distribution, notwithstanding that it can be mistaken for neurological diseases. Pain in depression can appear isolated or in combination with other symptoms. Other patients express rather a painful feeling of their whole body, either permanent or wandering pain (as in neuritis migrans). Sometimes the paraesthesic feelings are described as cold sensations (crypt-aesthesiae) affecting the limbs or the head.

(b) Psychosensorial disorders: dizziness and vertigo (thymopathic vertigo: López-Ibor, 1950) and disturbances of the vision, which sometimes are described as painful (dysopsia algica). It consists of a disturbance in the perception of space. The vertiginous sensation, changeable in intensity and in its quality (it goes from 'feel dizzy' up to a sudden and violent crisis), is the expression of an anxious perception of space. The symptoms may be identical with those of panic disorder. The transition of these phenomena with depersonalization and derealization is fluid.

(c) Other neurological symptoms: akathisia, manifested through inability to remain quiet or a compulsive impulse to be constantly moving (tasikinaesia). The restless legs syndromes (leg jitters, fidgety legs, anxietas tibiarum, syndrome of Ekbom, illness of Wittmaack–Ekbom) consists of a paraesthesic or disaesthesic feeling which goes along the tibial crest, accompanied by small muscle contractions. It has been described as a manifestation of depression (López-Ibor, 1950).

(d) Psychosomatic symptoms in a strict sense (Table III): the first group includes subjective symptoms without objective findings of an organic disorder. The second group is constituted by functional disorders. In a third group psychosomatic disorders with damage to the affected organs are included.

Table III. Possible psychosomatic symptoms of the depressions.

Gastrointestinal
Nausea, vomiting, gastralgia, meteorism, aerophagia, hickup, constipation, diarrhoea, bulimia, anorexia, ulcers, colitis (ulcerative)

Respiratory
Dyspnea, vasomotor rhinitis, asthma

Genitourinary
Dysuria, nervous bladder, impotence, premature ejaculation, hypersexuality, menorrhea, frigidity

Cardiovascular
Tachycardia, palpitations, extrasystoles, precordial pain, cardiac phobia

Skin
Itching, eczema, neurodermatitis, alopecia

Metabolic
Obesity, thinness

The behavioural masks of depression

Depressive mood can be hidden behind the mask of other psychiatric disorders or behaviour (Table IV). Lesse (1974) introduced the term behavioural masks. They are frequent in the history of adult patients suffering from depressive disorders, and they take the form of antisocial behaviour, fugues, small robberies, school phobia or learning difficulties in childhood (Table I). These behavioural masks are the consequence of individual ways of elaborating the experience of a long-lasting depressive mood which cannot be interpreted in another way.

The association of mood disorders with personality disorders suggests more similarities than differences in this field. Mood disorders are associated with substance abuse disorders, borderline personality disorder (Akiskal *et al.*, 1985; Gunderson and Elliot 1985; Alnaes and Torgersen, 1988a, b), or with other 'eccentric' or 'dramatic' personality disorders (Alnaes and Torgersen, 1988a, b, 1989). The association of mood disorders and borderline personality disorder has even been found when studying biological markers (Lahmeyer *et al.*, 1988, 1989). The reverse is also frequent—the association of personality disorders with anxiety and depressive disease (Klass *et al.*, 1989). Nevertheless, these associations are sometimes difficult to interpret as, for instance, a mood disorder may increase the relevance of pre-existing personality traits (Joffe and Regan, 1988).

Alexithymia has been described in masked depression in holocaust survivors (Fisch, 1989). A masked depression can also take the form of a personality disorder. The relationship of a common disorder to depression is often confusing. Novac (1986) identified a group of patients with borderline personality,

Table IV. Behavioural masks of depression (Lesse, 1974).

Suicide
Self-destructive behaviour
Sexual deviations
Twilight states
Alcoholism, addictions
Pathological gambling
Phobias, obsessions, dysmorphophobias
Kleptomania, theft, criminality
Hypochondria
Delusions (of reference, jealousy, etc.)
Depersonalization and derealization
Confabulation
School phobia, learning difficulties, behaviour disorders in children
Sadistic and masochistic behaviours
Accident proneness
Other psychiatric disorders

characterized by later development in life, a pre-morbid history of high social function and the presence of long-lasting stresses (such as migration) or multiple losses before onset, which he calls pseudoborderline syndrome. It is a form of masked depression and not a personality disorder although the symptoms are those of borderline personality disorder. These characteristics allow this syndrome to be differentiated from the subaffective disorders, characterological depression and the personality sequelae of affective disorders as described by Akiskal (1982).

Diagnosis

About one-half of all depressions seen by primary care physicians initially present predominantly or exclusively with somatic symptoms (Kielholz, 1973). Many of these depressions are not recognized or are misdiagnosed and mistreated. The proportion of depressions that are masked is positively correlated to the patient's tendency to somatize and negatively correlated to the doctor's ability to recognize depressions that hide behind somatic complaints (Fisch, 1987).

Masked depression is not always masked. Very often clear mood abnormalities are present, but physicians overlook them or consider them 'secondary' to another diagnosis or irrelevant for treatment. Patients with hypochondriasis have overt anxiety and depressive symptoms, something which has been interpreted against them being masked depression (Kellner et al., 1989). Pinard et al. (1986) compared two small samples of overt and masked depression. The scores on the Beck Depression Scale, Hamilton Depression Scale and other instruments were essentially the same. The only difference was that the patients with masked depression were more anxious and less inhibited than the endogenous ones. This fact has been used against the notion of masked depression (Kellner et al., 1989). Nevertheless in many neurotic patients there is a need for a multidimensional diagnosis and for target symptoms to treat, differentiating clearly what is to be expected from an antidepressant and what requires other therapeutic interventions.

The isolated symptoms described have no diagnostic value. Some patients turn up after having consulted other doctors without success. The absence of sufficient findings in the clinical examinations, an atypical symptomatology, poor precision in the description of the symptoms, failure of medical or surgical treatment, stressful or conflict situations, excessive anxiety or brooding with preoccupations or hypochondriac gestures, do turn the patient into a 'problem' who as a last resort is referred to the psychiatrist. Sometimes even a suicide attempt is necessary to make this decision. The task of the clinician is to make a positive diagnosis. The first step is the correct evaluation of the somatic findings. Eighteen per cent of my patients suffered from somatic disorders, of which the most important were focused in the spinal column (irrelevant degenerative malformations) and the electroencephalogram, mainly theta waves in the left temporal lobes, unrelated to epilepsy.

The second source of error consists of an exaggerated importance given by the physician to the psychological condition of the patient, based on an insufficient clinical examination (Ayuso and López-Ibor Jr, 1973), and inability to diagnose an underlying medical condition.

In the third place, depression (a very common disorder) can coincide not only with an unimportant finding but with another disease.

The diagnosis of masked depression relies on clinical skills. The first objective is to think about the possibility of a depression (Kielholz, 1973).

The second is to analyse the symptoms meticulously, looking for the presence of some depressive characteristics (the term microphenomenological analysis has been used in this context). The characteristics of the symptoms or complaints participate, so to say, in the general characteristics of the depressive mood. The symptom has a shade of anguish or of affliction. In general, the symptom is not concrete, but it has a certain vague or diffuse character. However, after the evolution of the illness it may remain more rigidly fixed. The patient may use neologisms which express the difficulties in describing the symptoms in everyday language.

Symptoms of masked depression are often accompanied by a minor depressive mood. Some patients know when a symptom is depressive because they grasp the 'atmosphere' which involves them (Walcher, 1970). This underlying depression can be interpreted wrongly by the patient and his or her doctor, who attribute it, sometimes obstinately, to the symptom itself. In the case of acute pain depression can be judged to be secondary. But an acute pain leads to irritability, never to depression.

The presence of some symptoms of depression has to be carefully investigated, such as sleep and appetite disturbances, loss of normal interests, inability to make decisions, lack of sense in everyday life, difficulties in concentrating, asthenia, fatigue, irritability, sudden mood changes, or the expression and psychomotor activity of the patient and so on. These symptoms are mitigated and sometimes they have to be pointed out by comparing the present state of the patient with his or her condition before the illness. In this sense, the history becomes an important functional test.

Although expressions like 'monosymptomatic depressions' or 'isolated pains' are often used, reality is different. As a general rule, no depressive symptom appears isolated. The more intense and severe is a pathological process in organic medicine, the lesser is the number and intensity of the subjective discomfort, excepting for example cases like those where a tumour squeezes a nerve plexus (Jores, 1964). This same fact is also found in the evolution of the masked depressions in which different symptoms can appear in different episodes (syndrome variation: Spiegelberg, 1955).

References

Abbey SE and Garfinkel PE (1990) Chronic fatigue syndrome and the psychiatrist. *Can J Psychiatry* **35**, 625–633.

Akiskal HS (1982) Factors associated with incomplete recovery in primary depressive illness. *J Clin Psychiatry* **43**, 266–271.

Akiskal H, Yerevanian B, Davies GC *et al.* (1985) The nosological status of borderline personality: Clinical and polysomnographic study. *Am J Psychiatry* **142**, 192–198.

Alnaes R and Torgersen S (1988a) The relationship between DSM-III symptom disorders (Axis I) and personality disorders (Axis II) in an outpatient population. *Acta Psychiatr Scand* **78**, 485–492.

Alnaes R and Torgernsen S (1988b) DSM-III symptom disorders (Axis I) and personality disorders (Axis II) in an outpatient population. *Acta Psychiatr Scand* **78**, 348–355.

Alnaes R and Torgernsen S (1989) Personality and personality disorders among patients with major depression in combination with dysthymic or cyclothymic disorders. *Acta Psychiatr Scand* **79**, 363–369.

Angst J (1973) Die larvierte Depression in Transkultureller Sicht. In: Kielholz P (ed.) *Die larvierte Depression.* Bern: Huber.

Angst J and Dobler-Mikola A (1985) The Zurich study: a prospective epidemiological study of depressive neurotic and psychosomatic syndromes IV. Recurrent and non-recurrent brief depression. *Eur Arch Psychiatry Neurol Sci* **234**, 408–416.

Ayuso JL and López-Ibor JL Jr (1973) Una nueva forma de iatrogenia: Los abusos de la hospitalizacion psiquiátrica en un hospital general. *Actas Luso Esp Neurol Psiquiatr* **1**, 571–577.

Ayuso JL and Saiz J (1981) *Las depresiones. Nuevas perspectivas clinicas, etiopatogenicas y terapiuticas.* Madrid: Interamericana.

Berrios GE (1990) Feelings of fatigue and psychopathology: A conceptual history. *Compr. Psychiatry* **31**, 140–151.

Burton R (1977) *The Anatomy of Melancholy.* New York: Vintage Books.

Burtsev EM and Molokov DD (1986) Diagnostika i sanatornoe lechenie nachal'nykh proiavlenii nedostatochnosti krovos—nabzhaneiia golovnogo mozga. [Diagnosis and sanatorium treatment of the initial manifestations of inadequate blood supply to the brain]. *Zh Nevropatol Psikhiatr* **86**, 1305–1310.

Campbell JD (1950) Mild manic-depressive psychosis, depressive type: Psychiatric and clinical significance. *J Nerv Ment Dis* **112**, 206–236.

Chamberlain OB (1949) Cryptic depressive states. *South Med J* **42**, 1078–1090.

Chen XS (1986) Masked depression among patients diagnosed as neurosis in general hospitals. *Chung Hua I Hsueh Tsa Chih* **66**, 32–33.

Cheung FM (1989) The indigenization of neurasthenia in Hong Kong. *Colt Med Psychiatry* **13**, 227–241.

Chkikvishvili TS and Somundzian AA (1987) The clinical picture of information neurosis. *Acta Nerv Super (Praha)* **29**, 109–111.

Cimbal M (1923) Vegetative Aquivalente der Depressionszustande. *Zbl Nevr* **34**, 321–325.

Davis DL (1989) Georg Beard and Lydia Pinkham: Gender, class, and nerves in late 19th century America. *Health Care Women Int* **10**, 93–114.

Fernandes Da Fonseca A (1973) Basic concepts of affective equivalents. In: De La Fuente R and Weisman M (eds) *Psychiatry 1. Proc 5th Wld Congr Psychiatry*, p. 627. Amsterdam: Excerpta Medica.

Fisch RZ (1987) Masked depression: Its interrelations with somatization, hypochondriasis and conversion. *Int J Psychiatry Med* **17**, 367–379.

Fisch RZ (1989) Alexithymia, masked depression and loss in a holocaust survivor. *Br J Psychiatry* **154**, 708–710.

Flodin U, Ekberg K and Andersson L (1989) Neuropsychiatric effects of low exposure to styrene. *Br J Ind Med* **46**, 805–808.

Glatzel J (1967) Uber zylothyme Depressionen mit vegetativer Symptomatik. *Fortschr Neurol Psychiatr* **35**, 441–452.

Goldberg DP and Bridges K (1987) The determinants of somatization. *9th World Congress of the International College of Psychosomatic Medicine* (Sydney, Australia), Book of Abstracts, p. 65. Royal Australian and New Zealand College of Psychiatrists.

Gorchakova LN (1988) Vialotekushchaia shizofreniia s preobladaniem astenicheskikh rasstroistv. [Torpid schizophrenia with a predominance of asthenic disorders]. *Zh Nevropatol Psikhiatr* **88**, 76–82.

Grassler W (1989) Zur Differentialdiagnose des sog. vorzeitigen Leistungsversagens oder der vorzeitigen Alterung. [Differential diagnosis of so-called premature performance failure or premature aging]. *Z Gesamte Inn Med* **44**, 370–373.

Greenberg DB (1990) Neurasthenia in the 1980s: Chronic mononucleosis, chronic fatigue syndrome, and anxiety and depressive disorders. *Psychosomatics* **31**, 129–137.

Gunderson J and Elliot G (1985) The interface between borderline personality disorder and affective disorder. *Am J Psychiatry* **142**, 277–288.

Hempel J (1937) Die vegetativ-dystone Depression. *Nervenarzt* **10**, 22–26.

Holland RG (1988) Virus of the year? [letter]. *Can Med Assoc J* **139**, 198–199.

Ierodiakonou CS and Iacovides A (1987) Somatic manifestations of depressive patients in different psychiatric settings. *Psychopathology* **29**, 136–143.

Insel T, Mueller EA and Alterman I (1985) Obsessive-compulsive disorder and serotonin: Is there a connection? *Biol Psychiatry* **20**, 1174–1188.

Jakubik A (1988) Leczenie astenii poobozowej. [Treatment of post-concentration camp asthenia]. *Przegl Lek* **45**, 21–24.

Janet P (1903) *Les Obsessions et la Psycasthenie*. Paris: Alcan.

Joffe RT and Regan JJ (1988) Personality and depression. *J Psychiatr Res* **22**, 279–286.

Jores A (1964) Symptom und Organbefund. In: Burger-Prinz H and Winzenried FJM (eds) *Befinden und Symptom*. Stuttgart: Schattauer.

Kellner R, Abbot P, Winslow WW and Pathak D (1989) Anxiety, depression, and somatization in DSM-III hypochondriasis. *Psychosomatics* **30**, 57–64.

Kessel A (1968) The borderlands of the depressive states. *Br J Psychiatry* **114**, 1135–1140.

Kielholz P (1973) *Die larvierte Depression*. Bern: Huber.

Kielholz P (1964) *Depressions in everyday practice*. Bern: Huber.

King CR (1989) Parallels between neurasthenia and premenstrual syndrome. *Women Health* **15**, 1–23.

Klass ET, Dinardo PA and Barlow DH (1989) DSM-III-R personality diagnoses in anxiety disorder patients. *Compr Psychiatry* **30**, 251–258.

Kohn R, Flaherty JA and Levav I (1989) Somatic symptoms among older Soviet immigrants: An exploratory study. *Int J Soc Psychiatry* **35**, 350–360.

Kranz H (1955) Das Thema des Wahns im Wandel der Zeit. *Fortschr Neurol Psychiatr* **23**, 58–72.

Labhardt F (1986) Psychosomatics and depression. *Psychopathology* **19** (Suppl.), 162–164.

Lahmeyer HW, Val E, Gaviria FM *et al.* (1988) Sleep, lithium transport, dexamethasone suppression, and monoamine oxidase activity in borderline personality disorder. *Psychiatry Res* **25**, 19–30.

Lahmeyer HW, Reynolds CF III *et al.* (1989) Biologic markers in borderline personality disorder: A review. *J Clin Psychiatry* **50**, 217–225.

Lang YY (1986) [Observations on the effects of exposure to methyl methacrylate on workers' health]. *Chung Hua Yu Fang I Hsueh Tsa Chih* **20**, 344–347.

Lange J (1928) Die endogenen und reaktiven Gemutserkrankungen und die manisch-depressive Konstitution. In: *Handbuch der Geisteskrankheiten*, spez. Teil, Vol. 2. Berlin: Springer.

Lemke R (1949) Über die vegetative Depression. *Psychiatr Neurol Med Psychol* **1**, 161–179.

Lesse S (1974) *Masked Depression*. New York: Aronson.

Lindberg N and Lindberg E (1988) Painter's syndrome. *Am J Ind Med* **13**, 519–520.

Loas G and Samuel-Lajeunesse PB (1989) Personnalites psychasthenique de P. Janet et sensitive d'E. Krestchmer: deux entites distinctes? *Ann Med Psychol (Paris)* **147**, 825–829.

López-Ibor JJ (1950) *La angustia vital*. Madrid: Paz Montalvo.

López-Ibor JJ (1966) *Las neurosis como enfermedades del inimo*. Madrid: Gredos.

López-Ibor JJ (1972) Masked depressions. 45th Maudsley Lecture. *Br J Psychiatry* **120**, 245–258.

López-Ibor JJ Jr (1972) *Los equivalentes depresivos*. Madrid: Pax Montalvo.

López-Ibor JJ Jr (1973) Clinical aspects of depressive equivalents. In: R De La Fuente and M Weisman (eds) *Psychiatry 1. Proc 5th Wld Congr Psychiatry*. Amsterdam: Excerpta Medica.

López-Ibor JJ Jr (1988) The involvement of serotonin in psychiatric disorders and behaviour. *Br J Psychiatry* **153**, 26–39.

López-Ibor JJ Jr (1989) Impulsive control in obsessive-compulsive disorder: A bio-psychopathological approach. *Prog Neuro-Psychopharmacol Biol Psychiatry* **14**, 709–718.

López-Ibor JJ Jr (1990) The spectrum of mood disorders. *J Clin Psychiatry* **51** (Suppl 9), 62–64.

López-Ibor JJ Jr and Lozano M (1987) Depression and pain. In: Biziere K, Garattini S and Simon P (eds) *Diagnosis and Treatment of Depression*. 'Quo Vadis?' Symposium. Montpelier: Sanofi.

Lozano M (1989) Aspectos psiquiitricos del dolor crónico no neoplásico. Doctoral thesis, Salamanca.

Magiera P (1986) Przypadek zaborzen neurastenicznych i psychotycznych w przebiegu niedokrwistosci zosliwej. [A case of neurasthenic and psychotic disorders in pernicious anaemia]. *Pol Tgy Lek* **41**, 249–250.

Makanjuola JD and Olaifa EA (1987) Masked depression in Nigerians treated at the Neuro-Psychiatric Hospital Aro, Abeokuta. *Acta Psychiatr Scand* **76**, 480–485.

Montgomery SA and Montgomery DB (1982) Pharmacological prevention of suicidal behaviour. *J Affect Dis* **4**, 291–398.

Morozov AM (1987) Psikhoterapiia nevrastenopodobnykh rasstroistv v otdalennom periode cherpno-mozgovoi travmy. [Psychotherapy of neurasthenia-like disorders in the late period of craniocerebral injuries]. *Vrach Delo* 101–102.

Munakata T (1989) The socio-cultural significance of the diagnostic label 'neurasthenia' in Japan's mental health care system. *Cult Med Psychiatry* **13**, 203–213.

Murphy DL, Siever LJ and Insel TR (1985) Therapeutic responses to tricyclic antidepressants and related drugs in non-affective disorder patient populations. *Prog Neuro-psychopharmacol Biol Psychiatry* **9**, 3–13.

Nissen G (1973) Die larvierte Depression bei Kindern und Jugendlichen. In: Kielholz P (ed.) *Die larvierte Depression*. Bern: Huber.

Nitka J (1986) Incidence of neuroses and neurotic syndromes in seamen and workers ashore with gastric and duodenal ulcer. *Boll Inst Marit Trop Med Gdynia* **37**, 165–173.

Novac A (1986) The pseudoborderline syndrome: A proposal based on case studies. *J Nerv Ment Dis* **174**, 84–91.

Orbaek P and Nise N (1989) Neurasthenic complaints and psychometric function of toluene-exposed rotogravure printers. *Am J Ind Med* **16**, 67–77.

Orelli A von (1954) Der Wandel des Inhaltes der depressiven Ideen bei der reinen Melancholie. *Schweiz Arch Neurol Psychiatr* **73**, 217–287.

Oxman TE, Posenberg SD, Schnurr PP and Tucker GJ (1985) Linguistic dimensions of affect and thought in somatization disorder. *Am J Psychiatry* **142**, 1150–1155.

Peng C (1990) [A comparative study of the clinical features of neurosis in urban and rural areas]. *Chung Hua Shen Ching Ching Shen Ko Tsa Chih* **23**, 6–8.

Petrilowitsch N (1961) Zur Problematik depressiver Psychosen. *Arch Psychiatr Nerv Krankh* **202**, 244–265.

Pfeiffer WM (1971) *Transkulturelle Psychiatrie. Ergebnisse und probleme.* Stuttgart: Thieme.

Pichot P (1985) *Un siècle de psychiatrie.* Paris: Poche.

Pinard G, Desmarais PA, Cormier H *et al.* (1986) Comparaison de la depression masquie et de la depression endogène a l'aide d'echelles psychometriques, de marqoeurs endocrinologiques et de reponses pharmacologiques. Depression masquiée versus depression endogène. *Encephale* **12**, 99–103.

Priori R (1962) La 'Depressio sine depressione' e le sue forme cliniche. In: Kranz H (ed.) *Psychopathologie Heute.* Stuttgart: Thieme.

Richmond C (1989) Myalgic encephalomyelitis, Princess Aurora, and the wandering womb. *Br Med J* **298**, 1295–1296.

Rin H and Huang MG (1989) Neurasthenia as nosological dilemma. *Cult med Psychiatry* **13**, 215–226.

Russell, JG (1989) Anxiety disorders in Japan: A review of the Japanese literature on shinkeishitsu and taijinkyofusho. *Cult Med Psychiatry* **13**, 391–403.

Ryn Z (1988) Psychpathology in mountaineering: Mental disturbances under high-altitude stress. *Int J Sports Med* **9**, 163–169.

Sartorius N (1985) ICD-10 and depression. In: Pichot P, Berner P, Wolf R and Than K (eds) *Psychiatry: The State of the Art*, Vol. 1, pp. 661–663. New York: Plenum.

Schneider K (1962) *Klinische Psychopathologie*, 8th edn. Stuttgart: Thieme.

Sokolovskaia LV (1989) Tipologiia astenicheskikh sostoianii (raektsii, fazy) pri psikhopatiiakh. [Classification of asthenic conditions (reactions, phases) in psychopathy]. *Zh Nevropatol Psikhiatr* **89**, 110–114.

Solms M (1989) Three previously untranslated reviews by Freud from the Neue Freie Presse. *Int J Psychoanal* **70**, 397–400.

Spiegelberg U (1955) Über Beziehungen endogener Psychosen zu psychosomatische Krankheiten. *Fortschr Neurol Psychiatrie* **23**, 221–248.

Stewart DE (1990) The changing faces of somatization. *Psychosomatics* **31**, 153–158.

Stornstein J and Stahell K (1986) Lsemiddelskader. Yrkesmedisinsk og neuropsykologisk underskelse av Isemiddeleksponerte arbeidstakere i en hyttalerfahrikk. [Toxic effects of solvents. An occupational medical and neuropsychological study of workers exposed to solvents in a loudspeaker factory]. *Tidsskr Nor Laegeforen* **106**, 1132–1135.

Stoudemire A, Kahn M, Brown JT *et al.* (1985) Masked depression in a combined medical–psychiatric unit. *Psychosomatics* **26**, 221–224; 227–228.

Straus SE (1988) The chronic mononucleosis syndrome. A. *J Infect Dis* **157**, 405–412.

Suzuki T (1989) The concept of neurasthenia and its treatment in Japan. *Cult Med Psychiatry* **13**, 187–202.

Tseng WS, Di X, Ebata K *et al.* (1986) Diagnostic pattern for neuroses in China, Japan, and the United States. *Am J Psychiatry* **146**, 1010–1014.

Van Amberg RJ (1990) Idiopathic chronic fatigue: A primary disorder. *N Engl J Med* **87**, 319–324.

Van Vliet C, Swaen GM, Meijers JM *et al.* (1989) Prenarcotic and neuraesthenic symptoms among Dutch workers exposed to organic solvents. *Br J Ind Med* **46**, 586–590.

Voloshina VM (1989) Astenicheskie rasstroistva u moriakov v period dlite'lnykh reisov. [Asthenic disorders in sailors during long sea voyages]. *Zh Nevropatol Psikhiatr* **89**, 60–65.

Walcher W (1970) *Die larvierte Depression.* Vienna: Hollinek.

Wang HL (1989) [Preliminary investigation of neurasthenic syndrome induced by occupational hazards]. *Chung Hua Shen Ching Ching Shen Ko Tsa Chih* **22**, 278–281; 317–318.

Watts CAH (1966) *Depressive Disorders in the Community.* Bristol: Wright.

Wessely S (1990) Old wine in new bottles: Neurasthenia and 'ME'. *Psychol Med* **20**, 35–53.

World Health Organization (1990) *International Classification of Diseases.* 1988 Draft of Ch V, Categories F00–F99, Mental, Behavioural and Developmental Disorders. Clinical Description and Diagnostic Guidelines. Geneva: WHO, Division of Mental Health (MNH/MEP/87.1 Rev. 4).

Zhang MY (1989) The diagnosis and phenomenology of neurasthenia: a Shanghai study. *Cult Med Psychiatry* **13**, 147–161.

Zohar J, Insel TR, Zohar-Kadouch RC *et al.* (1988) Serotonergic responsivity in obsessive-compulsive disorder: Effects of chronic clomipramine treatment. *Arch Gen Psychiatry* **45**, 162–172.

8

Recurrent brief depression

S.A. Montgomery

Introduction

The development of effective drugs for the treatment of depression has helped define the illness. The identification of features common to patients who respond to standard antidepressants rather than to placebo has brought about a consensus for definition. Depression is a syndrome characterized by a number of features in addition to the depressed mood which is generally considered to be a necessary but not sufficient indicator for the diagnosis. The most widely accepted definition emphasizes dysphoric mood plus a number of accompanying features taken from a list of core symptoms. This list is somewhat biased towards the more obviously biological symptoms.

The number of symptoms required to make a diagnosis is still debated. There is also disagreement since there are significant cultural differences in the presentation of the depressive illness. Eastern and African cultures, for example, report more somatic symptoms whereas Western cultures report more dysphoria and guilt. There is also good evidence that men report fewer symptoms than women even when the level of social or occupational impairment is the same (Angst and Dobler-Mikola, 1984). A syndromal definition that does not take this sex difference into account will under-represent male depression. In spite of these difficulties there is reasonable agreement and the operational criteria for conventional depression or major depression are similar in the Feighner criteria (Feighner *et al.*, 1972), the Research Diagnostic Criteria (RDC) (Spitzer *et al.*, 1978), the DSM-III, DSM-III-R (APA, 1980, 1987) and the International Classification of Diseases (ICD-10).

The Diagnosis of Depression. Edited by J.P. Feighner and W.F. Boyer
© 1991 John Wiley & Sons Ltd

These diagnostic schedules include a minimum duration of illness criterion to identify persistent illness. There is a fair degree of accord on the duration of illness that is required in order to meet diagnostic criteria for major depression. Most systems require a minimum of two weeks; the more stringent Feighner criteria require four.

Although shorter-duration depressions have been reported, much biological research has concentrated on persistent or major depression. Investigators take pains to exclude patients with brief episodes from efficacy studies for major depression. Some early placebo responses seen in conventional efficacy studies may be attributed to these spontaneously remitting brief depressions and this can make for difficulties in establishing the efficacy of antidepressants. There is also the suggestion, not yet systematically investigated, that these brief depressions do not respond well to conventional antidepressants (Montgomery *et al.*, 1983). Since one of the aims of the diagnosis of major depression is to identify those patients who are likely to respond to conventional antidepressant treatment it is not surprising that a duration of illness criterion that excludes brief episodes of depression has been adopted. Depressions lasting less than two weeks have been ignored, excluded from studies, and, until recently, formed a somewhat neglected category of illness.

Brief depressions

In establishing a relatively new illness concept such as brief depression it is important to consider the evidence from different perspectives. A careful clinical description of the distinctive features is the prime essential. This description should convey the severity, psychopathology, duration and pattern of recurrence, which allow other clinicians to recognize the condition. The effect of treatment in altering the course of the disorder also helps validate the illness concept. It is necessary to turn to well-conducted epidemiological studies to obtain some idea of the incidence of the disorder and its relative importance. If the features of the illness identified in clinical studies match the data from epidemiological field work the illness will have strong claims for recognition.

Clinical characteristics of brief depression

The features of brief depressions have been examined in clinical studies which have been able to record the brevity of the episodes, their severity, and the similarity of the symptomatology to major depression (Montgomery *et al.*, 1983, 1989, 1990).

Duration

A cohort of patients suffering from brief depressions has been investigated with frequent follow-up in a series of prospective studies in London. In this group of patients, two-thirds of brief depressive episodes were found to last between two and four days, with a median of three days (Montgomery *et al.*, 1989, 1990). This is in accord with the two to three-day duration reported in the epidemiological studies of Angst and Dobler-Mikola (1985).

The duration of the episodes (Figure 1) shows an obvious normal distribution which centres on a three-day median. Eighty-one per cent of the episodes had a duration of less than five days. Of those episodes which lasted less than 14 days 97% lasted one week or less. Some patients tended to have shorter and others longer episodes but the duration of the brief episodes was not constant for each individual. The episodes varied in length in individual patients in a way which suggested that this may be one measure of severity.

A small number of episodes occurred which lasted nine days or more and seemed therefore to be more closely related to major depression. The studies have not been designed to establish whether the small number of brief depressions lasting between nine and 13 days fit better within brief depression or major depression. However, the number of such episodes is small and it is

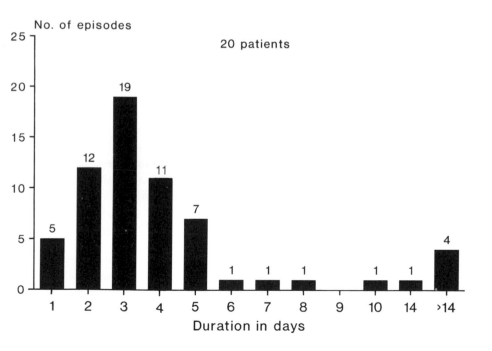

Figure 1. Duration of brief depressive episodes.

convenient for now to leave them outside the category of major depression and within the spectrum of brief depression.

There is similar doubt about the place of those depressions which fulfil criteria for major depression, but which last only two to four weeks. A substantial number of such patients in a study of major depression would increase the potential for early placebo response, thereby jeopardizing the ability of the study to determine efficacy. The common practice of excluding major depression which does not persist for four weeks or more from efficacy studies is designed to avoid this group and increase the chance of detecting a drug placebo difference.

Almost all the brief depressions reported lasted less than one week, so that there is some similarity to the intermittent depressions defined by the RDC. This diagnostic category cannot, however, be applied appropriately to the brief depressions described in this chapter. In RDC intermittent depression is a category of minor depression and is perceived as a mild form of depression (Williams and Spitzer, 1982), whereas the recurrent brief depression discussed here is a severe illness associated with significant morbidity.

The duration of the episodes as reported by patients can be affected in a number of ways which are often overlooked. The effect of memory and retrospective distortion of reporting by patients (Parker, 1987) is a well-discussed problem in studies investigating the lifetime prevalence of depression. Since patients tend to forget or distort early episodes, this can lead to substantial differences in the mean age of onset of major depression recorded by prospective and retrospective studies. In the short term patients have a tendency to remember severe symptoms more accurately than mild symptoms (Schrader *et al.*, 1990).

The duration of brief depressions in some patients seemed longer in retrospect than they actually were at the time. This difficulty appears to increase with the length of the period of recall. It therefore becomes difficult to be sure of the precise duration of very distant episodes. This inherent unreliability of the memory of the exact duration means that some individuals with brief depression may report these episodes as having been major depression when giving a history some years later.

Symptoms and severity

There is an unfortunate tendency to assume that if an episode of depression does not fulfil criteria for major depression it is automatically mild and minor. This approach has been reinforced to some degree by the catergorization of depression into major and minor implied in the DSM-III diagnostic system. Minor depression is perceived as chronic and mild (Williams and Spitzer, 1982) although there are few data from prospective community studies to indicate that mild depression is at all common or that minor depression is necessarily mild (Angst *et al.*, 1988).

The prospective clinical studies of brief depressions showed a marked severity of illness (Montgomery *et al.*, 1989, 1990). The mean severity of depression, measured on the Montgomery and Asberg Depression Rating Scale (MADRS) (Montgomery and Asberg, 1979), was around 30. This is well above the criterion of 24 adopted to select patients with moderate or greater severity for entry into studies of major depression. Two-thirds of individual episodes were severe enough to qualify for entry. 25% of episodes had a severity score greater than 35 on the MADRS, which is a criterion for severe depression. This level of severity emphasizes the disabling nature of the episodes and argues strongly for the separation of the illness from the minor depression category.

Epidemiological studies concentrate on the occurrence of illness and tend not to use adequate measures to comment on the severity of illness. Indirect measures of severity such as occupational or social impairment were, however, used to identify illness in the Zurich study (Angst and Dobler-Mikola, 1985). These indicate the same level of impairment as was seen in major depression.

In the clinical studies the severity of the episodes varied in any individual from one episode to the next. It was not possible to identify any factors that predicted whether the next episode would be mild, moderate or severe.

The symptomatology of the brief depressions is very similar to that seen in major depression. In both the clinical studies and the epidemiological studies brief depressions satisfied the syndromal definition of major depression except for the duration of illness criterion. The pattern of symptomatology recorded on the MADRS in the clinical studies was very similar to major depression, which suggests that the two disorders have much in common.

The pattern of symptomatology in brief depression did, however, vary from one episode to another. Some individuals switched, for example, from a melancholic pattern to an atypical pattern and back again. There are few data on the constancy of the pattern of symptomatology from one episode to the next in major depression, although there is an assumption that the patterns are relatively constant for any individual. The variability of symptoms sometimes seen from one episode to another makes it unlikely that individual symptoms would be helpful in identifying a favourable or unfavourable outcome. Formal studies to elucidate this point have still to be carried out.

Intervals and periodicity
In both the clinical and the epidemiological studies brief depressive episodes recurred frequently over the period of observation. In the clinical cohort the median interval between the beginning of one episode and the beginning of the next was 18 days, but this was variable. The intervals were irregular, with roughly equal numbers lasting between one and five weeks and only 14% lasting longer than five weeks. From these data it appears that the median number of episodes expected in a year would be 20. This is in agreement with

the data from the epidemiological studies, which indicate 12 or more episodes a year (Angst *et al.*, 1985).

In the epidemiological studies social and occupational impairment was concentrated in the group who had either at least one episode a month or 12 or more episodes a year. This led to the recommendation by Angst *et al.* (1988) that a criterion of at least monthly recurrence be adopted for the definition of the illness.

The clinical data, however, do not support the use of this criterion since it implies a greater regularity of recurrence than was observed. In the highly recurrent group followed up in the clinic the recurrences were irregular and unpredictable. Twenty-five per cent of the intervals between episodes were longer than four weeks. This irregularity also argues against a relationship with menses. Indeed only 15% of the episodes observed in the clinic occurred in the week prior to menses. There was no relationship between episodes and the menstrual cycle in the epidemiological study. There was, moreover, no obvious difference in pattern between male and female brief depressions.

Individuals who suffer from recurrent brief depression complain that they do not know when the next episode will strike or whether it will be particularly incapacitating or not. It is the combination of unpredictable occurrence and unpredictable severity which patients report as most distressing. They find it difficult to readjust their social life and occupational commitments at short notice. To accommodate to the unpredictable nature of the disorder a number of patients followed up in the clinic reported that they have changed to work which allows more erratic work practices.

Recurrent brief depressions: a common and stable illness

The epidemiological studies emanate from Zurich, where a normal population sample has been regularly followed up over ten years (Angst *et al.*, 1984). This study has established that recurrent brief depressions occur very commonly in the general population with an incidence reported between 5% and 8%, which is similar to, or slightly higher than, the rate of major depression (Angst and Dobler-Mikola, 1985; Angst *et al.*, 1988). A criterion of social or occupational impairment was used to define caseness and brief depressions were seen to be as disruptive and impairing as major depression. There was therefore some epidemiological justification for considering these brief episodes as an illness separate from, but as serious as, major depression.

A further validation of a diagnostic entity is the stability of the illness in the individual. If the same illness is reported over time in an individual, without changes that would lead to a different diagnosis, it adds substantially to the specificity of the diagnosis. Brief depression recurred in this epidemiological study with a stability similar to that of major depression, so that both forms of depression therefore appear to have equivalent diagnostic specificity. Recurrent brief depression was also similar to major depression in the stability of diagnosis over the ten-year follow-up period (Angst *et al.*, 1990a). In this it differs from the anxiety disorders, which were relatively unstable and had a greater tendency to evaporate or to develop into major depression (Vollrath and Angst, 1989). The incidence and stability of other diagnoses reported in the Zurich study are in accord with other epidemiological data and this strengthens the finding that recurrent brief depression is a stable illness.

Suicidal behaviour and brief depression

One of the most dramatic measures of the serious nature of recurrent brief depression is the relationship with suicide. The association of brief depressions with suicidal behaviour was identified during an investigation of treatments to reduce suicide attempts among frequent attempters without major depression (Montgomery *et al.*, 1979, 1983; Montgomery and Montgomery, 1982). In a series of studies examining the effect of treatment with a neuroleptic, an anti-depressant or placebo the best predictor of suicidal behaviour was a depressive episode lasting less than two weeks. The MADRS score during the first month predicted subsequent suicide attempts during the six-month prophylactic study. Moreover, six out of ten items on the MADRS individually predicted a subsequent suicide attempt. It appeared therefore that the recurrence of the brief depression brought a risk of subsequent suicide attempt. In later prospective cohort follow-up studies with frequent observations it appears that suicidal attempts occur almost entirely during episodes of brief depression rather than during the interval phase (Montgomery *et al.*, 1989).

Clinical experience has found more suicide attempts in patients with brief depressions than in major depression, but it was thought that this could be a reflection on sampling bias. However, more patients with brief depression are seen in hospital following suicide attempts than patients with major depression. This strongly suggests that suicide attempts are more frequent in patients with brief depression, since the incidence of the two illnesses is similar. Independent confirmation of the relationship between brief depression and suicidal attempts comes from a reanalysis of epidemiological data, which showed the suicide attempt rate to be significantly higher in the brief depression group than in the non-depressed normal population sample (Angst, 1990a). More recently, using a different epidemiological cohort the Zurich group reported that suicide attempts were more numerous in those with brief depressions than in those with major depression (Angst *et al.*, 1990b). The percentage of those with suicide attempts was twice as high in the brief depression group as in the major depression group, although the difference was not statistically significant.

Quite why patients with brief depressions should be more at risk has not been adequately discussed but there are several possible explanations. One of the factors may be the amount of time a patient with brief depression spends in the ill state. Brief depression appears to be a stable illness with a continuing high risk of frequent depressive episodes persisting over years. In the clinical sample studied, the illness is present in a depressive phase some 20% of the time and the risk for a suicide attempt is substantial. The proportion of time spent depressed is often much lower with major depression, at least until the condition becomes highly recurrent or chronic.

The speed of onset of the episodes of brief depressions may also contribute to the risk of suicidal behaviour. There is a much more marked and rapid change from well to severely ill with brief depressions than usually occurs with major depression. The effect of this sudden change may make it difficult to cope with suicidal urges and the rapidity of the change makes it difficult to take appropriate precautions. The usual techniques for managing suicidal risk in major depression, such as the mobilization of friends or family or hospital admission, are difficult to arrange at such short notice. One further reason why brief depression may be at particular risk of suicide attempts is that the depressive phase appears to be associated with increased hostility, aggression (Angst and Dobler-Mikola, 1985) and probably increased impulsivity.

Combined depression: brief and major depression together

A proportion of those with brief depressions develop a longer episode of 14 days or more, which therefore satisfies the duration criterion for major depression. The term chosen to describe this overlapping group of major and brief depressions in the clinical sample was combined depression (Montgomery *et al.*, 1989) and this term has been adopted for the epidemiological reports. In the clinical series 8% of patients with brief depression developed an episode of major depression during the follow-up period. This combined depression group had brief depressions with a slightly longer mean duration. Because the number of such individuals in the clinical sample is small it is difficult to be sure that their features are representative of this group. They do, however, appear to have more severe depressions.

The occurrence of a major depressive episode does not appear to change the pattern of subsequent brief depressions. As the episode of major depression resolves, the pattern of brief depressions reasserts itself. The median duration of the brief depressions is still three days, but there are more episodes lasting between one and two weeks.

The recurrent brief depression does not appear to be a prodromal phase of major depression nor to represent a secondary illness. The ten-year follow-up data in the epidemiological study show that recurrent brief depression is as stable a diagnosis as major depression. The number of people with recurrent brief depressions who later develop major depression is very similar to the number of major depression who develop recurrent brief depression (Angst *et al.*, 1990).

It is particularly interesting to note that the development of combined depression is associated with a markedly increased suicide attempt rate in the epidemiological cohort. In the group with combined depression the percentage of individuals with a suicide attempt was significantly higher than in either the major depression group or the brief depression group taken separately. Of those in the general population who developed combined depression some 30% had already attempted suicide by the age of 28 (Angst, 1990a). This high rate of suicidal behaviour makes combined depression the best clinical predictor of suicide attempts. In those with combined depression and a previous suicide attempt the risk would be expected to be even higher.

Individuals with combined depression appear to form a severely disordered group. In addition to the suicide attempts, drug and alcohol-related problems are reported to be more frequent. Panic disorder, which is associated with major depression and more particularly brief depression, also has a much higher incidence in the combined depression group. This reinforces the view that combined depression is a group with significant morbidity.

Overlap with dysthymia

It is possible to mistake recurrent episodes of brief depression for dysthymia. Dysthymia is a controversial category of depression perceived as minor or mild but present for more than half the time over a two-year period. The epidemiological catchment area (ECA) study carried out in the USA, relying on retrospective data collected by untrained raters, reports a surprisingly high prevalence of dysthymia without major depression (1.7%) (Burke *et al.*, 1988). It is unfortunate that this study failed to ask about brief depressions.

The inherent unreliability of memory for duration of illness over such a long period sometimes coalesces distant episodes of brief depression. This makes it seem that what had been discrete episodes were more chronic, and had been present for longer than was actually the case. The overlap between dysthymia and brief depression in the Zurich epidemiological data is some 30%. Although this is lower than the 50% overlap with major depression it is still substantial (Angst, 1990b). Pure dysthymia, i.e. dysthymia not overlapping with either major depression or brief depression, is rare in the Zurich epidemiological data and may turn out to be a misleading diagnosis. In the prospective clinical data dysthymia has a much lower overlap with recurrent brief depression than in the retrospectively collected epidemiological data.

The difficulty in identifying pure dysthymia is seen in drug studies for the treatment of this condition. For example, in the study of Kocsis *et al.* (1988) only

4% of patients diagnosed as suffering from dysthymia were found to have pure dysthymia. The overwhelming majority satisfied criteria for major depression and responded better to imipramine than placebo, as might be expected. This response to imipramine is much more likely to be due to an antidepressant effect on the major depression rather than on the mild symptoms. There has been an unfortunate tendency in some studies of dysthymia not to quantify concomitant major depression and thereby give the impression that pure dysthymia is commoner than it is.

Dysthymia, as the term is currently used, is mostly double depression, i.e. major depression with a background of low-grade, chronic mild depressive symptoms (Keller and Shapiro, 1982; Keller et al., 1983). Pure dysthymia is a difficult concept to maintain as it is very close to major depressive illness and is susceptible, more than other diagnosis, to the risk of over-diagnosis due to poor history taking and the distortions of retrospective memory.

Confusion with borderline personality disorders

Borderline personality disorder is a comparatively recent construct which attempts to define a longstanding unstable character flaw. In DSM-III the diagnostic criteria concentrate largely on depressive phenomena or on behavioural features which may often be secondary to recurrent brief depression (Table I). This has the unfortunate effect of implying that an individual who may have a primary depressive illness should be regarded as having a defective character not amenable to or requiring treatment.

The DSM-III criteria for borderline personality disorder, which have changed little for DSM-III-R, require five out of eight phenomena which include depressive features such as affective instability, suicide attempts and inappropriate control of anger. Affective instability describes the intermittent nature of brief depressions rather well and it is difficult therefore for those with recurrent brief depression to fail to satisfy this criterion.

Table I. Affective features defining DSM–III borderline personality disorders.

Borderline personality disorder is defined by depressive features which are either part of
    sudden brief depression, e.g.:
        Affective instability
        Self-damaging acts
        Impulsivity in two areas potentially self-damaging
        Anger or lack of control of anger
or possibly secondary to long-standing recurrent depressive illness:
        Chronic feelings of emptiness
        Unstable and intense relationships
        Identity disturbance
        Problems tolerating being alone

Similarly suicidal or aggressive acts are integral to depressive illness. Suicidal acts are, for example, used in the Hamilton Depression Rating Scale (Hamilton, 1967) to measure the severity of depression. Why this should be used as a criterion of a personality disorder rather than a measure of depressive illness has not been adequately explained. Suicide attempts are more common in brief depression than in major depression, which may increase the bias towards diagnosing brief depressions as borderline personality disorder. Suicidal acts in depressed patients often have an impulsive quality. It is therefore difficult to understand why this impulsive act should be considered as evidence of a personality disorder rather than depression. Similarly, anger cannot be considered specific to borderline personality disorder since it is also a feature of depression. Indeed in the Zurich study the Hopkins Symptom Check List (SCL 90) (Derogatis, 1977) measure of anger and hostility is significantly elevated in major depression and recurrent brief depression compared with normals (Angst *et al.*, 1990a). The clinical impression remains that both impulsivity and anger are more severe or common in brief than in major depression but this is not yet properly established.

Some of the criteria for the borderline personality disorder in DSM-III may be behavioural consequences secondary to longstanding recurrent depressive illness. These include chronic feelings of emptiness, unstable relationships, identity disturbance and problems in tolerating being alone. Many of the features which define borderline personality may occur in a longstanding recurrent depressive illness that is rapidly changing and disruptive.

It is therefore not surprising that a substantial overlap is reported between brief depressions and borderline personality disorder, particularly in the setting of a suicide prevention clinic. Many patients with borderline personality disorder have been found to have a primary depressive illness. It was indeed in this group of patients that the importance of brief depressions as predictors of suicide attempts was first identified (Montgomery *et al.*, 1979, 1983). Recurrent brief depression is also found in a large number of people who do not satisfy criteria for borderline personality disorder. The question which has not been addressed is whether borderline personality disorder defined using non-depressive criteria is an important group or not. At the moment this personality disorder construct is interfering with recognition of an important depressive illness, particularly if the indivdual has attempted suicide.

Possible links with bipolar illness

Because of the rapid shifts from well to ill seen with recurrent brief depression it is natural to speculate on a possible link with bipolar illness. However, neither the clinical nor the epidemiological studies support an association between recurrent brief depression and bipolar illness. In the clinical cohort approximately 3% of those with brief depressions developed hypomania or mania. The prospective follow-up on this group varies, so that it is not possible to be sure that the data are representative. In the ten-year epidemiological follow-up study the incidence of mania or hypomania in the 'no depression' group was 4.9%, which illustrates that bipolar disorder emerges in a small number of normals with the passage of time. The incidence of mania or hypo-mania in the recurrent brief depression group was 2.8%—somewhat lower than expected in the normal population (Angst *et al.*, 1990b). This might suggest, if anything, a negative relationship, with brief depression protecting against the development of mania.

A higher rate of manic or hypomanic symptoms was seen in those with combined depression in the clinical sample. In some of these patients a pattern of three-day hypomanic symptoms has occasionally been seen. The impression from the clinical data is that manic or hypomanic symptoms may be concen-trated in the combined depression group, rather than in pure recurrent brief depression. This is in accord with the ten-year follow-up epidemiological study, which reports double the incidence of mania or hypomania in the combined depression group compared with the normal population, although this dif-ference is not significant (Angst, 1990b).

The clinical database is still too small properly to test a possible relationship between combined depression and bipolar disorder. Combined depression is an interesting illness concept and larger studies in this group are needed before an association with manic or hypomanic symptoms can be established.

Life events and brief depressions

The nature of recurrent brief depression, with rapid relapse and remission, may lead to the onset of the remission being attributed, without much basis, to situational factors. However, brief depression, which in the clinical series had on average 20 episodes a year, is unlikely to be linked to major life events which are much less common. Patients themselves describe the episodes of brief depression as unpredictable and not related to external events. The epidemiological data support this view. Life events, measured on standard scales, were linked with episodes of major depression but no significant rela-tionship was reported between life events and brief depression (Angst and Dobler-Mikola, 1985).

The clinical data and the epidemiological data agree that major life events are not important in the aetiology of brief depression. The question remains about minor events. Brief depression is frequently accompanied by aggression and hostility, which are reflected in increased arguments with family, friends and colleagues. It therefore becomes difficult to disentangle minor events as the possible cause of depression from the secondary effects of the episode. In the absence of reports from sufferers that minor events are important in the provocation of episodes of illness, attempts to link the two are unlikely to be successful and other possible provoking factors should be sought. The most likely associations will probably be biological.

Establishing efficacy

There are no established treatments for recurrent brief depression, and the nature of the condition presents particular problems in establishing the efficacy of a treatment. Since the episodes are so brief and are expected to remit spontaneously in three days it is difficult to find efficacy with drugs that have a delayed onset of action. A more promising approach is to adopt a medium or long-term strategy over a sufficient period of time to modify the duration, severity and number of depressive episodes. Since suicide attempts are associated with brief depressions the number of attempts may be a subsidiary measure of efficacy.

The most appropriate design for testing long-term efficacy would be a double-blind parallel group comparison of active treatment and placebo. To avoid any confusion with carryover effects the patient population needs to be carefully selected as suffering from brief recurrent depression without major depression in the previous four to six months, in line with the evidence from the continuation treatment studies in major depression (Montgomery, 1989). Prophylactic studies of this type depend on adequate morbidity in the sample, and the previous recurrence rate in the selected patients is therefore important. Establishing the rate of recurrence retrospectively over a prolonged period such as a year is difficult, as has been discussed. For practical purposes the history over the past three months might prove to be a more reliable and useful measure. The clinical data suggest that the episodes occur rather frequently and a recurrence rate of at least three episodes in the previous three months appears an adequate selection criterion.

It is preferable that patients with an episode of at least moderate severity are included, so that comparisons of the mean episode severity between groups can be assessed. Measuring the severity of episodes of brief depression is somewhat different from studies of major depression, where an overall assessment over a period is made. With brief depression the individual episodes, whether current or retrospective, need to be assessed separately. Scales that rely heavily on observer items, such as the Hamilton Depression Scale, are obviously less useful in this context. The Montgomery and Asberg Depression Rating Scale (Montgomery and Asberg, 1979) may be more reliable, especially for the rating of episodes that have resolved.

The criterion used in the epidemiological study of a monthly recurrence with 12 episodes a year is not recommended for clinical studies. The monthly criterion is particularly inappropriate since it excludes 25% of the clinical sample who have a high but erratic recurrence rate (Montgomery *et al.*, 1989). The clinic patients have a relatively high recurrence rate but are sometimes unclear about the number of episodes judged retrospectively over a year. Both the epidemiological data and the clinical data suggest that the recurrent pattern persists throughout the year, therefore it seems logical to establish the specific pattern over a shorter period with resulting greater reliability. An additional precaution might be to require that individuals have a general history of a recurrent pattern of brief depressions for at least a year.

Patients do appear to go into remission in the long-term follow-up studies for periods of several months. In our follow-up some remissions have lasted as long as 18 months. There is some suggestion in the epidemiological studies that periods of remission were seen but the data are not published in sufficient detail to indicate the length of the periods. To select a sample with a high projected recurrence rate the most important factor would be a high recurrence rate immediately before entering the study.

There are clear indications from early studies that recurrent brief depression is susceptible to treatment, though formal prophylactic studies in patients suffering from the illness, as described here, are still to be completed. The placebo-controlled studies of suicidal behaviour in patients without major depression (Montgomery *et al.*, 1979, 1983), in whom brief depressive episodes were important, had a significant response to low doses of the neuroleptic flupenthixol. Monoamine oxidase inhibitors (MAOIs) are thought to be effective in patients suffering from 'atypical depression' (Quitkin *et al.*, 1979). It is possible that some of these patients are, in fact, suffering from recurrent brief depression since many are reported to have an intermittent (less than seven days) pattern of illness (Montgomery *et al.*, 1989; Liebowitz and Klein, 1979). Suicidal behaviour, aggression and impulsivity are all characteristics of brief depression (Montgomery *et al.*, 1989; Angst *et al.*, 1990). There are consistent reports in the literature of a link between these phenomena and a dysfunction in the serotonin (5-hydroxytryptamine, 5-HT) system (Asberg *et al.*, 1976; Traskman *et al.*, 1980; Lidberg *et al.*, 1985; Linnoila *et al.*, 1983). This suggests that a fruitful approach to treatment might be the use of drugs affecting the 5-HT system.

Conclusion

The epidemiological and clinical data have a high level of agreement. Both show that recurrent brief depression is a common, disruptive and potentially dangerous illness. The greatest obstacle to identifying the illness in clinical practice is the mind set that depression should be persistent. Once a clinician learns to look for this brief and recurrent pattern it becomes much easier to identify patients.

There are indications at the moment that this illness responds in the long term to different kinds of treatment that have been effective in short-term studies of major depression. Low doses of neuroleptics, 5-HT uptake inhibitors and MAOIs are the most likely candidates. The results from well-conducted formal treatment studies are awaited.

References

American Psychiatric Association (1980) *Diagnostic and Statistical Manual of Mental Disorders* (DSMM-III) (3rd edn). Washington, DC: American Psychiatric Association.

American Psychiatric Association (1987) *Diagnostic and Statistical Manual of Mental Disorders* (DSM-III-R) (3rd edn, revised). Washington, DC: American Psychiatric Association.

Angst J (1990a) Recurrent brief depression: A new concept of depression. *Pharmacopsychiatria* **23**, 63–66.

Angst J (1990b) Natural history and epidemiology of depression. In: Cobb J and Goeting NLM (eds) *Prediction and Treatment of Recurrent Depression*, pp. 1–9. Duphar Medical Publications.

Angst J and Dobler-Mikola A (1984) The Zurich Study: III. Diagnosis of depression. *Eur Arch Psychiatr Neurol Sci* **234**, 30–37.

Angst J and Dobler-Mikola A (1985) The Zurich Study: A prospective epidemiological study of depressive, neurotic and psychosomatic syndromes. IV. Recurrent and non-recurrent brief depression. *Eur Arch Psychiatr Neurol Sci* **234**, 408–416.

Angst J, Vollrath M and Koch R (1988) New aspects on epidemiology of depression. In: Angst J and Woggon B (eds) *Lofepramine in the Treatment of Depressive Disorders*, pp. 1–14. Braunschweig: Vieweg.

Angst J, Merinkangas K and Scheidegger P (1990a) Recurrent brief depression: A new subtype of affective disorder. *J Affect Dis* **19**, 87–98.

Angst J, Wicki W and Merinkangas K (1990b) Recurrent brief depression. Presented at Royal College of Psychiatrist's Annual Meeting, Birmingham.

Asberg M, Traskman L and Thoren P (1976) 5-HIAA in the cerebrospinal fluid: A biochemical suicide predictor? *Arch Gen Psychiatry* **33**, 1193–1197.

Burke JD, Regier DA and Christie KA (1988) Epidemiology of Depression: Recent findings from the NIMH epidemiologic catchment area program. In: Swinkels JA and Blijleven W (eds) *Depression, Anxiety and Aggression*, pp. 23–38. Houten: Medidact.

Derogatis LR (1977) *SCL-90 Administration Scoring and Procedures Manual for the R (Revised) Version and other Instruments of the Psychopathology Rating Scales Series.* Baltimore, MD: Johns Hopkins University School of Medicine.

Feighner JP, Robins E, Guze SB *et al.* (1972) Diagnostic criteria for use in psychiatric research. *Arch Gen Psychiatry* **26**, 57–63.

Hamilton M (1967) Development of a rating scale for primary depressive illness. *Br J Social Clin Psychol* **6**, 278–296.

Keller MB and Shapiro RW (1982) 'Double depression': Superimposition of acute depressive episodes on chronic depressive disorders. *Am J Psychiatry* **139**, 438–442.

Keller MB, Lavori PW, Endicott J *et al.* (1983) 'Double depression': Two year follow-up. *Am J Psychiatry* **140**, 689–694.

Kocsis JH, Frances AJ, Voss C *et al.* (1988) Imipramine treatment for chronic depression. *Arch Gen Psychiatry* **45**, 253–257.

Lidberg L, Tuck JR, Asberg M *et al.* (1985) Homicide, suicide and CSF 5HIAA. *Acta Psychiatr Scand* **71**, 23–26.

Liebowitz MR and Klein DF (1979) Hysteroid dysphoria *Psychiatr Clin North Am* **2**, 555–575.

Linnoila M, Virkkunen M, Scheinin M *et al.* (1983) Low cerebrospinal fluid 5-hydroxyindoleacetic acid concentration differentiates impulsive from non-impulsive violent behaviour. *Life Sci* **33**, 2609–2614.

Montgomery SA (1989) Prophylaxis in recurrent unipolar depression: A new indication for treatment studies. *J Psychopharmacol* **3**, 47–53.

Montgomery SA and Asberg M (1979) A new depression scale designed to be more sensitive to change. *Br J Psychiatry* **134**, 382–389.

Montgomery SA and Montgomery D (1982) Pharmacological prevention of suicidal behaviour. *J Affective Disorders* **4**, 291–298.

Montgomery SA, Montgomery D, McAuley R *et al.* (1979) Maintenance therapy in repeat suicidal behaviour: A placebo controlled trial. *Proceedings 10th International Congress for Suicide Prevention and Crisis Intervention*, 227–229.

Montgomery SA, Roy D and Montgomery DB (1983) The prevention of recurrent suicidal acts. *Br J Clin Pharmacol* **15**, 183S–188S.

Montgomery SA, Montgomery D, Baldwin D and Green M (1989) Intermittent 3-day depressions and suicidal behaviour. *Neuropsychobiology* **22**, 128–134.

Montgomery SA, Montgomery D, Baldwin D and Green M (1990) The duration, nature and recurrence rate of brief depressions. *Neuro-psychopharmacol Biol Psychiatry* **14**, 729–735.

Parker G (1987) Are the lifetime prevalence estimates in the ECA study accurate? *Psychol Med* **17**, 275–282.

Quitkin FM, Rifkin A and Klein DF (1979) Monoamine oxidase inhibitors: A review of antidepressant effectiveness. *Arch Gen Psychiatry* **36**, 749–760.

Schrader G, Davis A, Stefanovic S and Christie P (1990) The recollection of affect. *Psychol Med* **20**, 105–109.

Spitzer RL, Endicott J and Robins E (1978) Research diagnostic criteria: Rationale and reliability. *Arch Gen Psychiatry* **35**, 773–785.

Trasman L, Tybring G, Asberg M *et al.* (1980) Cortisol in the CSF of depressed and suicidal patients. *Arch Gen Psychiatry* **37**, 761–766.

Vollrath M and Angst J (1989) Results of the Zurich cohort study: Course of anxiety and depression. *Psychiatry Psychobiol* **4**, 307–313.

Williams JBW and Spitzer RL (1982) Research diagnostic criteria and DSM-III: An annotated comparison. *Arch Gen Psychiatry* **39**, 1283–1289.

Zimmerman NM and Coryell W (1986) Reliability of follow-up assessments of depressed inpatients. *Arch Gen Psychiatry* **43**, 468–470.

9

Seasonal affective disorder

J. Wålinder

Introduction

For a long time a relationship between the seasons and mood has been recognized. Seasonality is also present in many aspects of human behaviour and central nervous physiology and biochemistry, for instance neurotransmitter function, thermoregulation and sleep. The observation that some types of affective disorders occur with a striking regularity has initiated research into the cyclic aspects of these conditions.

It has been speculated that rhythmic fluctuations in affective disorders may be caused by endogenous biological cycles in systems regulating mood (Sack *et al.*, 1987) or a combination of endogenous and environmental factors or cycles.

There is much evidence that circadian rhythms are endogenous and self-sustaining. These observations have been corroborated when studying subjects who are allowed a free-run in temporal isolation (Sack *et al.*, 1987).

When a period of an endogenous circadian rhythm differs from an environmental cycle it must be supposed that there is a mechanism for synchronizing these two rhythms—a process which is called entrainment. Light–dark transitions, the duration of daylight, changes in temperature in the environment and social events (Ehlers *et al.*, 1988) may be examples of such signals that entrain biological rhythms.

A factor speaking in favour of the influence of seasonal factors on the course of affective syndromes comes from studies of suicide rates. A seasonal variation in suicide has been found (Durkheim, 1897), with a peak in the spring in the

The Diagnosis of Depression. Edited by J.P. Feighner and W.F. Boyer
© 1991 John Wiley & Sons Ltd

northern hemisphere. Studies on suicide rates south of the equator have revealed a peak in November, i.e. late spring on the southern hemisphere. It has been summarized that these data indicate that biological factors rather than cultural influences may be responsible for these season-bound suicides. Träskman-Bendz (1980) noted in her study on depression and suicidal behaviour that changes occurred in brain neurochemistry in impulsive suicidal behaviour and were not specifically related to the affective disorder as such. These recent findings may somewhat obscure the relevance of suicide data as markers for seasonal factors influencing the course of affective disorders.

Other studies focusing on finding a marker for seasonal factors have included, for example, birth patterns, epidemiological studies of seasonality in depression and hospital admissions. However, these studies have so far not produced any conclusive data.

In the early 1920s (Kraepelin, 1921) it was observed that some types of depressive disorders seemed to start in a regular way in the fall, remit in spring and follow a rather benign course compared to other types of bipolar affective disorder. These observations stimulated research into what is now known as seasonal affective disorder (SAD).

The concept of seasonal affective disorder

Some affective disorders peak in spring and fall. However, it seems as if the majority of affective disorders start during late fall, continue during wintertime and end in spring or summer, not seldom after a period of hypomania. This group of affective disorders represent what is called SAD.

Usually the depressive phase starts when days get shorter. In the northern hemisphere this means approximately in November–February and in the southern hemisphere in June–September. The depressive period goes on for approximately four months. Onset and severity of depression seem to depend on the actual latitude. Some people suffering from SAD can, by going south, postpone the onset of a depressive period. Spring and summer is characterized by a normal mood or a mild hypomanic state. A period of cloudy and rainy weather can, however, precipitate a short depressive spell even during summer.

Rosenthal *et al.* (1984) were those who first drew attention to this type of depressive syndrome and also described the clinical picture and course of the disease. Interest in the disorder has increased considerably during the 1980s and there seems to be good agreement between investigators about the clinical profile of SAD.

DSM-III-R has recognized SAD as a clinical entity and presents the diagnostic criteria as follows:

A. There has been a regular temporal relationship between the onset of an episode of Bipolar Disorder (including Bipolar Disorder NOS) or Recurrent

Major Depression (including Depressive Disorder (NOS) and a particular 60-day period of the year (e.g., regular appearance of depression between the beginning of October and the end of November).

Note: Do not include cases in which there is an obvious effect of seasonally related psychosocial stressors, e.g., regularly being unemployed every winter.

B. Full remissions (or a change from depression to mania or hypomania) also occurred within a particular 60-day period of the year (e.g., depression disappears from mid-February to mid-April).

C. There have been at least three episodes of mood disturbance in three separate years that demonstrated the temporal seasonal relationship defined in A and B; at least two of the years were consecutive.

D. Seasonal episodes of mood disturbance, as described above, outnumbered any nonseasonal episodes of such disturbance that may have occurred by more than three to one.

SAD patients often complain of sadness, decreased libido, social withdrawal and diminished functioning. However, these symptoms are not always severe enough to lead to a contact with the medical profession. These patients manage in some way or another to 'survive' until spring comes along.

The depressive phase of SAD may take on the characteristics of a melancholia. The hypothalamic symptoms that go with a 'true' melancholic syndrome are, however, reversed: the patients complain of hypersomnia instead of hyposomnia, hyperphagia (in particular carbohydrate craving) instead of anorexia, weight gain, and a diurnal rhythm with worsening of symptoms in afternoons and nights.

Patients suffering from the SAD syndrome show normal dexamethasone suppression test (DST) and normal response to thyrotrophin-releasing hormone (TRH) challenge test. Rapid eye movement (REM) latency is normal (not shortened as found in severe depressive disorders).

SAD may begin in childhood or adolescence, during which time fatigue, irritability, anxiety, various school problems, headache, acting out and tendency to isolation are prominent features. In approximately 15% of SAD cases there is a familial occurrence of the syndrome (Thompson, 1989).

In Tables I and II are presented clinical and demographic features of SAD as well as family history and the profile of depressive symptoms of SAD patients (after Sack *et al.*, 1987).

As can be seen the female to male ratio is approximately 6 : 1. About 90% of the patients had a history of bipolar affective disorder and one-third of the patients were treated for their depression. It should be noted that when estimating the frequency of bipolar disorder the Research Diagnostic Criteria (Spitzer *et al.*, 1978) was used. When using the Structured Clinical Interview for DSM-III-R (SCID) (Spitzer *et al.*, 1986) the figure dropped from 90% to 57% (Rosenthal *et al.*, 1989a). Some 10% had received hospital treatment and a family history of

Table I. Clinical and demographic features and family history of patients with SAD[a] (Reproduced with permission from H.Y. Meltzer (ed.) *Psychopharmacology: The Third Generation of Progress*, Biological rhythms in psychiatry, by D.A. Sack *et al.*, Raven Press, 1987, p. 678).

Feature	Finding
Sex	F, 86%; M, 14%
Mean ± SD age (years)	36.5 ± 11.2
Mean ± SD age at onset (years)	26.9 ± 13.2
Mean ± SD no. of seasonal cycles	9.5 ± 7.4
Depression milder near equator	83%
RDC diagnosis	Bipolar II, 76%
	Bipolar I, 17%
	Unipolar, 7%
Previous treatment (%)	
Antidepressants	24
Lithium carbonate	17
Thyroid	21
Hospitalization	10
ECT	0
No treatment	31
Family history[b]	
Affective disorder	69
Alcohol abuse	7
SAD	17

[a] Percentage of patients is given throughout, except as noted. Abbreviations: SAD, seasonal affective disorder; RDC, Research Diagnostic Criteria; ECT, electroconvulsive therapy.
[b] First-degree relative.

affective disorder was noted in nearly 70%, a history of alcohol abuse in 7% and of SAD in 17%.

As to depressive symptoms, sadness, decreased physical activity and interpersonal difficulties were present in all patients. Irritability, increased sleep time and change in sleep quality also ranked high.

In Table III (after Thompson, 1989) a comparison of SAD characteristics from three different series of patients are presented. There is a fair degree of agreement between the three series regarding age, the excess of women, age of onset and duration of episodes. Two series reported 10–17 episodes per patient. Frequencies of various depressive symptoms are similar in the three series, as are other features and family history of SAD in first-degree relatives. Rosenthal *et al.* (1989a) argue that the validity of SAD as a specific syndrome is still under debate. New subgroups of SAD begin to emerge and come into focus of research. One subgroup, the 'reverse-SAD', is characterized by recurrent summer

Table II. Depressive symptoms of patients with SAD (Reproduced with permission from H.Y. Meltzer (ed.) *Psychopharmacology: The Third Generation of Progress*, Biological rhythms in psychiatry, by D.A. Sack *et al.*, Raven Press, 1987, p. 678).

Symptom	Percentage of patients
Affect	
Sadness	100
Anxiety	72
Irritability	90
Physical activity decreased	100
Appetite	
Increased	66
Decreased	28
Mixed	3
No change	3
Carbohydrate craving	79
Weight	
Increased	76
Decreased	17
Mixed	3
No change	3
Sleep	
Earlier onset	79
Later waking	76
Increased sleep time	97
Change in quality (interrupted, not refreshing)	90
Daytime drowsiness	72
Decreased libido	69
Difficulties around menses	71
Work difficulties	97
Interpersonal difficulties	100

depression and normal mood during winter. Factors other than light may be of importance in this type of SAD, e.g. temperature conditions.

Another question of interest is whether SAD is just a subgroup of unipolar or bipolar affective disorder. As mentioned above, some 60% of SAD patients have according to DSM-III-R a history of bipolar disorder. Thus so far it seems justified to conclude that the issue of SAD as a distinct and specific syndrome is still not settled.

Finally it is of interest to note that 50% of SAD women also suffer from a pre-menstrual syndrome (PMS) which is a rapid-cycling mood disturbance occurring in association with the menstrual cycle (Rosenthal *et al.*, 1984).

Table III. Characteristics of a seasonal affective disorder group and comparisons with other series (Reproduced with permission from Thompson and Silverstone, 1989).

	UK $N = 51$	Swiss $N = 22$	USA $N = 29$
Mean age (years)	42	42	37
Sex ratio (F : M)	9 : 1	2.7 : 1	6.1 : 1
Depression			
Mean age at first episode	24	27	27
Mean number of episodes	17	Not given	10
Mean duration of episodes	18 weeks	23 weeks	17 weeks
Affect (% reporting present)			
Sadness	96	91	100
Anxiety	86	86	72
Irritability	77	82	90
Vegetative symptom (% reporting change)			
Appetite increased	74	45	66
Appetite decreased	16	45	23
Weight increased	84	55	76
Weight decreased	6	23	3
Carbohydrate craving	82	77	79
Sleep increased			
Duration of sleep in winter	8.8 hours	Not given	Not given
Duration of sleep in summer	6.9 hours	Not given	Not given
Other features (% reporting feature)			
Reduced physical activity	100	100	100
Reduced social function	98	100	100
Work difficulties	100	100	97
Time off work last 5 years	47		
Interpersonal difficulties	98	86	
RDC diagnosis (% sample)			
Bipolar I	20	18	17
Bipolar II	51	77	76
Unipolar	29	5	7
Family history in first-degree relatives			
Affective disorder	25	67	69
Alcoholism	8	28	7
Seasonal affective disorder	14	17	17
Previous treatment (% sample)			
In-patient	18	14	10
ECT	8	Not given	0
Lithium	16	Not given	Not given
Antidepressants	49	68	42
Benzodiazepines	40	Not given	Not given
No drug treatment	51	27	31

How common is SAD?

The exact prevalence of SAD is still unknown. There are so far a rather limited number of studies that have attempted to determine the frequency of seasonal disturbance of mood and behaviour in the general population.

In a Manhattan survey Terman (see Rosenthal *et al.*, 1989a) observed that rhythms in mood, energy, weight and social activity were present in 30–50% of the population. Twenty-five per cent of the actual population claimed that seasonal changes were a problem.

In a survey in Montgomery County (Kasper *et al.*, 1989) the percentages of subjects reporting seasonal changes in some variables were similar to what was found in the Manhattan study. These included sleep and weight, as 42% and 47%, respectively, reported seasonal changes as compared to 42% and 49%, respectively, in the Manhattan study. The corresponding figures for changes in energy, mood and social activity were 66%, 63% and 60%, respectively, compared to 50%, 31% and 31%, respectively, in the Manhattan study. Potkin *et al.* (1986) found a correlation between the percentage reporting winter problems and latitude.

The findings from the three studies referred to above must, however, be viewed with caution. Prevalence estimates in the general population are still lacking. In the Terman study a questionnaire was sent to 400 randomly chosen subjects, in the Kasper study a telephone version of the Seasonal Pattern Assessment Questionnaire (SPAQ) was used and in the Potkin study readers of a nationwide US newspaper were asked to fill out a checklist.

Rosenthal *et al.* (1989a) estimates a prevalence of SAD in the northern USA of 3–8% in the general population, although he stresses that the exact figure is still not known.

Two preliminary epidemiological studies from Norway (Lingjaerde *et al.*, 1986) seem to confirm the higher frequency of SAD in northern areas, especially north of the Arctic Circle.

In 1990 Haggag *et al.* published a study on seasonal mood variation in northern Norway. An extensive questionnaire was sent twice, in summer and winter, to 1000 subjects to investigate the degree of symptoms of mood changes during the polar winter and midnight sun season. The authors were able to define two subgroups: the first, a winter subgroup of patients, reported feeling more energetic (7%), very satisfied with their lives (37%) and optimistic (24%), compared to a summer subgroup showing 28%, 46% and 30%, respectively. The second group, a summer subgroup, reported feeling sad and depressed (13%), tired (33%), insomnia (23%), lack of interests (21%) and pessimism about the future (15%), compared to a winter subgroup reporting 27%, 61%, 24%, 34% and 21%, respectively.

The authors conclude that the general population north of the Arctic Circle shows considerable seasonal mood changes during winter and summer seasons and the observed mood variations from depression to hypomania or euphoria suggest an individual vulnerability to extreme light variation.

Thompson and Silverstone (1989) summarize that there emerges a picture of normal mood and major affective disorders having a tendency to entrain to a yearly cycle preferentially in a summer-mania and winter-depression relationship. Patients suffering from major affective disorders have an exaggeration of this effect compared to normal subjects and SAD patients are at the extreme end showing the greatest effect.

Mechanisms

One of the most striking features of SAD is the prompt response to treatment with light. Many studies have confirmed this observation (for overviews see Rosenthal *et al.*, 1989b and Terman *et al.*, 1989). It has also been noted that only a weak antidepressant response is obtained when patients with non-seasonal affective disorder are treated with phototherapy (Stinson and Thompson, 1990). These differences may indicate differences in the pathophysiology of these two groups of affective disorders.

It has been proposed that the clinical symptoms of SAD may be due to a circadian abnormality. Lewy *et al.* (1987) suggested a delay in the onset of melatonin secretion in SAD and that a phase delay in circadian rhythms was in some way related to the pathophysiology of the SAD syndrome. The phototherapy was accordingly supposed to work by inducing a phase advance effect.

Murphy *et al.* (1989) claim, however, that secretion of melatonin in SAD subjects is normal both regarding phase and amplitude. Melatonin secretion normally peaks at about 0200 hours and is suppressed by light. Using a combination of evening and morning light the authors failed to produce a phase advance in melatonin rhythm but the antidepressant effect of the phototherapy was still significant. They conclude that the mechanism of action of bright light in the treatment of SAD does not involve circadian phase mechanisms and that suppression of melatonin does not seem to be the mechanism by which phototherapy works. If melatonin is involved in any way in the pathogenesis of SAD it is at most indirect and is unlikely to be crucial. The negative effect on SAD symptoms after oral melatonin medication (Wirz-Justice *et al*, 1990) seems to corroborate this assumption.

However, recently Sack *et al.* (1990) maintain that patients suffering from winter depressions have circadian rhythms that are abnormally delayed and that bright light benefits this type of depression by providing a corrective advance. In this context the studies by Beck-Friis (1983) and Beck-Friis *et al.* (1985) showing a 'low melatonin syndrome' in patients with major depressive disorders must be remembered. Low melatonin correlated with sadness, lassitude and inability to feel emotions. Patients with no reported diurnal variation of depressive symptoms and with ongoing depressions during summer had lowered melatonin, indicating that depressed patients with low nocturnalmelatonin have a less pronounced daily and annual cyclic variation in symptomatology.

What implications these findings may have for the biochemical basis of SAD subjects is still open to discussion. Further well-designed studies are certainly needed to shed light on the many contradictory findings within this field of pathogenesis.

Another issue as to the pathophysiology of SAD that has been much under debate is whether these patients have a change in their sensitivity to light compared to normals and subjects with different types of affective syndromes. Changes in light intensity is relayed from the retina to the circadian pacemaker nucleus suprachiasmaticus. A pathway from this nucleus then extends via the superior cervical ganglion to the pineal gland. A change in light sensitivity could therefore be due to an abnormality at any point between retina and pineal gland. It has been claimed that manic-depressive patients may be supersensitive to light. This poses the question whether SAD patients are supersensitive to light just like manic patients, or the opposite: are they subsensitive, which would explain their need for light during wintertime? However, Murphy *et al.* (1989) after studying melatonin suppression in response to light found no evidence of light insensitivity in SAD subjects. Recently Thompson *et al.* (1990) claimed that 12 patients with SAD but not a group of 11 controls showed a significant seasonal variation in sensitivity to light during summer. Thus the question of changes in sensitivity to light in SAD subjects does not seem to be settled.

There is support for the notion that therapy with light influences central serotoninergic and noradrenergic (NA) neurotransmission (Mason, 1989). It is interesting to note that these effects are very similar to those obtained after a couple of weeks' treatment with antidepressant drugs, i.e. an increased sensitivity to postsynaptic serotoninergic receptors and a downregulation of β-adrenoceptors.

Today there is an impressive body of evidence indicating that monoamines, in particular serotin (5-hydroxytryptamine 5-HT) and noradrenaline (NA), play important roles in the causation of mood disorders. Many studies suggest that 5-HT neurotransmission is decreased during an episode of depression. There are also some indications that this weakness in the 5-HT system persists to some extent even after the patient has recovered from the depressive illness. This change in central 5-HT neurotransmission may also be present among first-degree relatives of depressed patients.

Studies using 5-HT-active drugs, e.g. 5-HT reuptake inhibitors (paroxetine, fluvoxamine, fluoxetine), indicate that these drugs particularly have an effect on symptoms of anxiety. It is also of interest to note the role of 5-HT in aggressive disorders, suicidal behaviour, phobic conditions, alcoholism, and, in this particular context, the effect on eating disorders (Turner et al., 1988).

As has been pointed out one characteristic feature of the depressive phase of SAD is the increased desire for sweets (carbohydrate craving). Drugs that selectively block 5-HT neurotransmission lead to a significant rise in the intake of sweet foods (Silverstone, 1989). On the other hand, drugs that selectively enhance central 5-HT neurotransmission often lead to a decrease in appetite (Wålinder et al., 1983; Silverstone, 1989).

It is also of interest to note that there is evidence that seasonal variations of 5-HT occur in humans, Thus, Wirz-Justice and Richter (1979) observed changes in platelet 5-HT concentrations, values peaking in May and November—times when mood changes are most prominent. Another observation of importance is a marked seasonal and circadian variation of 5-HT in the hypothalaus of human post-mortem brains. A maximum level was noted in brains of humans who had died in October and November and a minimum in December and January (Carlsson et al., 1980). Hypothalamic 5-HT levels also showed a circadian variation, with lowest values between 0600 and 1500 hours. A rapid fall was reported to occur between 0500 and 0800 hours. It is also reported that the 5-HT metabolite 5-hydroxyindoleacetic acid shows seasonal variation in cerebrospinal fluid (see Sack et al., 1987).

One study (Skwerer et al., 1988) shows that plasma NA levels in SAD subjects are inversely related to the severity of the depressive symptoms and that treatment with bright light increases the NA plasma levels in a way that is directly proportional to mood improvement.

What concerns abnormalities in other CNS neurotransmitters, e.g. dopamine, acetylcholine, γ-aminobutyric acid, the situation is more unclear. It is uncertain how closely laboratory observations from depressive disorders of the non-seasonal type apply to SAD. More research is needed to get a better understanding of any biochemical abnormality in the pathogenesis of SAD.

From the observations mentioned above there seems, however, to be evidence in favour of 5-HT being more involved in the pathogenesis of SAD than other neurotransmitters.

As mentioned in the introduction to this chapter Ehlers et al. (1988) published a paper on 'Social Zeitgebers and biological rhythms'. They suggested that a disruption of social rhythms, resulting in instability in biological rhythms, could be responsible for triggering the onset of depressive episodes in vulnerable individuals (Figure 1). The light/dark changes may fit this concept of 'Zeitgebers'. It seems reasonable to suppose that light changes as well as other environmental factors, e.g. temperature, may be the trigger for biological changes at the molecular level, leading to disrupted brain rhythms which in turn will induce the clinical profile of SAD. Patients at risk are supposed to exhibit a genetically controlled vulnerability to these trigger mechanisms.

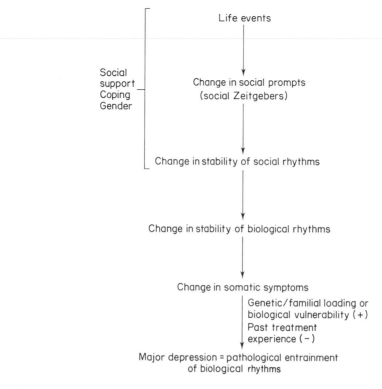

Figure 1. Schema for Zeitgeber theory. (Reproduced with permission from *Archives of General Psychiatry*, 1988, **45**, 951. Copyright 1988, American Medical Association).

Treatment

As the concept of SAD is of fairly recent date it must be supposed that most SAD patients receive conventional antidepressant treatment, i.e. by antidepressant drugs or electroconvulsive therapy (ECT). Whether the antidepressant response in SAD subjects differs from that in non-SAD patients has not been extensively investigated. In an attempt to assess responsiveness of winter depression to a standard treatment for depression Dilsaver and Jaeckle (1990) found, however, that 14 patients suffering from winter depression responded to treatment with tranylcypromine.

Since Rosenthal and coworkers described the clinical syndrome of SAD some five years ago this mood disorder has been ultimately linked to therapy with bright light. There is now good agreement that best results are obtained by using 'full spectrum light' at an intensity of 2500 lux. Clinical improvement usually occurs within the first four days, with a full remission of symptoms after about seven days. Relapse may occur within several days if light treatment is discontinued. Although phototherapy is helpful in most SAD subjects some patients do not respond. So far no predictors for the antidepressant response have been identified. The presence of increased sleep and appetite may, however, indicate a good therapeutic effect. There seems to be good agreement that the best response when treating winter depression is obtained by giving morning treatment sessions for about one week. Thus Sack *et al.* (1990) found that morning light treatment for 2 hours (0600–0800 hours) was significantly better than evening light (1900–2100 hours) in reducing depressive symptoms. The same result was reported by Avery *et al.* (1990) in a randomized cross-over study comprising seven patients with winter depression. Concomitant medication with an antidepressant drug seems to enhance the therapeutic response to light (Rosenthal *et al.*, 1989b). There are, however, observations that indirectly raises the question of whether patients who are on long-term treatment with a lithium salt should be recommended light therapy. These patients take a longer time to improve and require higher doses. In animal studies it has been found that lithium and light both increase retinal phospholipid metabolism, which may indicate similar mechanisms at the membrane (Remé *et al.*, 1987). These observations need further exploration before any firm conclusions can be drawn.

The fact that the antidepressant effect of light therapy is evident after three to four days, the effect of sleep deprivation after one to two days and the effect of antidepressant drugs after some 14 days speaks in favour of different mechanisms of action. From what is said above it may be suggested that the beneficial effect of phototherapy is mediated mainly via serotoninergic mechanisms. If and how melatonin is involved is not known. Further research on the treatment of SAD patients may hopefully help in uncovering any underlying mechanism in this puzzling, cyclic mood disorder.

References

Avery DH, Khan A, Dager SR *et al.* (1990) Bright light treatment of winter depression: Morning versus evening light. *Acta Psychiatr Scand* **82**, 335–338.

Beck-Friis J (1983) *Melatonin in depressive disorder, a methodological and clinical study of the pineal–hypothalamic–pituitary–adrenal cortex system.* Stockholm: Thesis.

Beck-Friis J, Kjellman BF, Aperia B *et al.* (1985) Serum melatonin in relation to clinical variables in patients with major depressive disorders: A hypothesis of a low melatonin syndrome. *Acta Psychiatr Scand* **71**, 319–330.

Carlsson A, Svennerholm L and Winblad B (1980) Seasonal and circadian monoamine variations in human brains examined postmortem. In: Svensson TH and Carlsson A (eds) *Biogenic Amines and Affective Disorders. Acta Psychiatr Scand* **61** Suppl. 280, 75–83.

Dilsaver SC and Jaeckle RS (1990) Winter depression responds to an open trial of tranylcypromine. *J Clin Psychiatry* **51**, 326–329.

Durkheim E (1897) *Suicide: A Study in Sociology.* London: Routledge & Kegan Paul.

Ehlers CL, Frank E and Kipfer DJ (1988) Social Zeitgebers and biological rhythms. *Arch Gen Psychiatry* **45**, 948–952.

Haggag A, Eklund B, Linaker O and Götestam KG (1990) Seasonal mood variation: An epidemiological study in northern Norway. *Acta Psychiatr Scand* **81**, 141–145.

Kasper S, Wehr TA, Bartko JJ *et al.* (1989) Epidemiological findings of seasonal changes in mood and behaviour: A telephone surgery of Montgomery County, Maryland, USA. *Arch Gen Psychiatry* **46**, 823–833.

Kraepelin E (1921) In: Robertson GM (ed.) *Manic Depressive Insanity and Paranoia.* Edinburgh: Livingstone.

Lewy AJ, Sack RL, Miller LS and Hoban TM (1987) Antidepressant and circadian phase shifting effects of light. *Science* **235**, 352–354.

Lingjaerde O, Bratlid T, Hansen T and Götestam KG (1986) Seasonal affective disorder and midwinter insomnia in the far north: Studies on two related chronobiological disorders in Norway. *Proc Coll Int Neuropsychopharmacol* **15**, 187–189.

Mason R (1989) The effect of light on neuronal sensitivity to noradrenaline and serotonin (5-HT). In: Thompson C and Silverstone T (eds) *Seasonal Affective Disorder,* pp. 243–258. London: CNS (Neuroscience).

Murphy DGM, Abas M, Winton F (1989) Seasonal affective disorder: A neurophysiological approach. In: Thompson C and Silverstone T (eds) *Seasonal Affective Disorder,* pp. 233–242. London: CNS (Neuroscience).

Potkin SG, Feltin M, Stamenkovic V *et al.* (1986) Seasonal affective disorder: prevalence varies with latitude and climate. *Clin Neuropharmacol* **9** (suppl.), 181–183.

Remé C, Federspiel E, Pfeilschifter J and Wirz-Justice A (1987) Lithium damages the rat retina: Potentiation by light. *N Engl J Med* **317**, 1478.

Rosenthal NE, Sack DA, Gillin JC *et al.* (1984) Seasonal affective disorder: A description of the syndrome and preliminary findings with light therapy. *Arch Gen Psychiatry* **41**, 72–80.

Rosenthal NE, Kasper S, Schultz PM and Wehr TA (1989a) New concepts and developments in seasonal affective disorder. In: Thompson C and Silverstone T (eds) *Seasonal Affective Disorder,* pp. 97–130. London: CNS (Neuroscience).

Rosenthal NE, Skwerer RG, Jacobsen FM *et al.* (1989b) Phototherapy: The NIMH experience. In: Thompson C and Silverstone T (eds) *Seasonal Affective Disorder,* pp.145–158. London: CNS (Neuroscience).

Sack DA, Rosenthal NE, Parry BL and Wehr TA (1987) Biological rhythms in psychiatry. In: Meltzer HY (ed.) *Psychopharmacology: The Third Generation of Progress,* pp.669–685. New York; Raven Press.

Sack RL, Lewy AJ, White DM *et al.* (1990) Morning vs evening light treatment for winter depression. *Arch Gen Psychiatry* **47**, 343–351.

Silverstone T (1989) The clinical psychopharmacology of seasonal affective disorder. In: Thompson C and Silverstone T (eds) *Seasonal Affective Disorder,* pp. 259–268. London: CNS (Neuroscience).

Skwerer RG, Duncan C, Jacobsen FM *et al.* (1988) Neurobiology of seasonal affective disorder and phototherapy. *J Biol Rhythms* **3**, 135–154.

Spitzer RL, Endicott J and Robins E (1978) Research diagnostic criteria: Rationale and reliability. *Arch Gen Psychiatry* **35**, 773–782.

Spitzer RL, Williams JB and Gibbon M (1986) *Instruction Manual for the Structured Clinical Interview for DSM-III-R.* Biometrics Research Department, New York State Psychiatric Institute.

Stinson D and Thompson C (1990) Clinical experience with phototherapy. *J Affect Dis* **18**, 129–135.

Terman M, Terman JS, Quitkin FM *et al.* (1989) Dosing dimensions of light therapy: Duration and time of day. In: Thompson C and Silverstone T (eds) *Seasonal Affective Disorder*, pp.187–204. London: CNS (Neuroscience).

Thompson C (1989) The syndrome of seasonal affective disorder. In: Thompson C and Silverstone T (eds) *Seasonal Affective Disorder*, pp. 37–57. London: CNS (Neuroscience).

Thompson C and Silverstone T (eds) (1989) Conclusions. In: *Seasonal Affective Disorder*, pp. 269–273. London: CNS (Neuroscience).

Thompson C, Stinson D and Smith A (1990) Seasonal affective disorders and season-dependent abnormalities of melatonin suppression by light. *Lancet* **336**, 703–706.

Träskman-Bendz L (1980) *Depression and Suicidal Behaviour: A Biochemical and Pharmacological Study.* Stockholm: Thesis.

Turner P, Wålinder J and Dunbar GC (eds) (1989) The antidepressant paroxetine: A specific 5-HT uptake inhibitor. *Acta Psychiatr Scand* (Suppl. 350), **80**.

Wirz-Justice A and Richter (1979) Seasonality in biochemical determinations. *Psychiatr Res* **1**, 53–60.

Wirz-Justice A, Graw P, Kräuchi K *et al.* (1990) Morning or night-time melatonin is ineffective in seasonal affective disorder. *J Psychiatr Res* **24**, 129–137.

Wålinder J, Åberg-Wistedt A, Jozwiak H *et al.* (1983) The safety of Zimeldine in long-term use in depressive illness. *Acta Psychiatr Scand* **68**, 147–160.

10

Clinical subtypes of chronic-resistant depression

H.S. Akiskal

Introduction

The delineation of unambiguous criteria for major psychiatric disorders (Feighner *et al.*, 1972) provided new momentum to rigorous clinical reearch during the 1970s and 1980s. However, many patients—especially those with chronic affective complaints—do not easily meet the criteria for rigorously defined depression. Conventional clinical wisdom includes patients with such complaints under the general category of neurotic depression. This is widely believed to be the expression of a 'character neurosis' or a 'characterologic depression' (Bonime, 1966; Arieti and Bemporad, 1978). Recent systematic clinical observations, family history and laboratory findings allow the re-classification of many such patients into clinically meaningful subtypes of mood disorder (Akiskal *et al.*, 1981; Akiskal, 1983). The new diagnostic rubric of dysthymic disorder was introduced into DSM-III-R to include this hetero-geneous realm of mixed characterologic and low-grade affective pathology. This chapter reviews the rationale—modified from the Washington University Schema (Feighner *et al.*, 1972)—for the inclusion of dysthymic and other chronic affective subtypes within the general class of mood disorders. In other words, new evidence based on familial aggregation, selected laboratory mark-ers, and prospective follow-up supports considering many of these chronic conditions as variants of affective disorders.

Chronic depressives are often prematurely considered 'resistant' to

The Diagnosis of Depression. Edited by J.P. Feighner and W.F. Boyer
© 1991 John Wiley & Sons Ltd

antidepressant somatotherapy. However, the emerging systematic clinical experience in differential thymoleptic responsiveness is an eloquent argument for the utility of the proposed chronic-depressive subtypes. As the primary goal of this chapter is clinical subtyping of these depressions, the discussion of therapeutic considerations is illustrative rather than exhaustive.

Prevalence and patterns of chronicity

That clinical depression spontaneously remits after five to six months (Angst, 1973), is among the few facts with which psychiatrists can comfort victims of this illness. Unfortunately this comfort does not apply to 15% (Robins and Guze, 1972). In some, this continuing depressive suffering is due to undertreatment; in others, it represents resistance to first-line interventions. Neither explanation, however, is adequate for those patients whose illness presents with established chronicity before any attempts at treatment.

The US National Institute of Mental Health epidemiological catchment area study (Regier *et al.*, 1988) revealed that 3.3% of the population reports depressive symptoms. Given an 8–9% lifetime risk for mood disorders in the general population, it follows that one out of three individuals with these disorders will develop *chronic* depression. In epidemiological samples, about half of all chronic cases occur without coexisting major depression (Weissman *et al.*, 1991). However, in clinical samples, 80–90% either have coexisting major depression or have had such episodes in the past (Akiskal, 1983; Keller and Sessa, 1990). This suggests that low-grade chronic misery is prevalent in the community, but does not get much psychiatric attention until such suffering progresses to major depressive episodes. However, these chronically depressed patients are major utilizers of the general medical care system. Despite the low-grade nature of their symptomatology, their suffering and disability is greater than that of most chronic physical conditions (Wells *et al.*, 1989).

In view of its prevalence and clinical significance, DSM-III-R (1987) now recognizes chronicity of depression either as residual symptomatology following incomplete recovery from a syndromal depressive episode, or as early-onset low-grade subsyndromal dysthymia. Research at the University of Tennessee (Akiskal *et al.*, 1981; Akiskal, 1983), which provided much of the database for this classification, has shown that pharmacological interventions are regrettably often used half-heartedly in the clinical management of these patients.

Adequacy of treatment, 'resistance' and chronicity

There is no universal agreement on what is 'chronic' or 'resistant' depression. Any discussion of definitional issues must first consider the adequacy of treatment provided to the patient. As already pointed out, chronicity may pre-date clinical referral. DSM-III-R defines chronicity as either persistent or inter-mittent depression for at least two years. For many patients, duration of illness is much longer, sometimes for a lifetime (Akiskal *et al.*, 1981). Optimally all treatments found effective in randomized trials—such as classic or tricyclic antidepressants (TCAs), new-generation cyclic antidepressants, monoamine ox-idase inhibitors (MAOIs) or electroconvulsive therapy (ECT)—should be given a fair trial before considering the patient 'resistant' (Akiskal, 1985a). The min-imum standard (Freyhan, 1974; Sartorius, 1974) would be a trial of at least two classic antidepressants—provided they were well tolerated by the patient and were given in adequate doses—for four to five weeks each, with a supportive psychotherapeutic relationship and education about the illness to the patient and the family (Akiskal, 1985b). Even with this minimum standard, Figure 1 shows that nearly all patients referred to our service were inadequately treated during the 1970s. Such undertreatment was prevalent then, at least in North America (Keller *et al.*, 1982), and probably elsewhere in the world. In the 1980s this proportion dropped to an average of 40% in Memphis. It is our impression that this reflects greater recognition in North America of the importance of treating clinical depression early and energetically. The conclusion that depres-sion remains an undertreated disorder has also been echoed from Europe (Scott, 1988).

Among the factors contributing to inadequate treatment (Akiskal, 1985a),

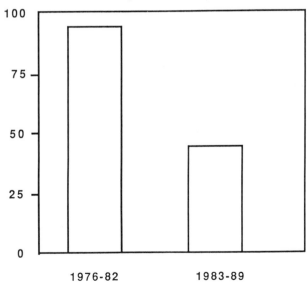

Figure 1. Percentage of undertreated depressed patients in two time periods (data based on evaluation of more then 500 patients referred to the Mood Clinic, University of Tennessee).

subtherapeutic blood levels of antidepressants account for no more than 5% of therapeutic failures in our experience. Instead, such failure is typically due to low doses of TCAs and short duration of treatment. Underdosing itself often reflects patients' reluctance or fear to take medication—and subtle physician attitudes, mainly ambivalence about the use of somatic interventions for chronic depressions. This last factor is particularly operative for psychiatrists who equate chronic depression with 'character pathology'. Price (1978) has pointed out that frustration in the face of an unresponsive patient may lead some clinicians to change the diagnosis from affective to personality disorder based on the stereotypic view that patients with personality disorder do not suffer.

Spontaneous remission is known to occur in acute or subacute depressives resistant to pharmacotherapy. However, most resistant depressives may have already entered a phase of chronicity by the time they come to the attention of psychiatrists in specialized affective disorder units. After excluding those patients who were inadequately treated prior to referral to our university-based mood clinic from 1976 to 1989, systematic longitudinal observations led to the categorization of chronic-resistant patients into four groups (Akiskal et al., 1989). The first of these categories (atypical depression) has been known for at least three decades. The others have been largely delineated during the past decade and represent North American clinical research contributions:

1. *Atypical depression*: fatigue and fluctuating depressive symptomatology of adult onset with reverse vegetative signs (e.g., feeling worse in the evening, initial insomnia, over-sleeping and over-eating), against a background of panic–phobic symptomatology.

2. *Dysthymic disorder*: low-grade depressive symptomatology of childhood or adolescent onset without antecedent panic and related symptomatology. Although fatigue, hypersomnia and over-eating are not uncommon, *reversed diurnality in mood is uncharacteristic*; many dysthymics actually experience greater depressive suffering in the morning.

3. *Residual depression*: or incomplete remission from one or several unipolar episodes without antecedent dysthymia, nor of a frank neurotic disorder. The key distinction from dysthymia is historical in that low-grade depression follows, rather than precedes, depressive episodes.

4. *Protracted mixed state*: as with residual depression, this category refers to those who do not recover from depressive episodes, but against a background of subtle signs of bipolarity as described in this chapter.

This is a heuristic classification in that it organizes a large body of complex clinical data. Each subgroup has its special psychopathological features, aetiological correlates and therapeutic interventions. Detailed accounts of our findings on these chronic-resistant depressive subtypes have appeared elsewhere both as research reports (Akiskal et al., 1980, 1981, 1984; Akiskal and Mallya, 1987) and systematic reviews of clinical experience (Akiskal, 1983,

1985a, 1985b, 1990; Akiskal and Simmons, 1985; Links and Akiskal, 1987; Akiskal and Haykal, 1988; Akiskal *et al.*, 1989). The present chapter derives from these prior attempts to delineate chronic-resistant depressive subtypes. It focuses on those aspects that are of the greatest relevance to clinical practice.

Atypical depression

Although historically atypical depression was among the first of the chronic affective states to be described, there is no standard definition of this entity. As developed in the UK (West and Dally, 1959; Sargent, 1961), this rubric referred to patients—with low-grade depression—who had previously attended cardiology clinics because of autonomic nervous system hyperactivity and varying degrees of phobic avoidance; the concept of reverse vegetative signs was expounded later (Pollitt, 1965). More recently, clinical research at the New York Psychiatric Institute (Liebowitz and Klein, 1979) emphasized 'hysteroid' features such as extreme reactivity to romantic disappointment, but with essentially unimpaired hedonic capacity. Table I summarizes the core features of atypical depression as described by these groups of investigators. Atypicality emerges as a short-hand description for depressed patients with a strong reactive component, past—and often current—somatic anxiety and phobic features, and reverse vegetative signs. Although its nosological validity is still a matter of debate, the concept of atypical depression has survived in the psychopharmacological literature (Davidson *et al.*, 1982).

Research conducted in our sleep laboratory (Akiskal *et al.*, 1984) has shown that atypical depressions in the British sense are more like anxiety states than primary depressions. The initial insomnia with multiple awakenings in the first part of the night in many anxious patients leads to a tendency to over-sleep in the morning. However, practical demands of life are such that many have to get up early in the morning. The resultant sleep deprivation leads to daytime hypersomnolence, fatigue and irritability (Akiskal and Lemmi, 1987)—hence the

Table I. Features of atypical depression derived from the literature.

Fluctuating depression
Hedonic capacity often preserved
Rejection-sensitive with reactivity of mood
Worse in evening
Initial insomnia
Fatigue and lethargy
Hypersomnia and weight gain
Past history of somatic anxiety and phobias
Craving for sweets and chocolate

genesis of some symptoms considered characteristic of atypical depressions. It is not surprising then that such patients appear exhausted and fatigued after many years of neurotic suffering characterized by panic attacks or lesser degrees of somatic anxiety and phobic avoidance. These features are reminiscent of the older American concept of neurasthenia (Beard, 1880). Other observations (Cassano *et al.*, 1990) suggest that leisure—and hedonic—functions are relatively preserved in atypical depressives. This is consistent with Klein's (1974) earlier suggestion that 'consummatory' reward is preserved in atypical depressions. Strictly speaking, this group of patients is best considered a variant of panic disorder complicated by depression, rather than belonging to primary mood disorders. This suggestion also accords with the original British concept, and accounts for the intermittent chronicity of the disorder. However, as discussed in the next section, other intermittent depressions with prominent lethargy and hypersomnia overlap with dysthymic and bipolar II disorders (Davidson *et al.*, 1982).

MAOIs are generally considered superior to TCAs for many of these 'atypical' patients (Liebowitz *et al.*, 1988), though not all investigators agree (Paykel *et al.*, 1983). The higher level of the enzyme MAO in the brains of females (Robinson *et al.*, 1971) may, in part, account for the higher prevalence of atypical depression in women and their preferential response to MAOIs (Davidson and Pelton, 1986). This provocative idea deserves further research validation.

Dysthymic disorder

This disorder, which refers to patients with low-grade subsyndromal depressive symptomatology, typically begins early in life (i.e., late childhood or adolescence) and pursues a course of intermittent—and less commonly, of persistent—chronicity (Akiskal, 1983). The validity of this disorder has been questioned, especially in Europe where neurotic depression is the preferred concept. However, there is recent British interest in this construct as summarized in Burton and Akiskal (1990). To be meaningful, this DSM-III-R category should not be secondary to other neurotic—such as panic—disorders. Otherwise it would degenerate into a synonym for all low-grade protracted dysphoric states (Akiskal, 1990). Primary dysthymia pursues a fluctuating course and most patients eventually, albeit briefly, meet criteria for syndromal depressions. Such patients have been dubbed 'double depressives' (Keller *et al.*, 1983).

Table II summarizes the core defining features of dysthymia. The sombre personality profile of these patients is a central characteristic of dysthymia, and contrasts with the more lively ('hysteroid') traits observed in atypical depressives. Furthermore, the habitual gloominess, pessimism and low self-esteem of these patients is hard to separate from their low-grade depressive symptomatology—hence the designation of 'characterologic depression', a

Table II. Definitional and clinical characteristics of dysthymia.

Low-grade chronic depression (>2 years) which is not residual of a major depressive
  episode
Insidious onset typically <21 years, without antecedent panic and phobic features
Persistent or intermittent in course
Ambulatory disorder with several of the following features:

1. Gloomy or anhedonic mood, typically worse in the morning
2. Low self-esteem, guilty ruminations, pessimistic outlook and suicidal ideation
3. Insomnia, hypersomnia or over-eating
4. Fatigue and tendency for social withdrawal

clinical colloquialism that carries the connotation of characterologic origin of
the disorder. Although such formulations are still fashionable in some circles,
recent North American research reviewed below provides evidence that many
dysthymics represent variants of primary mood disorders.

Encouraged by sleep electroencephalographic findings of short rapid eye
movement (REM) latency (Akiskal *et al.*, 1980) and bipolar family history
(Rosenthal *et al.*, 1981) in some dysthymic patients, our mood clinic has given
these patients therapeutic trials with secondary amine TCAs such as desipramine. We have seen gradual decrease of the chronic depressive inertia in
many of these patients, and brief hypomanic responses in about a third of TCA-
responsive patients. Hypomanic features have also been observed in the prospective follow-up of both dysthymic children (Kovacs and Gastsonis, 1989) and
adults (Klein *et al.*, 1988; Rihmer, 1990). Such data provide an explanation for
the potential usefulness of lithium carbonate with or without desipramine in
some dysthymic patients (Akiskal, 1983). MAOIs may benefit still others (Valejo
et al., 1987). Low-dose stimulants (e.g., ritalin 5–10 mg b.i.d.) could be useful
for those few dysthymics whose intermittent dysphoria occurs with residual
attention deficit disorder (Wood *et al.*, 1976). Finally, we have recently observed even more dramatic normalization of a variety of dysthymic manifestations with the new serotonergic antidepressant fluoxetine (Haykal and Akiskal,
unpublished data). Whether serotonergic antidepressants work on the core
depressive features, or 'co-morbid' avoidant, eating, sleep and alcohol problems, is uncertain (Akiskal, 1991). It is nevertheless impressive that some young
to middle-aged adults—patients whose existence had been immersed in perpetual low-grade gloom, lack of confidence, anhedonia, fatigue and
hypersomnia—have reversed their habitual selves in the direction of mildly
hypomanic tendencies. The positive response of dysthymic patients to chemo-
therapy as originally reported by our group (Akiskal *et al.*, 1980) was replicated
in part by Rihmer (1990), who has also reported that these patients respond to
sleep deprivation. This is of theoretical interest because it contrasts with the
worsening of anxious–depressive symptoms in panic disorder after sleep deprivation (Roy-Byrne *et al.*, 1986).

Residual chronic depressions

Primary unipolar depressions with onset after age 50 often have a protracted course, with depressive residua following one or several clinical episodes that fail to remit fully (Akiskal *et al.*, 1981). During this protracted residual phase (Cassano *et al.*, 1983), 'characterologic' manifestations—passivity, a sense of resignation, generalized fear of inability to cope, adherence to rigid routines, interpersonal sensitivity and inhibited communication—can dominate the clinical picture. Depressive symptoms may be pushed to the background (Table III). Rather than frank depressive affect, many of these patients exhibit deficits in leisure (Delisio *et al.*, 1986; Perugi *et al.*, 1988) and an attitude of irritable moroseness. These leisure deficits and irritable humour tend to poison conjugal life: the marriage is typically in a state of chronic deadlock, culminating neither in divorce nor in reconciliation. In other patients, the residual phase is dominated by somatic manifestations; sleep and other vegetative or autonomic irregularities may mimic anxiety symptoms, and self-treatment with ethanol or iatrogenic benzodiazepine dependence is commonly observed (Weissman and Klerman, 1977; Akiskal, 1982). That these interpersonal, conjugal and autonomic manifestations represent unresolved depression is shown by persistent sleep electroencephalographic—especially REM and delta phase—abnormalities which are indistinguishable from their acute counterparts (Akiskal,1982).

Failure to recover from clinical depression is associated with increased familial loading for depression, disabled spouses, death of immediate family members, concurrent disabling medical disease, use of depressant antihypertensive agents and excessive use of alcohol and sedative–hypnotic agents. Most of these findings from the Memphis study (Akiskal, 1982) have been replicated in Newcastle (Scott *et al.*, 1988) and Pisa (Musetti *et al.*, 1989).

Social support is often eroded in residual depressives either through death or disease of significant others. Therefore social supportive interventions are an essential ingredient of the overall therapeutic approach to these patients (Weissman and Akiskal, 1984). One also must eliminate contributory drug factors (e.g., depressant antihypertensives, benzodiazepines or alcohol) before embarking upon a *vigorous* chemotherapeutic regimen (Akiskal, 1985a, 1985b) such as nortriptyline, which can be easily given in effective doses because its

Table III. The clinical picture of residual unipolar depression.

Diminished joie de vivre with impaired leisure
Irritable morosity
Signs of vegetative irregularity—sleep disturbance and monosymptomatic pain
Sedativism as self-treatment
Marital deadlock and post-depressive personality disturbances

---

pharmacokinetics are well established. This can be coupled, if needed, with a relatively low-dose of a high potency neuroleptic such as thiothixene, 2–10 mg per day in those with delusional features; for those with severe insomnia, trimipramine often improves sleep without adverse effects on REM parameters. We also recommend one of the new cyclic antidepressants with purely serotonergic profile based on experimental data implicating the serotonin (5-hydroxytryptamine, 5-HT) system in treatment resistance (see Akiskal, 1991). Residual symptoms respond to a course of ECT in most of the remaining unresponsive patients. In our experience, most residual unipolar depressives ultimately respond to the foregoing interventions. The few who remain refractory often prove to have endocrine abnormalities, occult malignancies or neurological disease (Akiskal, 1985a; Akiskal *et al.*, 1989). Thus, clinicians faced with ultra-refractory depressives must seriously consider the possibility that intractability might be due to hypothyroidism, Addison's or Cushing's disease, an abdominal malignancy, brain tumour or a 'silent' (frontal) stroke; an early phase of Binswanger's or Parkinson's disease, another CNS degenerative disorder; sleep apnea or nocturnal myoclonus.

Protracted mixed states

In the 1970s, inadequate antidepressant treatment was a major contributor to residual depressions. Recent clinical observations, however, suggest that continued TCA treatment in young and middle-aged depressives may lead not only to rapid cycling (Kukopoulos *et al.*, 1980; Wehr and Goodwin, 1987), but also to a chronic denouement (Akiskal and Mallya, 1987).

In our experience, TCAs are more likely to favour such an unfavourable outcome in the presence of other risk factors (Akiskal and Mallya, 1987). The most important of these are female gender, pre-morbid cyclothymic or hyperthymic temperament—borderline hypothyroid indices that are best elicited with the thyrotropin-releasing hormone (TRH) test, and substance abuse.

As shown in Table IV, these highly dysphoric residual states are characterized by psychomotor inertia alongside intense emotional arousal, anxiety, agitation, insomnia, racing thoughts and other evidence of subtle hypomanic intrusions such as intense sexual appetite and extraverted behaviour. These occur against a background of genuine expressions of depressive suffering. Thus, the residual symptomatology in some recurrent depressions in reality represent a protracted mixed state. These mixed states are distinguished from Kraepelin's (1921) original description—which was based on in-patients—in that they are of non-psychotic intensity. Nevertheless they are greatly disruptive because of their subacute or even chronic course. Therefore, the intense emotionality, and the labile and seemingly inconsistent (mixed) clinical picture puts these patients at risk of being labelled 'character disordered'.

Table IV. Clinical features suggestive of a pseudo-unipolar mixed state.

Unrelenting dysphoria with irascibility
Agitation against a background of retardation
Extreme fatigue with racing thoughts
Intractable panic and insomnia
Suicidal obsessions and impulses
Unendurable sexual excitement
'Histrionic'—yet genuine expression of intense suffering

Protracted mixed states represent a complex therapeutic challenge. We believe that lithium augmentation as championed by deMontigny *et al.* (1981) is particularly useful for such pseudo-unipolar depressions. (We doubt if lithium augmentation is ever useful in strictly unipolar patients.) In our view, once lithium augmentation converts a TCA non-responder to a responder, the TCA should be discontinued within a week or two and the patient maintained on lithium. MAOIs are not entirely benign from the standpoint of rapid cycling or chronicization. However, in at least some patients—when combined with lithium—they are a better alternative to TCAs (Himmelhoch and Neil, 1980). Some patients can be maintained on lithium alone; others require low-dose neuroleptics for brief periods—certainly no more than two to three weeks—superimposed on a lithium maintenance regimen. Thyroid augmentation of lithium (Extein and Gold, 1986) and carbamazepine or valproate augmentation of lithium (Post *et al.*, 1986; Emrich *et al.*, 1985) especially benefit those with thyroid disturbances and/or cycling with mixed features, respectively. Finally, our recent experience (Haykal and Akiskal, 1990) suggests that bupropion, a newly released—possibly dopaminergic and noradrenergic—antidepressant in the USA, might offer freedom from cycling to some of the most refractory pseudo-unipolar depressives or those with depressive rapid cycling from a bipolar II base. Bupropion can also be combined with lithium.

Philosophy of clinical management

This chapter reflects clinical experience that has shown a vast heterogeneity of chronic-resistant depressions. The categorization into the four types offered here is not meant to provide a validated nosology of these depressions. It is intended to provide the practitioner with a tool to bring order into this complex universe of chronic affective suffering—a tool that can enhance clinical management.

The central thesis of this chapter is that chronic depressive suffering is prevalent in both community and clinical samples. It is often misdiagnosed as character disorder and therefore undertreated. The first step in the proper management of these patients is to recognize that repeated attacks of depression may coalesce into protracted low-grade depressive symptomatology. This can seriously disrupt vocational, conjugal and interpersonal functioning. That is, characterological disturbances in many, if not most, chronic depressives represent post-affective complications. In those with early-onset dysthymia, affective and characterologic manifestations appear intimately woven. In both situations, however, competent pharmacotherapy geared to the affective disorder subtype is often successful in attenuating the characterologic disturbances (Akiskal *et al.*, 1989). The recognition of several varieties of chronic depression with relatively distinct clinical features and course is thus a crucial step toward rational treatment.

Psycho-educational and supportive psychotherapeutic measures are useful in enhancing rapport, compliance and hope. However, by themselves they do not represent adequate treatment for this difficult group of patients. Long-term psychotherapy targeted to the interpersonal difficulties of these patients represents an ambitious aim that is not of proven efficacy.

This chapter has emphasized the clinical utility of tailoring pharmacological interventions to the clinical subtype of chronic-resistant depression. Treating depressed individuals who have been chronically ill is a long-term challenge that requires sophistication in nosology, competence in neuropsychiatry and general medicine, as well as mastery of the art and science of psychopharmacotherapy. Above all, the clinician must possess the stamina to withstand frustration in the face of protracted human suffering that resists all conventional and many unconventional psychopharmacological strategies. The clinical subtypes of chronic-resistant depression described in this chapter are meant to aid the proper matching of interventions for a given patient. The physician will then experience the gratification of not only alleviating the patient's depressive anguish, but also the attenuation of the most pernicious characterologic distortions produced by protracted depressive suffering. Few professional activities in medicine provide the gratification of saving a hopelessly and chronically depressed patient from the malignant transformation that depression brings in the lives of 15% of its sufferers. The arrival of the new class of serotonergic antidepressants and atypical antidepressants such as bupropion provide physicians with new optimism to comfort such patients.

References

Akiskal HS (1982) Factors associated with incomplete recovery in primary depressive illness. *J Clin Psychiatry* **43**, 266–271.
Akiskal HS (1983) Dysthymic disorder: psychopathology of proposed chronic depressive subtypes. *Am J Psychiatry* **140**, 11–20.
Akiskal HS (1985a) A proposed clinical approach to chronic and 'resistant' depressions: evaluation and treatment. *Psychiatry* **46** (Sec. 2), 32–36.

Akiskal HS (1985b) The clinical management of affective disorders. In: Michels RR, Cooper AM, Guze SB, Judd LL and Klerman GL (eds) *Psychiatry*, Vol. 1, pp. 1–27. Philadelphia: JB Lippincott.

Akiskal HS (1990) Toward a definition of dysthymia: boundaries with personality and mood disorders. In: Burton SW and Akiskal HS (eds) *Dysthymic Disorder* pp. 1–12. London: Royal College of Psychiatrists.

Akiskal HS (1991) Chronic-resistant depressions: are serotonergic mechanisms relevant? In: Cassano GB and Akiskal HS (eds) *Serotonin-Related Psychiatric Syndromes— Clinical and Therapeutic Links*, pp. 171–174. London: Royal Society of Medicine.

Akiskal HS and Haykal RF (1988) Dysthymic and chronic depressive conditions. In: Georgotas A and Cancro R (eds) *Depression and Mania: A Comprehensive Textbook*, pp. 96–103. New York: Elsevier.

Akiskal HS and Lemmi H (1987) Sleep EEG findings bearing on the relationship of anxiety and depressive disorders. In: Racagni G and Smeraldi E (eds) *Anxious Depressions: Assessment and Treatment*, pp. 153–159. New York: Raven Press.

Akiskal HS and Mallya G (1987) Criteria for the 'soft' bipolar spectrum: Treatment implications. *Psychopharmacology Bull* **23**, 68–73.

Akiskal HS and Simmons R (1985) Chronic and refractory depressions: Evaluation and management. In: Beckham E and Leber W (eds) *Handbook for the Diagnosis and Treatment of Depression*, pp.587–605. Homewood, IL: Dorsey.

Akiskal HS, Rosenthal TL, Haykal RF *et al.* (1980) Characterological depressions: Clinical and sleep EEG findings separating 'subaffective dysthymias' from 'character-spectrum' disorders. *Arch Gen Psychiatry* **37**, 777–783.

Akiskal HS, King D, Rosenthal TL *et al.* (1981) Chronic depressions: Part 1. Clinical and familial characteristics in 137 probands. *J Affect Dis* **3**, 297–311.

Akiskal HS, Walker PW, Puzantian VR *et al.* (1983) Bipolar outcome in the course of depressive illness: Phenomenologic, familial and pharmacologic predictors. *J Affect Dis* **5**, 115–128.

Akiskal HS, Lemmi H, Dickson H *et al.* (1984) Chronic depressions: Part 2. Sleep EEG differentiation of primary dysthymic disorders from anxious depressions. *J Affect Dis* **6**, 287–295.

American Psychiatric Association (1987) *Diagnostic and Statistical Manual of Mental Disorders* (3rd edn, revised). Washington, DC: American Psychiatric Press.

Angst J (1973) The etiology and nosology of endogenous depressive disorders. *Foreign Psychiatry* **II** (Spring), 1–108.

Arieti S and Bemporad J (1978) *Severe and Mild Depression.* New York: Basic Books.

Beard GM (1880) *A Practical Treatise on Nervous Exhaustion (Neurasthenia): Its Nature, Sequences, and Treatment.* New York: Wood.

Bonime W (1966) The psychodynamics of neurotic depression. In: Arieti S (ed.) *American Handbook of Psychiatry*, pp. 239–255. New York: Basic Books.

Burton SW and Akiskal HS (eds) (1990) *Dysthymic Disorder.* London: Royal College of Psychiatrists.

Cassano GB, Maggini C and Akiskal HS (1983) Short-term, subchronic, and chronic sequelae of affective disorders. *Psychiatr Clin North Am* **6**, 55–67.

Cassano GB, Perugi G, Maremmani I and Akiskal HS (1990) Social adjustment in dysthymia. In: Burton WS and Akiskal HS (eds) *Dysthymic Disorder.* London: Royal College of Psychiatrists.

Davidson J and Pelton S (1986) Forms of atypical depression and their response to antidepressant drugs. *Psychiatry Res* **17**, 87–95.

Davidson JRT, Miller RD, Turnbull CD and Sullivan JL (1982) Atypical depression. *Arch Gen Psychiatry* **39**, 527–534.

DeLisio G, Maremmani I, Perugi G *et al.* (1986) Impairment of work and leisure in depressed outpatients: A preliminary communication. *J Affect Dis* **10**, 79–84.

deMontigny C, Grunberg P, Mayer A and Deschennes J (1981) Lithium induces a rapid relief of depression in tricyclic antidepressant drug non-responders. *Br J Psychiatry* **138**, 252–256.

Emrich HM, Dose M and von Zerssen D (1985) The use of sodium valproate, carbamazepine and oxcarbamazepine in patients with affective disorders. *J Affect Dis* **8**, 243–250.

Extein I and Gold M (1986) Psychiatric applications of thyroid tests. *J Clin Psychiatry* **47** (Suppl. 1), 13–16.

Feighner JP, Robins E, Guze SB *et al.* (1972) Diagnostic criteria for use in psychiatric research. *Arch Gen Psychiatry* **26**, 57–63.

Freyhan FA (1974) Contributions to the definition of therapy-resistance and the therapy-resistant depressions. *Pharmakopsychiatr Neuro-psychopharmakol* **7**, 70–75.

Haykal RF and Akiskal HS (1990) Bupropion as a promising approach to rapid-cycling bipolar II patients. *J Clin Psychiatry* **51**, 450–455.

Himmelhoch JM and Neil JF (1980) Lithium therapy in combination with other forms of treatment. In: Johnson FN (ed.) *A Handbook of Lithium Therapy*, pp. 51–67. Lancaster: MTP Press.

Keller MB, Klerman GL, Lavori PW *et al.* (1982) Treatment received by depressed patients. *JAMA* **248**, 1848–1855.

Keller MD and Sessa FM (1990) Dysthymia: Development and clinical course. In: Burton SW and Akiskal HS (eds) *Dysthymic Disorder*, pp. 13–23. London: Royal College of Psychiatrists.

Klein DF (1974) Endogenomorphic depression: A conceptual and terminological revision. *Arch Gen Psychiatry* **31**, 447–454.

Klein DN, Taylor EB, Harding K and Dickstein S (1988) Double depression and episodic major depression: Demographic, clinical, familial, personality, and socio-environmental characteristics and short-term outcome. *Am J Psychiatry* **145**, 1226–1231.

Kovacs M and Gastsonis C (1989) Stability and change in childhood-onset of depressive disorders: Longitudinal course as a diagnostic validator. In: Robins LN and Barrett JE (eds) *The Validity of Psychiatric Diagnosis*, pp. 57–73. New York: Raven Press.

Kraepelin E (1921) *Manic-Depressive Illness and Paranoia.* Edinburgh: Livingstone.

Kukopoulos A, Reginaldi R, Floris G *et al.* (1980) Course of the manic-depressive cycle in changes caused by treatment. *Pharmakopsychiatr Neuropsychopharmakol* **13**, 156–167.

Liebowitz MR and Klein DF (1979) Hysteroid dysphoria. *Psychiatr Clin North Am* **2**, 555–575.

Liebowitz MR, Quitkin FM, Stewart JW *et al.* (1988) Antidepressant specificity in atypical depression. *Arch Gen Psychiatry* **45**, 129–137.

Links P and Akiskal HS (1987) Chronic and intractable depressions: Terminology, classification, and description of subtypes. In: Zohar J and Belmaker RH (eds) *Treating Resistant-Depressions*, pp.1–12. New York: PMA.

Musetti L, Perugi G, Soriani A *et al.* (1989) Depression before and after age 65. *Br J Psychiatry* **155**, 330–336.

Paykel ES, Parker RR, Rowan PR *et al.* (1983) Nosology of atypical depression. *Psychol Med* **13**, 131–139.

Perugi G, Maremmani I, McNair DM *et al.* (1988) Differential changes in areas of social adjustment from depressive episodes through recovery. *J Affect Dis* **15**, 39–43.

Pollitt JD (1965) Suggestions for a physiological classification of depression. *Br J Psychiatry* **111**, 489–495.

Post RM, Uhde TN, Roy-Byrne PP and Joffe RT (1986) Antidepressant effects of carbamazepine. *Am J Psychiatry* **143**, 29–34.

Price JS (1978) Chronic depressive illness. *Br Med J* **2**, 1200–1201.

Regier DA, Boyd JH, Burke JD *et al.* (1988) One-month prevalence of mental disorders in the United States: Based on five epidemiological catchment area sites. *Arch Gen Psychiatry* **45**, 977–986.

Rihmer Z (1990) Dysthymia: A clinician's perspective. In: Burton S and Akiskal HS (eds). *Dysthymic Disorder*, pp. 112–125. London: Royal College of Psychiatrists.

Robins E and Guze SB (1972) Classification of affective disorders: The primary–secondary, the endogenous–reactive and the neurotic–psychotic concepts. In: Williams TA, Katz MM and Shields JA (eds) *The Psychobiology of the Depressive Illness.* Washington DC: US Government Printing Office.

Robinson DS, Davis JM, Nies A *et al.* (1971) Relation of sex and aging to monoamine oxidase activity of human brain, plasma, and platelets. *Arch Gen Psychiatry* **24**, 536–539.

Rosenthal TL, Akiskal HS, Scott-Strauss A *et al.* (1981) Familial and developmental factors in characterological depressions. *J Affect Dis* **3**, 183–192.

Roy-Byrne PP, Uhde T Jr and Post RM (1986) Effects of one-night's sleep deprivation on mood and behavior in panic disorder: Patients with panic disorder compared with depressed patients and normal controls. *Arch Gen Psychiatry* **43**, 895–899.

Sargent W (1961) Drugs in the treatment of depression. *Br Med J* **1**, 225–227.

Sartorius N (1974) Description and classification of depressive disorders: Contributions for the definition of the therapy-resistance and of therapy resistant depressions. *Pharmakopsychiatr Neuro-psychopharmakol* **7**, 76–79.

Scott J (1988) Chronic depression. *Br J Psychiatry* **153**, 287–297.

Scott J, Barker VA and Eccleston D (1988) The Newcastle chronic depression study: Patient characteristics and factors associated with chronicity. *Br J Psychiatry* **152**, 28–33.

Valejo J, Gasto C, Catalan R and Salamero M (1987) Double-blind study of imipramine vs phenelzine in melancholias and dysthymic disorder. *Br J Psychiatry* **151**, 639–642.

Wehr TA and Goodwin FK (1987) Can antidepressants cause mania and worsen the course of affective illness? *Am J Psychiatry* **136**, 502–507.

Weissman MM and Akiskal HS (1984) The role of psychotherapy in chronic depressions: A proposal. *Compr Psychiatry* **25**, 23–31.

Weissman MM and Klerman GL (1977) The chronic depressive in the community: Unrecognized and poorly treated. *Compr Psychiatry* **18**, 523–532.

Weissman MM, Bruce ML, Leaf PJ *et al.* (1991) Affective disorders. In: Robins LN, Regier DA (eds) *Psychiatric Disorders in America: The Epidemiologic Catchment Area Study*, pp. 53–80. New York: Free Press.

Wells KB, Stewart A, Hays RD *et al.* (1989) The functioning and well-being of depressed patients. *JAMA* **7**, 914–919.

West ED and Dally PJ (1959) Effects of iproniazid in depressive syndromes. *Br Med J* **1**, 1491–1494.

Wood DR, Reimherr FW, Wender PH and Johnson GE (1976) Diagnosis and treatment of minimal brain dysfunction in adults. *Arch Gen Psychiatry* **33**, 1453–1460.

11

The practical clinical diagnosis of depression in Japan

Y. Kasahara

A brief history of psychiatric diagnosis in Japan

Until around 1950, Japanese psychiatric diagnosis was under the strong influence of European, in particular German, psychiatry. Textbooks such as those by Karl Jaspers or Kurt Schneider were regarded as essential for a beginner in psychiatry. French psychiatry was also influential and many French articles were introduced and translated into Japanese. However, after 1950 Japanese psychiatrists started paying more attention to American diagnostic practice. Japanese psychiatrists began to be aware of the practical usefulness of American psychiatric concepts, particularly after the introduction of the concept of borderline conditions.

One of the strong leads from American psychiatry was the publication of DSM-III in 1980. For many Japanese it appeared fresh and novel, particularly because of its harmoniously well-balanced approaches of both traditional descriptive psychopathology and dynamic psychiatry. The impact of the American diagnostic system can be summarized by the following three points:

1. It stimulated the interest of Japanese psychiatrists in the operationalization of psychiatric diagnostic criteria and the quantitative measurement of symptoms and signs. Research groups on diagnosis were founded and methods of structured and semi-structured interviews were introduced and are being studied further. It also led many Japanese psychiatrists to review the British literature and to participate in nationwide trials of ICD-10 conducted by the Japanese National Institute of Mental Health in 1989.

The Diagnosis of Depression. Edited by J.P. Feighner and W.F. Boyer
© 1991 John Wiley & Sons Ltd

2. The second impact of DSM-III arose from its multi-axial evaluation approach. It goes without saying that this holistic viewpoint is very important in psychiatric practice. The multi-axial evaluation of DSM-III seems to be the only successful diagnostic system so far which concretely describes how it should be used in daily practice. There had been similar trial systems in Japan as well. In fact, in our school we had proposed a 'multidimensional diagnostic system' and established a concrete scheme of 'multidimensional diagnosis for depressive states' in 1975. It resembles the DSM-III multi-axial diagnostic system very much. This issue will be discussed further.

3. The third impact of DSM-III is closely connected to the second point; the refinement of the descriptions of personality disorders. In our study of the aforementioned multidimensional diagnostic system we attached high importance to the evaluation of personality attributes. Therefore we had a strong interest in the description of the personality disorders in DSM-III when it was published. Although we found some parts of Axis II, such as avoidant personality disorder and narcissistic personality disorder, to be not well defined, its systematized description and the substantial quality of the contents are, on the whole, satisfying. We hope that it will be further refined. Perhaps a few new categories should be added.

In summary, current Japanese psychiatry is evenly influenced by German, French, American and British psychiatry. In the diagnosis of depressive states, which is the title of this volume, we are well acquainted with: (1) the clinical entity of 'endogenous depression' that has been elegantly elaborated by German psychopathologists; (2) the subtle relationships between depressive states and anxious states discussed mainly by British psychiatrists; (3) the unique consciousness of depressive states of the neo-Jacksonian school of French psychopathology; and (4) the psychodynamic interpretations of depressive states mainly developed in the USA since Abraham.

Japanese psychiatry has also proposed several original concepts during its over 100-year history. These are still valid in current practice. For example, Morita (1874–1938) devised two important concepts of neuroses in the 1920s. These were 'Shinkeishitsu' and 'Taijin-phobia'. The latter is almost the same as social phobia in DSM-III (Kasahara, 1987). Shinkeishitsu will be discussed later.

Shimoda (1885–1980) proposed in 1941 that 'cohesive personality' (or 'immodithym personality') was the usual pre-morbid character of manic-depressive illness. Kretschmer's 'cycloid or cyclothymic personality' was already well known as a pre-morbid personality for certain mood disorders. Nevertheless, Shimoda found a higher frequency of the cohesive personality than cyclothymic personality among patients. Shimoda's hypothesis will also be discussed later because it plays an important role in our 'multidimensional diagnostic system'.

Mitsuda's 'atypical psychosis' (1942) has been frequently used in Japan in the diagnosis of schizophrenia and allied conditions. The concept is akin to schizo-affective psychoses, 'cykloid psychose' (Leonhard), 'psychose délirante', etc. I will also touch on this concept later because it is related to severe levels of mood disturbance.

A multidimensional system for diagnosis of depression

Bin Kimura and I devised a multidimensional diagnostic system of depressive disorders in 1975. We proposed this system because patients suffering from milder depression had increased in number in psychiatric out-patient clinics. This coincided with the nationwide spread of the national health insurance system in the 1960s. The conventional dichotomy of endogenous versus reac-tive, or psychotic versus neurotic, was inadequate for these milder depressions. Consequently, a new classification model was needed. In addition, clinical experience with the new pharmacotherapy stimulated psychiatrists to produce diagnostic schemes which could suggest not only classification but also therapy. The concept of 'Situagenie' coined by German psychopathologists (for instance, Baeyer, Pauleikoff) was helpful to our thinking because it transcended the simple and rigid dichotomy of endogenous versus reactive. Another closely related issue was the pre-morbid personality of depressive patients, particularly the description of Shimoda's cohesive personality. Without Shimoda's theory, our multidimensional scheme could not have been devised.

Five dimensions or five aspects were proposed:

1. Psychiatric symptoms.
2. Pre-morbid personality features.
3. Psychosocial stressors.
4. Level of social functioning prior to onset.
5. Attitude towards psychiatric treatment and course.

Interestingly, when we compared our system with the multi-axial system of DSM-III which came out several years later, we found that the first, second, third and fourth dimensions were nearly the same. Instead of having physical conditions (Axis III of DSM-III), our system has 'attitude towards psychiatric treatment' as the fifth dimension. However, there were more significant dif-ferences between the two methods. The multi-axial system of DSM-III was devised for promoting understanding among professionals in psychiatric prac-tice. It naturally covers all the fields of psychiatric disorders, whereas our multi-dimensional system was devised to assist the experienced psychiatrist in the proper choice of treatment for depressed patients.

Table I shows that our system classifies several types of depressive disor-ders according to combinations of the five dimensions. On the other hand DSM-III tries to describe and evaluate patients from a psycho-bio-social point of view.

Table I. Kasahara and Kimura's classification of affective disorders (1975).

	Type I	Type II	→	Type V
Dimension 1 Present state	———	———	. . .	———
Dimension 2 Personality	———	———	. . .	———
Dimension 3 Stressors	———	———	. . .	———
Dimension 4 Social functioning	———	———	. . .	———
Dimension 5 Attitude	———	———	. . .	———

Now, for example, I would like to explain the combination of features of 'type I' depression. This is the one most frequently seen among affectively ill patients in Japan during the past several years.

Dimension 1 (Symptoms): Typical unipolar features, almost identical to endogenous depressive symptoms, but of mild to moderate severity.

Dimension 2 (Personality): Cohesive personality (Shimoda) Typus Melancholicus (Tellenbach), Obsessoid personality (Kasahara).

Dimension 3 (Psychosocial stressors): (1) Changes in lifestyle, transfer to a new occupation, promotion, change of employment, change in constellation of family members, mild physical illness or injury, sudden increase or diminution of responsibility, changing residence, going abroad, etc. or (2) No psychosocial stressor.

Dimension 4 (Social functioning): Excellent or good functioning as businessman or housewife, no history of mania and few if any previous episodes of depression which were at most mild in severity.

Dimension 5 (Attitude toward treatment): Constant and positive relationship with therapists, coping with distress, good response to pharmacotherapy, one-third curable within three months, around 10% having a chronic course over two-year follow-up.

As indicated above, in a subtype of this type I depression there is a significant role for psychosocial stressors, even though the symptoms might be characterized as a mild endogenous depression. To understand the coexistence of endogenous and reactive features in these cases it is necessary to think of the pre-morbid personality (Dimension 2) as the key concept. In other words, personality and psychosocial stressors seem to be especially interrelated in this subtype. Therefore, type I might be called a 'personality-situation type'.

Therefore I will further discuss the relationship between the subtype and the personality attributes, particularly Shimoda's cohesive personality.

The Japanese concept of cohesive personality in depression

Shimoda investigated 92 subjects in 1950 in order to ascertain the frequency of cohesive personality among depressive patients. Eighty had unipolar depression, seven had a bipolar depression and five were in a manic episode. Cohesive personality was found in 86 cases (93.4%) whereas Kretschmer's cycloid (or cyclothymic) personality was seen in only 39 subjects (42.7%). According to Yamashita (1981), cohesive personality can be summarized by three types of character tendencies:

1. Orderly, perfectionistic, meticulous, scrupulous.
2. Conscientious, upright, dutiful, reliable.
3. Zealous, devoted, persistent, unshakeable to the end.

Shimoda's hypothesis was not well accepted by clinicians in his day. However, his theory was re-evaluated in the 1960s. Hirasawa (1966) particularly found orderliness and perfectionism among depressive patients with mild endogenous features.

Cohesive personality roughly corresponds to the concept of 'Typus Melancholicus' proposed by Tellenbach (1961). According to Tellenbach, the most fundamental component of this personality trait is 'love for orderliness'. He emphasized that this concept covers not only the ability to organize things at a materialistic level but also a deliberate attitude towards others which borders on an internalized feature such as 'conscience'. This concept of Typus melancholicus was well accepted in Japan because of its resemblance to the cohesive personality described by Shimoda.

These personality traits do not deal with personality disorder but rather with traits which stay within the realm of normalcy. The cohesive personality was described by Shimoda in ways such as 'possessing over-average ability', 'an ideal worker', or 'model soldier'. Some personality features like inclination to orderliness, perfectionism, conscientiousness and meticulousness are often seen and could be characterized under obsessive personality disorder. But the aggressiveness and egocentric stubbornness of patients with obsessive personality disorder are not seen in those with cohesive personality. Rather they show tendencies to avoid conflict and to seek harmonious and comfortable relationships with others.

More concretely speaking, these people sensitively monitor the feelings of others and tend to give in easily when they find it difficult to get along with others. They seldom say no when they are asked for a favour. When Tellenbach used the expression 'Sein für Andere' (to exist for others) it suggested the essential meaning of this concept.

A psychological disposition such as this may be an asthenic component of temperament which may occasionally show psychological transition towards avoidant characteristics with excessive fear of rejection. It can also show transition toward masochistic features, e.g. excessive self-demands and self-reproach. However, the fearful and masochistic traits found in the avoidant and masochistic personality disorders of DSM-III-R are much stronger than the traits of those with cohesive personality. In short, I would like to revise the description of the depression-prone 'normal' personality as follows:

1. Orderly, perfectionistic, duty-bound, achievement-oriented.
2. Longing for comfortable social relationships.
3. Quiet, non-aggressive.

I propose to call such a mild and non-aggressive type of obsessive-compulsive personality disorder 'Obsessoid personality' (1984).

This kind of 'other-person' orientation is also related to the syntonic or amiable character described by Kretschmer in the cyclothymic personality. In fact, it has often been pointed out that the cohesive personality is quite compatible with cyclothymic personality.

Where does such a characterological non-aggressiveness come from? Hirasawa (1966) hypothesized that cyclothymic personality is an inborn and biologically determined component whereas cohesive personality is acquired. Both personalities could also coexist on different levels. Based on studies of identical twins suffering from depressive disorders, Ihda and colleagues (1979) pointed out that cyclothymic personality is seen only when a healthy development of cyclothymic traits is disturbed during childhood or early adolescence. Traits such as fixation on orderliness and love for perfectionism then develop as secondary and compensatory.

Another speculation about the non-aggressiveness of cohesive personality relates to the psychological and behavioural characteristics of the Japanese. Generally speaking, the Japanese have an inclination to maintain their self-esteem predominantly by establishing harmonious relationships with others. The perpetual and excessive efforts to keep such harmonious relations are often converted into an achievement-oriented personality, conventional thinking and excellent levels of social functioning until the onset of depressive disorder, typically in middle age. It can easily be understood then that the psychosocial stressors prior to onset need not necessarily be marked life events, but rather may be mild enough to seem trivial.

In his original paper Shimoda (1941), postulated the following:

In the typical case, when he or she was distressed with an exhausting situation for a certain period of time, some signs of neurasthenia developed. However, a person with this personality is prevented from recuperating from the distress because of persisting emotional excitability. He continues to work actively despite the exhaustion. This produces a vicious cycle and makes him all the more exhausted. Only after the outbreak of depression can this person really retreat from the hectic situation.

Although this hypothesis may sound simple, it matched the situation preceding the outbreak of many cases of depressive disorders between 1960 and 1990 in Japan (Kasahara *et al.*, 1987). It holds true particularly well for unipolar depression among middle-aged people, for example the businessman in a big company or a middle-class office manager. Currently, mild depression, along with myocardial infarction and peptic ulcer, are considered the most common diseases among businessmen. Therefore, psychiatrists in industry are paying attention to the risk factors, psychosocial stressors and especially the pre-morbid personality of depression such as cohesive personality or typus melancholicus.

'Neurotic depression'

Type II depression, according to our system, corresponds almost exactly to the classical type of endogenous bipolar disorder, so detailed description will not be needed.

Dimension 1 (Psychiatric symptoms): Less typical and comprehensive than those in type I, episodes of mania or hypomania in the past, often pyknic body habitus.
Dimension 2 (Pre-morbid personality): Cycloid or cyclothymic personality, sometimes cohesive personality, typus melancholicus, obsessoid personality.
Dimension 3 (Psychosocial stressors): Unclear, sometimes a physical condition, for example, menstruation, seasonal factors, physical exhaustion.
Dimension 4 (Social functioning): Good or fair, difficult to evaluate because of insufficient social experience in a young adult.
Dimension 5 (Attitude toward treatment): Possibly an unstable relationship, moderate response to pharmacotherapy, longer course and tendency to relapse.

Both type III and type IV depression could be classified as 'neurotic' according to traditional systems. Studies on 'borderline conditions' and 'mild and oligosymptomatic schizophrenia' since the 1960s are a stimulus to discriminate these two types of depression. This may be done by comparing the individual axes for these types (Table II).

Dimension 1 (Psychiatric symptoms)
Type III: Long history of other neurotic symptoms such as agoraphobia, social phobia, obsessive-compulsive symptoms, hypochondriacal symptoms, more manifest other-critical than self-critical tendencies, even though suicidal ideas do exist.

Table II. Type III and type IV depression.

	Type III	Type IV
Dimension 1	So-called neurotic depressive features, chronic	Atypical features (dysphoric, apathetic pan-neurotic), sometimes impulsive dyscontrol symptoms, chronic
Dimension 2	Depressive (Schneider) Dependent (DSM-III) Histrionic (DSM-III) Narcissistic (DSM-III)	Borderline (DSM-III) Schizotypal avoidant (DSM-III)
Dimension 3	Persisting inner conflict (young and middle age)	Identity problems (late adolescent and young adult)
Dimension 4	Fair or poor	Fair or poor
Dimension 5	Poor response to pharmacotherapy, unstable relationship with therapists	Poor response to pharmacotherapy, unstable relationship with therapists

Type IV: Atypical depressive symptoms, i.e. dysphoric mood, apathetic and indifferent attitude, pan-neurotic symptoms, not infrequently impulse dis-control symptoms such as absenteeism, running away, excessive spending, shoplifting, sexual abuse, substance abuse, self-mutilating behaviours, etc.; often rapid mood swings from dysphoria to hypomania.

Ogawa (1986) elaborated a unique hypothesis on this classification in order to elim-inate the ambiguity of 'neurotic depression'. Kasahara (1984, 1989) described apa-thetic and indifferent conditions among highly educated young persons and called them 'retreat' or 'withdrawal' types of depression. It is characterized as follows:

1. Predominant symptoms of egosyntonic psychic inhibition rather than de-pressive mood.
2. 'Selective retreat' from the competitive aspects of life (i.e. major fields of study as a college student, work duties as a businessman), no problems in non-competitive aspects of life.
3. Indifference to conflicts, not because of psychotic loss of reality testing but from the psychic defences of denial and splitting.

Dimension 2 (Personality)

Type III: Depressive psychopath (Schneider), dependent personality disorder, histrionic personality disorder, avoidant, obsessive-compulsive personality disorder (DSM-III) and Morita's Shinkeishitsu.*

---

* Morita's Shinkeishitsu contains two opposite components—asthenic and sthenic—and therefore is always prone to inner conflicts. Persons with the Shinkeishitsu personality are meticulous, perfec-tionistic, idealistic, unyielding, excessively introspective, and egoistic. They have low self-confidence and a strong desire for life. This contrasts with the cohesive personality, which has an inclination to abandon life in the face of frustration (Kasahara, 1987).

Type IV: Avoidant, borderline, schizoid, schizotypal personality disorders (DSM-III).

Dimension 3 (Precipitating stress)
Type III: Persistent inner conflict, long-lasting excessive burdens of responsibility, crisis of psychic development during adolescence.
Type IV: Life events such as 'identity problems', i.e. difficult love affairs, unhappy sexual experiences, religious experiences, failure in career choice or important examinations, experience of isolation, long journey, etc.

Dimension 4 (Social functioning)
Both types: Fair or poor social functioning prior to onset, mainly from late adolescence to young adulthood, but in type III only, middle age or early senescence.

Dimension 5 (Attitude toward treatment)
Type III: Although response to pharmacotherapy is generally poor, the doctor–patient relationship remains stable. The course is often chronic. Not infrequently a differential diagnosis is required from the chronic and pseudo-neurotic features of type I.
Type IV: Unstable relationship with therapist, sometimes poor motivation to psychiatric treatment.

Type IV depression (borderline-schizoid type) has been increasing in number during the past twenty years. The closeness of depressive disorders to borderline personality disorder was pointed out by Stone (1979) and Gunderson (1985). Ogawa (1986) used the term 'type detache' for type IV, in contrast to 'type attache' for type III because detached types of personality such as avoidant, borderline or schizotypal are often found among patients with type IV depression.

Type V depression corresponds to grief reaction, adjustment disorder with depressed mood or post-traumatic stress disorders in DSM-III. Type VI is a residual category for any kind of depressive state which cannot be classified according to the five dimensions. These include, for example, organic depressive syndromes, depressive states in childhood, adolescence and senility.

In summary, each type could be termed as follows:

Type I: Personality–Situation Type.
Type II: Circular Type.
Type III: Conflict–Relation Type.
Type IV: Schizoid–Borderline Type.
Type V: Grief–Reaction Type.
Type VI: Miscellaneous.

Type I is, as mentioned above, the most frequent in Japan today. According to our experience, at least 40% of depressive patients visiting the psychiatric out-patient clinic of Nagoya University Hospital* in the past decade belong to type I. Type II is relatively uncommon whereas types III and IV account for approximately 10% each. Type V is also relatively rare.

Severity of illness

We propose to add another dimension to this diagnostic scheme, which is 'level of severity'. Four levels of severity for type I depression will be as follows:

1. Mild severity including masked depression or depressive equivalents.
2. Moderate severity including a single brief, one to two-week, hypomanic episode in the final stage of pharmacotherapy.
3. Chronic cases, including secondary manifestations of neurotic conflicts resulting from the chronic nature of the illness.
4. Transient psychotic features including mood-congruent psychotic features or atypical psychosis (Murakami, 1953).

As far as the case belongs to type I depression (the Personality–Situation type), the therapeutic manoeuvres should be essentially the same, regardless of the level of severity. Four principal methods are recommended:

1. Pharmacotherapy.
2. Supportive psychotherapy.
3. Counselling with the spouse of significant persons within the family.
4. Guidance for rehabilitation of social functioning.

Even if patients have a chronic course and complain of persistent neurotic or hysterical symptoms they should not be mistaken as type III or IV. According to our experience, many cases of type I depression of the third level of severity recover around two or three years after its onset. After recovering they are able to be as healthy as before the illness.

---

* The clinic has almost 1200 new patients a year. Almost all of them belong to the middle or upper social class and use the national health insurance. The percentage of affective disorders among these 1200 out-patients is uniformly 20–24%. The clinic is located in the central part of Nagoya, which is Japan's third largest city after Tokyo and Osaka. It is an industrial city which has experienced remarkable development during the last 100 years. Its population now is approximately two million.

Table III. Multidimensional diagnosis of depressive states (Kasahara).

	Type I	Type II	Type III	Type IV	Type V	Type VI
I. Present state	Depressive episode, unipolar, mild severity	Depressive episode, unipolar, recurrent	So-called neurotic, chronic	Atypical features (dysphoric, apathetic, impulse dyscontrol)	Repetitive thought of 'loss' or 'event'	Unspecified (organic depressive syndrome, depressive states in childhood, adolescence and senile persons, and others)
II. Pre-morbid personality	'Cohesive personality' (Shimoda) 'Typus melancholicus'	Cycloid (Kretschmer) (plus) Cohesive personality	Depressive personality (Schneider) dependent, histrionic (DSM-III)	Avoidant, borderline, schizotypal (DSM-III)	Unspecified	
III. Outbreaking situations (stressor)	Changes in way of life (new career, promotion)	Unclear, often no stressors	Persisting inner conflicts	Identity problems	Loss of close relatives, unusual psychic trauma	
IV. Pre-morbid social functioning	Very good or good (businessmen or housewives of middle age)	Good or fair (from adolescence to middle age)	Fair or poor (young and middle age)	Fair or poor (late adolescence and young adults)	Unspecified	
V. Attitudes towards treatment	Good relationship, good response to pharmacotherapy	Almost good, but sometimes unstable relationship	Poor response to pharmacotherapy	Poor response to pharmacotherapy, unstable relationship	Rarely visits psychiatrists	
Levels of severity	I—1 I—2 I—3 I—4	II—1 II—2 II—3 II—4	III—1 III—2 III—3 III—4	IV—1 IV—2 IV—3 IV—4	V—1 V—2 V—3 V—4	

I would like to add one more example of level of severity. This one is for type IV depression:

Level 1: Psychic inhibition or apathetic condition more predominant than the depressive mood, lack of responsibility in social life, complaints of identity problems.
Level 2: Transient hypomanic or manic episodes.
Level 3: Various or single symptoms of impulse discontrol.
Level 4: Short-lived psychotic experiences.

Table III illustrates the six types of depression and their levels of severity.

Plans for the future

The multidimensional diagnosis of depressive states is well accepted by many clinicians, particularly in the urban areas of Japan. It is not universally accepted because we cannot conduct a wide trial with this method. However, in our medical school, we make the diagnosis using both the international system (such as DSM-III-R or ICD-10) and our own. We use both standard and colloquial language at the same time, so to speak.

Needless to say, international methods have advantages for statistical and epidemiological studies, and local ones such as our six-type diagnosis may help clinicians to make precise selection of therapeutic manoeuvres for each patient. Our next plans for this system are to incorporate aspects of multi-axial diagnosis in order to make our diagnostic system more comprehensive and useful.

According to the review of Mezzic *et al.* (1987) nine aspects are important for a comprehensive description of depressed patients: symptoms, course, severity, personality, physical illness, psychosocial stressors, aetiology, social functioning and demographics. Among these items, symptoms, course and personality attract the most attention of researchers. I believe that three aspects are the minimum necessary for multi-axial characterization of mood disorders. If possible, social functioning prior to onset should be added. I also hope that knowledge of the relationship between personality and affective disorders will be further refined.

Akiskal (1981) adopted seven aspects when he classified three subtypes of chronic depression: onset, course, personality, developmental history, family history, rapid eye movement (REM) latency and pharmacological response. I have also been interested in adding to my table one or two aspects concerning biological markers such as the REM latency in Akiskal's table. Plasma biopterin levels (Hashimoto *et al.*, 1987, 1988) is the most likely one for us.

References

Akiskal HS (1981) Chronic depressions. *J Affect Dis* **3**, 297–315.

Gunderson JG (1985) The interface between borderline personality disorders and affective disorder. *Am J Psychiatry* **142**, 277–288.

Hashimoto R, Ozaki N, Ohta T *et al.* (1987) Total biopterin levels of plasma in patients with depression. *Neuropsychobiology* **17**, 176–177.

Hashimoto R, Ozaki N, Ohta T *et al.* (1988) Plasma biopterin levels of patients with affective disorders. *Neuropsychobiology* **19**, 61–63.

Hirasawa H (1966) *On Mild Forms of Endogenous Depression: Symptom and Outcome* [in Japanese]. Tokyo: Igakushoin.

Ihda S (1979) Discordance of identical twins suffering from depressive disorders: psychologial development of 'Typus Melancholicus' (Tellenbach) [in Japanese]. In Ihda S (ed.) *Psychopathology of Manic-depressive Illness*, pp.1–20. Tokyo: Kobundo.

Kasahara Y (1984) *Apathy Syndrome: Psychology of Highly-educated Young Persons* [in Japanese]. Tokyo: Iwanami-Shoten.

Kasahara Y (1987) Social phobia in Japan. In: *Social Phobia in Japan and Korea* (Proceedings of the 1st Cultural Psychiatry Symposium between Japan and Korea), pp. 3–14. Soeul: East Asian Academy of Cultural Psychiatry.

Kasahara Y (1989) Reflexions on school phobia. *Jpn J Child Adol Psychiatry* **30**, 242–251.

Kasahara Y and Kimura B (1975) Zur klassifizierung depressiver Zustände [in Japanese]. *Psychiatr Neurol Jpn* **77**, 715–735.

Kasahara Y and Sakamoto K (1971) Ereutophobia and allied conditions: A contribution toward the psychopathological and cross-cultural study of borderline states. In: Arieti S (ed.) *World Biennial of Psychiatry and Psychotherapy*, Bd. I, pp. 292–303. New York: Basic Books.

Kasahara Y, Fujita O and Sakai K (1987) Industrialization and mental health in Japan: Mental health of large enterprise employees in their 40s and 50s. *Jpn J Psychiatr Neurol* **41**, 179–185.

Mezzich JE, Fabrega H and Coffman GA (1987) Multiaxial characterization of depressive patients. *J Nerv Ment Dis* **175**, 339–346.

Mitsuda H (1965) The concept of 'atypical pscyhosis' from the aspect of clinical genetics. *Acta Psychiatr Scand* **41**, 372–379.

Morita H (1922) *Shinkeishitsu* [in Japanese]. Tokyo: Hakuyosha.

Murakami M (1953) Clinical observations on 'degeneration-psychosis' [in Japanese]. *Psychiatr Neurol Jpn* **55**, 22–32.

Ogawa T (1986) La dépression néurotique à la lumière du concept d'état limite. In: Bergeret J (ed.) *Narcissism et état limite*, pp. 121–127. Paris: Dunod.

Pauleikoff B (1958) Über die Bedeutung situaer Einflüsse bei der Auslösung genidogener depressiver Phasen. *Arch Psychiatr Nervenkr* **197**, 669–677.

Shimoda M (1941) Premorbid Character der Manisch-depressiver Irreseins [in Japanese]. *Psychiatr Neurol Jpn* **45**, 101–103.

Shimoda M (1950) Uber manisch-depressiver Irreseins [in Japanese]. *Yonago Med Sch* **2**, 1–5.

Stone MH (1979) Contemporary shift of the borderline concept from a subschizophrenic disorder to a subaffective disorder. *Clin North Am* **2**, 577–594.

Tellenbach H (1961) *Melancholie*. Berlin: Springer.

von Baeyer W (1966) Situation, Jetztsein, Psychose. Bemerkungen zum Problem der Komplementären Situagenie Endogener Psychosen. In: von Baeyer (ed.) *Conditio Humana*. Berlin: Springer.

Yamashita I (1981) Depression in Japan. In: Ban TA *et al.* (eds) *Prevention and Treatment of Depression*, pp. 39–94. Baltimore: New Port Press.

12

Nosology in the 1990s: an update on the diagnostic process and its application to depressive disorders

W.F. Boyer and J.P. Feighner

Introduction

The first question to ask in a book about diagnosis, even if rhetorical, is why diagnose? The answer to this has changed with time. The importance of diagnosis in the first half of the twentieth century was that diagnosis related to prognosis. Some disorders were associated with better outcomes than others. With the arrival of several classes of effective psychotherapeutic drugs and a broad spectrum of psychotherapies diagnosis has become even more important. Certain treatments are indicated and others are relatively contraindicated for certain disorders. For example, somatic therapy should almost always be part of the approach to moderate, marked or severe depression. Patients with affective disorders are probably more likely than others to develop tardive dyskinesia from neuroleptic medication and patients with panic disorder may initially get worse when started on an antidepressant. Some patients with severe character pathology may be less able to tolerate certain forms of psychotherapy because they elicit too much anxiety or aggressive feelings.

Diagnosis also has a crucial role in research. Without a reliable diagnostic system investigators cannot replicate experiments. Without replication the epidemiology, genetics, clinical course and biological markers of psychiatric disorders can never be established and the effectiveness of new treatments can never be adequately evaluated.

The Diagnosis of Depression. Edited by J.P. Feighner and W.F. Boyer
© 1991 John Wiley & Sons Ltd

The Feighner criteria, published in 1972, marked a turning point in the modern American approach to psychiatric diagnosis (Feighner *et al.*, 1972). It offered specific inclusion and exclusion criteria for 14 disorders, including major depression and mania. A diagnosis required a minimum number of symptoms for 'probable' and more for a 'definite' diagnosis. The authors based these criteria on a five-point approach to diagnostic validity. These were clinical description, differentiation from other disorders, laboratory tests, family history and course of illness. Later a sixth criterion, treatment response, was added (Feighner, 1981).

These criteria led to a dynamic, evolving approach to psychiatric nosology. For example, the results of a follow-up study may suggest that patients with a certain disorder can have multiple outcomes. This compels a re-examination of the original clinical description, family history and other variables. This characteristic of a data-oriented approach accounts for the rapid publication and revision of diagnostic systems over the past 20 years.

This chapter wil present a clinically oriented overview of the state of knowledge in these six areas as it relates to the diagnosis of depression. Whole volumes can and have been written about each of these subjects, so we will choose what we consider to be major points in each area. The reader will be able to appreciate how each of the areas impacts on the others.

Clinical description

The main challenge in clinical description is to present a disease in such a way that the features are 'reliable'. Reliability means that different raters are able to agree on the presence or absence of a feature. Efforts to reach this goal have led to the lessening of emphasis of more inferential psychodynamic characteristics in diagnosis. It is also important that the feature(s) be relatively stable over time. This is seen in phrases in DSM-III such as 'depressed mood most of the day'.

A good example of recent changes in clinical description is the transition from DSM-III to DSM-III-R. The DSM-III-R criteria for melancholia contain three new items which are significant because they depart from a strictly symptom-oriented approach. These are: no pre-morbid personality disorder; one or more previous episodes with complete, or nearly complete recovery; and history of good response to adequate somatic therapy. This is an excellent example of how clinical course and treatment response can be woven into the clinical description. A seasonal subtype of depression was also added in DSM-III-R in response to papers describing patients with seasonal affective disorder, the course of illness and response to treatment, especially phototherapy.

Criteria were added to DSM-III-R for schizoaffective disorder. This had been the only diagnostic category without specific inclusion criteria. Dysthymic disorder also became a narrower concept in DSM-III-R. This reflects progress in research in the diagnosis and treatment of less severe forms of depression. To illustrate this narrowing of focus consider that in DSM-III there were 8100 possible combinations of symptoms consistent with dysthymic disorder, compared to 56 in DSM-III-R.

The number of symptom combinations in dysthymic disorder brings up an important problem in clinical description. The major advantage of specific diagnostic criteria is increased homogeneity of patients within a diagnostic category. As the minimum number of symptoms required for a diagnosis decreases, heterogeneity increases dramatically, as reflected by the number of possible symptom combinations which can make a diagnosis (Figure 1). For example, when the minimum number of symptoms for major depression decreased from five of eight in the RDC to four of eight in DSM-III the number of possible symptom combinations jumped from 93 to 163. While 'common sense' suggests there is little difference between most of these combinations, there are so many that the suggestion is untestable. This is clearly not consistent with an empirical approach to diagnosis. On the other hand, if the minimum number of symptoms is too high a significant number of patients may not qualify for a specific diagnosis. This would be especially troubling for clinicians although it might be tolerated in a research setting.

Most clinicians probably work around this problem already with an informal 'double standard'. If a patient is significantly disabled with early morning

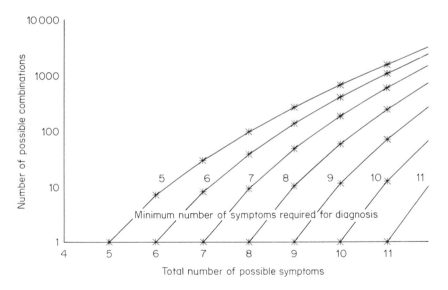

Figure 1. Number of possible symptom combinations as a function of total number of items and number required for diagnosis. For example, if a diagnosis requires at least nine of ten possible symptoms there are 11 possible symptom combinations; if it requires five of ten there are 638 possible combinations

awakening, weight loss and suicidal ideation most clinicians would approach that patient as though he or she had 'probable' major depression even if the required number of symptoms is not met.

The solution may lie in a formal 'double standard', narrow guidelines for research and more liberal ones for clinical work. This was anticipated in the Feighner and RDC criteria, which had separate cut-offs for 'definite' and 'probable' cases and in the development of ICD-10 (see Chapter 3). The initial plans for DSM-III called for the symptom criteria to be 'suggested' rather than required. The recognition of the differing needs and requirements of clinicians and researchers is one of the most pressing areas in clinical description.

Differentiation from other disorders

In addition to describing the features of an illness reliably it is important that some attributes separate the condition from other disorders. This is especially a problem in psychiatric disorders in which patients frequently have mixed presentations. A good example of these mixed presentations is a study by Hecht and von Wittchen. The investigators found that subjects with combined anxiety–depressive disorders were almost as common as those with depressive disorders alone (Hecht *et al.*, 1990), a fact appreciated by most clinicians.

An area of study which may help differentiation is the study of psychiatric comorbidity. By the study of comorbidity it may be possible to define new disorders which are now clinically seen as patients with various combinations of axis I and axis II disorders of the DSM-III-R. A number of studies have shown that the presence of another psychiatric disorder, especially personality disorder, is associated with greater disability, poorer treatment response, longer hospitalization and greater risk of relapse (Rounsaville *et al.*, 1986; Pfohl *et al.*, 1987; Andreoli *et al.*, 1989; Bossert *et al.*, 1989; Keller *et al.*, 1989; Nurnberg *et al.*, 1989; Hecht *et al.*, 1990; Kiesler *et al.*, 1990; Vollrath *et al.*, 1990).

'Double depression', or the coexistence of major depression and dysthymic disorder, may have special clinical significance. Klein and colleagues compared 31 out-patients with double depression to 50 out-patients with major depression alone. Patients with double depression had significantly greater impairment, more severe depressive symptoms, greater comorbidity, more personality disturbance, lower levels of social support, and higher rates of bipolar II and non-bipolar affective disorders in first-degree relatives. In a six-month follow-up the patients with double depression were significantly less likely to recover and a higher proportion experienced hypomanic episodes than did patients with episodic major depression (Klein *et al.*, 1988).

Patients with comorbid psychiatric disorders may be biologically different from those with single diagnoses. For example, Grunhaus and colleagues found that α-adrenergic receptors were significantly decreased in patients with both panic disorder and major depression compared to those with major depression alone (Grunhaus *et al.*, 1990). In another relevant study Frost, Moffitt and McGee assessed members of a birth cohort for psychopathology and neuro-psychological dysfunction at age 13. Subjects who met DSM-III-R criteria for a single disorder, multiple disorders, and no disorder were compared on five composite neuropsychological measures. The multiple disorders group performed significantly worse than the non-disordered group on the verbal, visuospatial, verbal memory, and visual-motor integration factors. They also showed the highest rate of neuropsychological impairment (Frost *et al.*, 1989).

Studies of comorbidity may lead to the development of new diagnoses which are now seen as multiple axis I or axis I–axis II diagnoses. If patients with these disorders have distinct biological characteristics, as some of the data implies, it will further support their validity.

Laboratory tests

A large number of laboratory tests have been reported to be abnormal in depressed patients. These are discussed in Chapter 6. They include sleep parameters, neuroendocrine function, circadian rhythms, regional cerebral blood flow, brain glucose metabolism, water and electrolyte balance, and immune system parameters (Pawlik *et al.*, 1986; Kishimoto *et al.*, 1987; Martinot *et al.*, 1987). Which tests will ultimately have the greatest clinical utility will depend on the replicability of findings and the ease with which they can be implemented in a clinical setting.

These findings have several important implications. One is that major depression is almost certainly a systemic medical illness, with widespread primary and secondary manifestations throughout the body. Viewed in this fashion depressed mood can be seen as a common but not invariant feature of major depression. This viewpoint supports the concept of masked depressions, discussed in Chapter 7.

Another implication is that depression may be caused by multiple biological pathways. The existence of multiple pathways is underlined by the number of physical illnesses and medications which may be associated with the disorder. Some of these are listed in Tables I and II (Cassem *et al.*, 1988). The fact that some medications implicated in causing depressed mood, such as thyroid hormone and bromocriptine, can also be used to treat some patients with affective illness further underscores the multiple aetiologies.

A third possible implication is that laboratory testing may lead to new psychiatric diagnoses that cross traditional boundaries. Studies which implicate serotonin (5-hydroxytryptamine, 5-HT), dysfunction in a wide variety of psychiatric disorders are a good example of this. The disorders include major depression, obsessive-compulsive disorder, panic disorder, bulimia, obesity,

Table I. Some medical illnesses associated with depression.

Circulatory	Infectious
Cerebral insufficiency or anoxia	Encephalitis
Hypertensive encephalopathy	Malaria
	Pneumonia
Endocrine	Mononucleosis
Hyperthyroidism	Brucellosis
Hypothyroidism	Tuberculosis
Hyperinsulinism	Sarcoidosis
Diabetes mellitus	
Addison's disease	Malignancies
Cushing's disease	Pancreatic carcinoma
Hyperaldosteronism	Disseminated carcinomatosis
	Carcinoid
Gastrointestinal	Oat cell carcinoma
Inflammatory bowel disease	
Cirrhosis	Neurological
Viral hepatitis	Parkinson's disease
	Tumour
Haematological	Multiple sclerosis
Anaemia	Wilson's disease
Polycythaemia vera	Huntingdon's chorea
	Temporal lobe epilepsy
	Post-concussive syndrome
	Stroke
	Other
	Nutritional deficiency
	Systemic lupus
	Acute intermittent porphyria
	Amyloidosis

aggression and both suicidal ideation and attempts (Brown *et al.*, 1982; Stanley and Mann, 1983; Borg *et al.*, 1985; Donders *et al.*, 1985; Edman *et al.*, 1986; van-Praag, 1986; Kay *et al.*, 1988; Lander and Schoemaker, 1988; Coccaro *et al.*, 1989; Schalling, 1989; Tollefson, 1989). Such an alternative diagnostic approach is discussed elsewhere in this volume.

Family history

There is currently a considerable amount of research and clinical interest in the contribution of family variables to psychopathology. The two traditional areas are psychiatric genetics (nature) and the effects of family environment (nurture).

Studies of affective disorders have shown a strong genetic contribution to bipolar and severe unipolar disorders (McGuffin *et al.*, 1987; Coryell and Zimmerman, 1988). This contribution appears to be a predisposition to the

Table II. Some medications associated with depressed mood.

Analgesics and anti-inflammatories	*Anticholinergics (numerous drugs)*
Morphine and derivatives	
Meperidine	*Antihypertensives*
Pentazocine	Hydrochlorothiazide
Indomethacin	Beta blockers
Naproxen	Furosemide
Phenylbutazone	
Propoxyphene	*Antihistamines*
Zomepirac sodium	Cimetidine
Tolmetin sodium	Promethazine
Ibuprofen	Ranitidine
Antiarrhythmics	*Antineoplastics*
Lidocaine	Fluorouracil
Procainamide	Aminogluthethimide
Disopyramide	Vinblastine
Mexilitene	Vincristine
	Azathioprine
Anticonvulsants	Asparaginase
Barbiturates	Bleomycin
Hydantoins	Mithramycin
Primidone	Trimethoprim
Sodium valproate	Azacytadine
Succinimide	Cytabarine (high dose)
	Dacarbazine
Antibiotics, antifungals, antihelminths	Methenamine
Ampicillin	Methotrexate (high dose)
Sulphonamides	Procarbazine
Clotrimazole	Tamoxifen
Cycloserine	Interferon
Dapsone	Interleukin-2
Ethionamide	Etopside
Griseofulvin	
Metronidazole	*Antiparkinsonians*
Nitrofurantoin	Anticholinergics
Nalidixic acid	Amantadine
Streptomycin	Bromocriptine
Aminoglycosides	Carbidopa
Amodiaquine	Levodopa
Amphotericin-B	
Cephalosporins	*Antivirals*
Chloramphenicol	Acyclovir
Chloroquine	Azidothymidine (AZT)
Cholistin sulphate	Suramin
Ethambutol	
Rifampin	*Endocrine*
Tetracycline	Adrenocorticosteroids
Ticarcillin	Oestrogens
Flucytosine	Thyroid
	Sympatholytics and sympathomimetics

development of disorder. The factors or factors which determine whether or not the illness actually occurs are unknown. It is often helpful for patients and families to draw parallels to better-known illnesses such as heart disease and breast cancer. These illnesses also seem to have a genetic component but not all family members are affected.

One of the more exciting developments in psychiatric genetics in the past several years was the report that a gene conferring a strong predisposition to manic-depressive illness had been localized to the tip of the short arm of chromosome 11 (Egeland et al., 1987). However, these findings were not replicated in subsequent studies (Hodgkinson et al., 1987). Bipolar illness has also been linked to the chromosome for deutan colour blindness and glucose 6-phosphate dehydrogenase (G6PD) deficiency in some families (Fieve et al., 1975; Mendlewicz et al., 1979, 1980; Baron et al., 1987). These findings suggest that multiple genetic pathways may lead to the expression of bipolar disorder.

Other studies suggest that bipolar I and bipolar II disorders may be genetically distinct from each other (Andreasen et al., 1987; Coryell, 1987). The validity of schizoaffective disorder (Abrams, 1984) and milder forms of depression from a genetic standpoint is more uncertain (Kringlen, 1985; Torgersen, 1986; Winokur et al., 1986; Edwards and Watts, 1989; McGuffin and Katz, 1989).

There are several methodological difficulties in studies of psychiatric genetics. Phenocopies pose one of the more serious problems. A phenocopy is an illness that clinically appears the same as a genetic one, but does not result from a genetic disturbance. A study by Cook and associates provides a case in point. The investigators examined the electroencephalograms (EEGs) and familial pattern of psychopathology in 46 patients with bipolar illness. Those patients with abnormal EEGs had a significantly negative family history of affective disorder when compared to the normal EEG group (Cook et al., 1986).

Another problem is that some illnesses may have variable expression. It may be important, for example, to include patients with affective-spectrum disorders in genetic studies (Gasperini et al., 1987). In one study Wender and associates compared the prevalence of mood disorders in the relatives of 71 affectively ill adult adoptees with the prevalence among relatives of a control group. Results showed a significantly increased frequency of not only unipolar depression, but also suicide and alcohol abuse or dependence among the biological relatives of patients (Wender et al., 1986).

Other clinical factors may also be important in genetic studies. These include age of onset, history of recurrence, and degree of incapacitation associated with the illness. In general the earlier the age of onset and more severe the incapacitation, the more likely the illness may be genetically transmitted. A study by Weissman and colleagues illustrates these points. The investigators found an inverse relationship between the rates of major depression among children and the age of onset of major depression in their parents (Weissman et al., 1988). Gershon and associates also found that relatives of affective patients were more likely to have had multiple episodes of depression and severe impairment in their major life role compared to the depressed relatives of normal controls (Gershon *et al.*, 1986). These studies suggest that the clinician may need to assess factors such as severity and age of onset of illness in the family history.

In general the literature suggests that severe affective illness and schizophrenic disorders occur in separate family pedigrees. If one family member has a well-established diagnosis of one of these types it strongly suggests that another family member, if ill, has a similar disorder.

Family environment, although long the subject of many theories in psychiatry, has been very difficult to study. However, recent research into 'expressed emotion' has revealed the importance of family environment in psychiatric disturbance. Expressed emotion is usually defined as a measure of the number of critical or intrusive comments made by family members toward the patient during an interview. Most of these studies have examined expressed emotion within the families of schizophrenic patients and show that this variable significantly predicts relapse independently of medication compliance.

Although patients with affective illness have not been studied as often as those with schizophrenia, there are indications that the level of expressed emotion within the family is a significant predictor of relapse for these disorders as well (Vaughn and Leff, 1976). Miklowitz and colleagues (1986) found that expressed emotion within the family, as well as a related measure termed affective style, helped predict relapse in bipolar disorder. Hooley and co-workers (1986) studied the relationship between spouses' levels of expressed emotion (EE) and relapse in a sample of 39 depressed inpatients. Over a nine-month follow-up 50% of patients with high-EE spouses relapsed compared to none of those living with a low-EE spouse.

These studies have measured illness relapse. It is likely that some of the same family conditions which predispose to relapse also influence the onset of the initial episode. These studies are much harder to do as they must either be retrospective, after the onset of illness, or rely on the identification of subjects who are at very high risk of illness in the near future. Even with these obstacles the expressed emotion field offers the promise of exposing psychosocial factors to rigorous scientific investigation.

Course of illness

Clinicians should be familiar with the natural course of depressive illness in order adequately to counsel their patients about treatment options and prognosis. There is certainly no fixed consensus on these issues, but some outlines may be sketched. For most individuals major depression is characterized by eventual remission. Therefore most depressions will get better with time, even untreated. However, this must be moderated by a full appreciation of the morbidity and mortality which may accompany depressive illness. The most dramatic example is that approximately 10% of patients with major depression will eventually suicide (Hamilton, 1985).

The average length of the first episode of depression is about three months, but there is considerable variation. Subsequent episodes tend to last somewhat longer and to occur more frequently (Hamilton, 1985). Patients with delusional or non-delusional depression tend to have the same type of illness when it recurs (Ayuso, 1984). The risk of relapse increases after each episode for both bipolar and unipolar depression. This may reflect a physiological process such as 'kindling' or may simply show that patients with chronic, recurrent forms of an illness gradually become apparent over time. The longitudinal course of schizoaffective disorder is probably midway between schizophrenia and bipolar disorder (Huba et al., 1976).

The diagnosis of bipolar disorder in a first-degree family member is a risk factor for relapse, as are the number of previous episodes, poor social adaptation, pathological personality and residual depressive symptoms such as underlying dysthymic disorder (Keller et al., 1983a, 1983b; Faravelli et al., 1986; Simons et al., 1986; Winokur et al., 1986; Coryell et al., 1987; Scott et al., 1988). Some laboratory markers may also help predict the course of illness. For example, continued dexamethasone non-suppression, abnormal thyrotrophin-releasing hormone (TRH) test, or shortened rapid eye movement (REM) latency may predict relapse (Green et al., 1983; Krog et al., 1984; Giles et al., 1987; Schweitzer et al., 1987).

A few studies have examined the efficacy of antidepressants in preventing relapse of depression. Those patients who relapse on placebo provide some information on the natural course of illness. In the typical study patients are successfully treated for the acute illness and are then maintained on either the same medication or placebo for a variable length of time. This length of time affects the relapse rate found. Georgotas and McCue (1989) found a placebo relapse rate of 15.8% in eight weeks. Rouillon and colleagues (1989) found a one-year relapse rate of 31.5–37.5%. Bialos and colleagues (1982) reported that eight of ten patients on long-term amitriptyline maintenance relapsed within 15 weeks after being switched to placebo under double-blind conditions. For the average patient the risk of relapse remains high until at least four months have passed with minimal symptoms of depression (Prien and Kupfer, 1986). This time may represent the average duration of the biological condition(s) which initiated or maintained the illness.

Treatment response

Treatment response is acknowledged as an important diagnostic criterion in DSM-III-R. One of the new criteria for major depression is 'history of good response to adequate somatic therapy'. Most of the data concerning treatment response come from psychopharmacological studies. Antidepressants and mood stabilizers have been found to be effective, at least in some patients, in a broad range of conditions. This prompts speculation as to whether some or all of these conditions may be variants of affective illness. For example, antidepressants, especially those with 5-HT reuptake blocking capacity, have been found to be effective in depression, obsessive-compulsive disorder, bulimia, generalized anxiety disorder, panic attacks, social phobia, and some substance use disorders, especially alcoholism. Unfortunately the most helpful type of data, which is the *relative* efficacy of antidepressants in each of these conditions compared to depression, is lacking.

It must also be remembered that mood stabilizers, such as lithium, carbamazepine and valproic acid, have been reported to be helpful not only in bipolar disorder, but in the treatment and prophylaxis of some cases of unipolar depression, hyperactivity, aggression and schizophrenia. Neuroleptics are efficacious not only in psychosis but also in anxiety and some cases of depression. Benzodiazepines are useful in anxiety and also have adjunctive use in psychotic agitation. Some benzodiazepines, especially alprazolam and adinazolam, also have antidepressant properties.

This discussion is not meant to devalue treatment response as a criterion for diagnostic validity. It is meant rather to point out that most of the crucial data, as in laboratory testing, are not yet available. In addition to clinical trials comparing different treatments it may be possible to utilize newer statistical techniques, such as meta-analysis, to gain some insight into the relative efficacy of different classes of medication within a given disorder.

Clinical application of the nosological process

The six points discussed in this chapter have direct application in clinical situations as well as in developing official diagnostic schemes. The first task in an initial interview is to obtain a description of the patient's symptoms and disturbed areas of functioning. Ideally there is a balance of observation by the clinician and historical data provided by the patient. Observation will include such items as predominant mood, psychomotor changes, and the style and substance of thought. Historical items involve factors such as sleep disturbance, weight loss, suicidal feelings and the presence or absence of hallucinations and delusions. More severely disturbed individuals may be unable to provide a coherent history or their history may be distorted (retrospective falsification). Then the observations of family members and hospital personnel are even more important than usual.

In addition to providing diagnostic information this process can furnish 'target' symptoms. These are prominent, easily measured symptoms, such as weight and sleep disturbance, which can serve as a barometer of treatment progress.

While the initial data are being gathered the clinician is also formulating diagnostic hypotheses and sharpening the areas of enquiry to 'rule out' (differentiate) other disorders. More than one disorder may also be 'ruled in', thereby disclosing psychiatric comorbidity. This will have implications for treatment and prognosis as discussed above.

Physical examination may help exclude organic factors as causing the patient's complaints, or may help confirm a diagnosis such as substance abuse. Laboratory testing may further these goals. The concept of psychiatric laboratory tests should be broad enough also to include psychological testing. Psychological tests can help formulate diagnostic hypotheses and may suggest the presence of psychiatric comorbidity. Neuropsychological testing may be helpful to document the presence of organic mental dysfunction and to plot its course over time.

Family history may suggest a genetic component to the illness. The presence of a family member with a well-established diagnosis of a major psychiatric disorder should weigh heavily in the diagnostic evaluation. Often times the patients may not know the family member's diagnosis, but may be able to provide information such as whether the family member was hospitalized, whether electroconvulsive therapy (ECT) or lithium was used. Markers of depression-spectrum disorders such as suicide attempts or alcoholism may also be significant. This data should be supplemented when possible with information from other family members.

In addition to the description of the patient's current symptoms it is important to appreciate the natural history of his or her illness. Is the affective disturbance seasonal? Is it related to menstrual function? Did the symptoms pre-date or follow periods of substance abuse? An accurate history from family members can again be crucial. Patients with affective disorders, even when accompanied by psychotic symptoms, usually make a full, or nearly full, recovery between episodes. Recovery from an exacerbation of schizophrenia is commonly incomplete and the overall course shows progressive dysfunction. A history of recovery between episodes provides evidence for an affective disorder and should influence the approach to treatment. If faced with a patient with an ambiguous clinical picture it is often better to diagnose the 'good prognosis' illness, affective disorder, than to risk prematurely burdening the patient and family with the poor prognosis associated with schizophrenia.

These basic considerations should be tempered with one more factor. It is not unusual for patients to become significantly 'demoralized' after a severe affective episode. This demoralization may take the form of constriction of social and vocational activities and may reflect an intense fear of relapse or the patient's pessimism about ever being 'the person I used to be'. This demoralization and withdrawal could be confused with the negative symptoms of schizophrenia.

The difference, however, is that the schizophrenic patient usually does not retain the same level of insight and does not appear to miss the former level of function the way an affectively disordered patient does.

The patient's family is usually in a better position to provide information about his or her early years. Possibly relevant information includes a history of complications in pregnancy or delivery. This includes maternal substance abuse. The patient may have experienced a significant illness or injury in childhood. 'Injury' of course includes both physical and emotional trauma. Symptoms of attention deficit disorder in primary school or antisocial traits during the teenage years may also be relevant. The family may be able to provide information about chronic patterns of behaviour which may rule in or out a substance abuse or an axis II diagnosis.

The clinical value of treatment response is a history, within an individual, of response to a particular type of treatment. History of improvement with a particular type of treatment strongly suggests that the patient will respond again to the same or a similar agent. A history of response to a particular agent in a family member also suggests that the same treatment may be effective for the patient. It is also important to consider the potential short and long-term side effects associated with a particular treatment.

Categorical and dimensional diagnoses

The title and contents of this chapter are concerned with the nosological approach to diagnosis. This can also be called a categorical system, since different illnesses are felt to represent separate categories. A dimensional approach is a different model in which a patient's condition is described by rating it on each of several scores, or dimensions. This is illustrated in Figure 2, which shows part of an MMPI profile for an imaginary patient.

A dimensional diagnosis is already used in some areas of medicine such as the staging of many cancers or rating the severity of a myocardial infarction. Psychiatric clinicians also informally use a dimensional model at times. An illness might be described as 'a major depression with obsessional features' or 'a bipolar illness with occasional panic attacks'.

It is important to understand that dimensional and categorical diagnoses are fundamentally related. The highest score of the imaginary MMPI profile in Figure 2 is depression. If one sets a threshold score of 80 for making a diagnosis from this profile then the patient will be diagnosed as being depressed. If one lowers the threshold a little an elevated score on 'Psychasthenia' becomes apparent. Since an elevated Psychasthenia scale often reflects anxiety and worry the patient's diagnosis then might be interpreted as depression with significant anxiety features. If one lowers the threshold still further an elevated 'Psychopathic deviate' scale is seen. This might suggest some unconventional

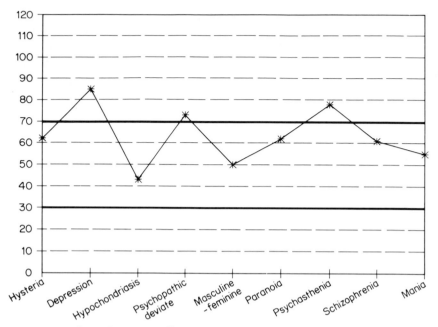

Figure 2. Hypothetical MMPI profile.

social attitudes, difficulty in interpersonal relations and perhaps a tendency to act out. While in actual practice the MMPI cannot be used directly to make diagnoses like this, this discussion illustrates how categorical and dimensional diagnoses are interrelated. The ideal diagnostic system will make use of both methods. Chapter 5 contains a fuller description of the potential advantages of dimensional diagnosis.

In summary, the six-point approach to diagnostic validity discussed in this chapter has provided an immensely useful approach to psychiatric nosology. Results in a particular area prompt research in one or more of the others. This has produced a rapidly growing amount of data and has prompted continued criticism and revision of official diagnostic systems. One of the current challenges is to utilize the best of both categorical and dimensional approaches to diagnosis.

Although the pace of change in diagnostic practice may be uncomfortable at times, the clinical and scientific value of continued research and revision more than compensate for it. As long as psychiatry continues to employ this data-oriented approach the rapid increase in knowledge and improvements in diagnosis are likely to follow.

References

Abrams R (1984) Genetic studies of the schizoaffective syndrome: A selective review. *Schizophr Bull* **10**, 26–29.

Andreasen NC, Rice J, Endicott J *et al.* (1987) Familial rates of affective disorder: A report from the National Institute of Mental Health Collaborative Study. *Arch Gen Psychiatry* **44**, 461–469.

Andreoli A, Gressot G, Aapro N *et al.* (1989) Personality disorders as a predictor of outcome. First International Congress on the Disorders of Personality (1988, Copenhagen, Denmark). *J Pers Dis* **3**, 307–320.

Ayuso GJL (1984) Melancolia delirante? Subtipo clinico o entidad autonoma? [Delusional depression: Clinical subtype or autonomous entity]. *Rev Dep Psiquiatr Fac Med Barcelona* **11**, 247–256.

Baron M, Risch N, Hamburger R *et al.* (1987) Genetic linkage between X-chromosome markers and bipolar affective illness. *Nature* **326**, 289–292.

Bialos D, Giller E, Jatlow P *et al.* (1982) Recurrence of depression after discontinuation of long-term amitriptyline treatment. *Am J Psychiatry* **139**, 325–329.

Borg S, Kvande H, Liljeberg P *et al.* (1985) 5-Hydroxyindoleacetic acid in cerebrospinal fluid in alcoholic patients under different clinical conditions. *Alcohol* **2**, 415–418.

Bossert S, Schnabel E and Krieg JC (1989) Effects and limitations of cognitive behavior therapy in bulimia inpatients. *Psychother Psychosom* **51**, 77–82.

Brown GL, Goodwin FK and Bunney WE (1982) Human aggression and suicide: Their relationship to neuropsychiatric diagnoses and serotonin metabolism. In Ho BT, Schoolar JC and Usdin E (eds) *Serotinin in Biological Psychiatry*, pp. 287–307.

Cassem EH, Lake CR and Boyer WF (1988) Psychopharmacology in the ICU. In: Chernow B (ed.) *The Pharmacologic Approach to the Critically Ill Patient*, pp. 491–510.

Coccaro EF, Siever LJ, Klar HM *et al.* (1989) Serotonergic studies in patients with affective and personality disorders: Correlates with suicidal and impulsive aggressive behaviour. *Arch Gen Psychiatry* **46**, 587–599.

Cook BL, Shukla S and Hoff AL (1986) EEG abnormalities in bipolar affective disorder. *J Affect Dis* **11**, 147–149.

Coryell W (1987) Outcome and family studies of bipolar II depression. *Psychiatr Ann* **17**, 28–31.

Coryell W and Zimmerman M (1988) The heritability of schizophrenia and schizoaffective disorder: A family study. *Arch Gen Psychiatry* **45**, 323–327.

Coryell W, Andreasen NC, Endicott J *et al.* (1987) The significance of past mania or hypomania in the course and outcome of major depression. *Am J Psychiatry* **144**, 309–315.

Donders SH, Pieters GF, Heevel JG *et al.* (1985) Disparity of thyrotropin (TSH) and prolactin responses to TSH-releasing hormone in obesity. *J Clin Endocrinol Metab* **61**, 56–59.

Edman G, Asberg M, Levander S *et al.* (1986) Skin conductance habituation and cerebrospinal fluid 5-hydroxyindoleacetic acid in suicidal patients. *Arch Gen Psychiatry* **43**, 586–592.

Edwards JH and Watt DC (1989) Caution in locating the gene(s) for affective disorder. *Psychol Med* **19**, 273–275.

Egeland JA, Gerhard DS, Pauls DL *et al.* (1987) Bipolar affective disorders linked to DNA markers on chromosome 11. *Nature* **325**, 783–787.

Faravelli C, Ambonetti A, Pallanti S *et al.* (1986) Depressive relapses and incomplete recovery from index episode. *Am J Psychiatry* **143**, 888–891.

Feighner JP (1981) Nosology of primary affective disorders and application to clinical research. *Acta Psychiatr Scand Suppl* **63**, 29–41.

Feighner JP, Robins E, Guze SB *et al.* (1972) Diagnostic criteria for use in psychiatric research. *Arch Gen Psychiatry* **26**, 57–63.

Fieve RR, Mendlewicz J, Rainer JD *et al.* (1975) A dominant X-linked factor in manic-depressive illness: Studies with color blindness. *Proc Annu Meet Am Psychopathol Assoc* **63**, 241–255.

Frost LA, Moffitt TE and McGee R (1989) Neuropsychological correlates of psychopathology in an unselected cohort of young adolescents. *J Abnormal Psychol* **98**, 307–313.

Gasperini M, Orsini A, Bussoleni C *et al.* (1987) Genetic approach to the study of heterogeneity of affective disorders. *J Affect Dis* **12**, 105–113.

Georgotas A and McCue RE (1989) Relapse of depressed patients after effective continuation therapy. *J Affect Dis* **17**, 159–164.

Gershon ES, Weissman MM, Guroff JJ *et al.* (1986) Validation of criteria for major depression through controlled family study. *J Affect Dis* **11**, 125–131.

Giles DE, Jarrett RB, Roffwarg HP *et al* (1987) Reduced rapid eye movement latency: A prediction of recurrence in depression. *Neuropschopharmacology* **1**, 33–39.

Green HS and Kane JM (1983) The dexamethasone suppression test in depression. *Clin Neuropharmacol* **6**, 7–24.

Grunhaus LJ, Cameron OG, Pande AC *et al.* (1990) Comorbidity of panic disorder and major depressive disorder: Effects on platelet aplha-sub-2 adrenergic receptors. *Acta Psychiatr Scand* **81**, 216–219.

Hamilton M (1985) Mood disorders: Clinical features. In: Kaplan HI and Sadock BJ (eds) *Comprehensive Textbook of Psychiatry*, pp. 892–913.

Hecht H, von Zerssen D and Wittchen HU (1990) Anxiety and depression in a community sample: The influence of comorbidity on social functioning. *J Affect Dis* **18**, 137–144.

Hodgkinson S, Sherrington R, Gurling H *et al.* (1987) Molecular genetic evidence for heterogeneity in manic depression. *Nature* **325**, 805–806.

Hooley JM, Orley J and Teasdale JD (1986) Levels of expressed emotion and relapse in depressed patients. *Br J Psychiatry* **148**, 642–647.

Huba GJ, Lawlor WG, Stallone F *et al.* (1976) The use of autocorrelation analysis in the longitudinal study of mood patterns in depressed patients. *Br J Psychiatry* **128**, 146–155.

Kaye WH, Gwirtsman HE, Brewerton TD *et al.* (1988) Bingeing behavior and plasma amino acids: A possible involvement of brain serotonin in bulimia nervosa. *Psych Res* **23**, 31–43.

Keller MB, Lavori PW, Endicott J *et al.* (1983a) 'Double depression': Two-year follow-up. *Am J Psychiatry* **140**, 689–694.

Keller MB, Lavori PW, Lewis C *et al.* (1983b) Predictors of relapse in major depressive disorder. *JAMA* **250**, 3299–3309.

Keller MB, Herzog DB, Lavori PW *et al.* (1989) High rates of chronicity and rapidity of relapse in patients with bulimia nervosa and depression. *Arch Gen Psychiatry* **46**, 480–481.

Kiesler CA, Simpkins C and Morton T (1990) Predicting length of hospital stay for psychiatric inpatients. *Hosp Community Psychiatry* **41**, 149–154.

Kishimoto H, Takazu O, Ohno S *et al.* (1987) 11C-glucose metabolism in manic and depressed patients. *Psych Res* **22**, 81–88.

Klein DN, Taylor EB, Harding K *et al.* (1988) Double depression and episodic major depression: Demographic, clinical, familial, personality, and socioenvironmental characteristics and short-term outcome. *Am J Psychiatry* **145**, 1226–1231.

Kringlen E (1985) Depression research: A review with special emphasis on etiology. World Psychiatric Association Regional Symposium: New perspectives in psychiatric research (1984, Helsinki, Finland). *Acta Psychiatr Scand* **71**, 117–130.

Krog MI, Kirkegaard C, Kijne B *et al.* (1984) Prediction of relapse with the TRH test and prophylactic amitriptyline in 39 patients with endogenous depression. *Am J Psychiatry* **141**, 945–948.

Langer SZ and Schoemaker H (1988) Effects of antidepressants on monoamine transporters. *Prog Neuropsychopharmacol Biol Psychiatry* **12**, 193–216.

Martinot JL and Peron-Magnan P (1987) [Cerebral imaging and depressive disorder]. *L'Encephale* **13**, 273–277.

McGuffin P and Katz R (1989) The genetics of depression and manic-depressive disorder. *Br J Pschiatry* **155**, 294–304.

McGuffin P, Katz R and Bebbington P (1987) Hazard, heredity and depression: A family study. Munich Genetic Discussion International Symposium (1986, Berlin, Federal Republic of Germany). *J Psychiatr Res* **21**, 365–375.

Mendlewicz J, Linkowski P, Guroff JJ *et al.* (1979) Color blindness linkage to bipolar manic-depressive illness: New evidence. *Arch Gen Psychiatry* **36**, 1442–1447.

Mendlewicz J, Linkowski P and Wilmotte J (1980) Linkage between glucose-6-phosphate dehydrogenase deficiency and manic-depressive psychosis. *Br J Psychiatry* **137**, 337–342.

Miklowitz DJ, Goldstein MJ, Nuechterlein KH *et al.* (1986) Expressed emotion, affective style, lithium compliance, and relapse in recent onset mania. *Psychopharmacol Bull* **22**, 628–632.

Nurnberg HG, Raskin M, Levine PE *et al.* (1989) Borderline personality disorder as a negative prognostic factor in anxiety disorders. 141st Annual Meeting of the American Psychiatric Association (1988, Montreal, Canada). *Journal of Pers Dis* **3**, 205–216.

Pawlik G, Beil C, Hebold I *et al.* (1986) Positron emission tomography in depression research: Principles—results—perspectives. *Psychopathology* **19** (Suppl. 2), 85–93.

Pfohl B, Coryell W, Zimmerman M *et al.* (1987) Prognostic validity of self-report and interview measures of pesonality disorder in depressed inpatients. *J Clin Psychiatry* **48**, 468–472.

Prien RF and Kupfer DJ (1986) Continuation therapy for major depressive episodes: How long should it be maintained? *Am J Psychiatry* **143**, 18–23.

Rouillon F, Phillips R, Serrurier D *et al.* (1989) Rechutes de depression unipolaire et efficacite del la maprotiline. *L'Encephale* **15**, 527–534.

Rounsaville BJ, Kosten TR and Kleber HD (1986). Long-term changes in current psychiatric diagnosis of treated opiate addicts. *Compr Psychiatry* **27**, 480–498.

Schalling D (1989) Biochemical correlates of temperament dimensions. *Biol Psychiatry Suppl* **25(7A)**, 139A–140A.

Schweitzer I, Maguire KP, Gee AH *et al.* (1987) Prediction of outcome in depressed patients by weekly monitoring with the dexamethasone suppression test. *Br J Psychiatry* **151**, 780–784.

Scott J, Barker WA and Eccleston D (1988) The Newcastle chronic depression study: Patient characteristics and factors associated with chronicity. *Br J Psychiatry* **152**, 28–33.

Simons AD, Murphy GE, Levine JL *et al.* (1986). Cognitive therapy and pharmacotherapy for depression: Sustained improvement over one year. *Arch Gen Psychiatry* **43**, 43–48.

Stanley M and Mann JJ (1983) Increased serotonin-2-binding sites in frontal cortex of suicide victims. *Lancet* **i**, 214–216.

Tollefson DG (1989) Serotonin and alcohol: Interrelationships. 16th collegium inter-
nationale neuropsychopharmacologicum congress satellite conference: New findings
with anxiolytic drugs (1988, Munich, Germany). *Psychopathology* **22**, 37–48.

Torgerson S (1986) Genetic factors in moderately severe and mild affective disorders.
Arch Gen Psychiatry **43**, 222–226.

van-Praag HM (1986) Affective disorders and aggression disorders: Evidence for a common biological mechanism. *Suicide Life Threat Behav* **16**, 103–132.

Vaughn CE and Leff JP (1976) The influence of family and social factors on the course of
psychiatric illness: A comparison of schizophrenic and depressed neurotic patients.
Br J Psychiatry **129**, 125–137.

Vollrath M, Koch R and Angst J (1990) The Zurich study: IX. Panic disorder and sporadic
panic: Symptoms, diagnosis, prevalence, and overlap with depression. *Eur Arch
Psychiatry Neurol Sci* **239**, 221–230.

Weissman MM, Warner V, Wickramaratne P *et al.* (1988) Early-onset major depression in
parents and their children. *J Affect Dis* **15**, 269–277.

Wender PH, Kety SS, Rosenthal D *et al.* (1986) Psychiatric disorders in the biological and
adoptive families of adopted individuals with affective disorders. *Arch Gen Psychiatry*
43, 923–929.

Winokur G, Crowe R and Kadrmas A (1986) Genetic approach to heterogeneity in
psychoses: Relationship of a family history of mania or depression to course in
bipolar illness. *Psychopathology* **19**, 80–84.

Index

Index compiled by Doreen Blake